UNTOUCHABLE SAINTS

An Indian Phenomenon

Untouchable Saints

An Indian Phenomenon

Edited by
ELEANOR ZELLIOT
ROHINI MOKASHI-PUNEKAR

MANOHAR
2026

First published 2005
Reprinted 2019, 2021, 2022, 2023, 2024, 2025, 2026

ISBN 978-81-7304-644-5

Published by
Ajay Kumar Jain *for*
Manohar Publishers & Distributors
4753/23 Ansari Road, Daryaganj
New Delhi 110 002

Printed at
Replika Press Pvt. Ltd.

Contents

Illustrations

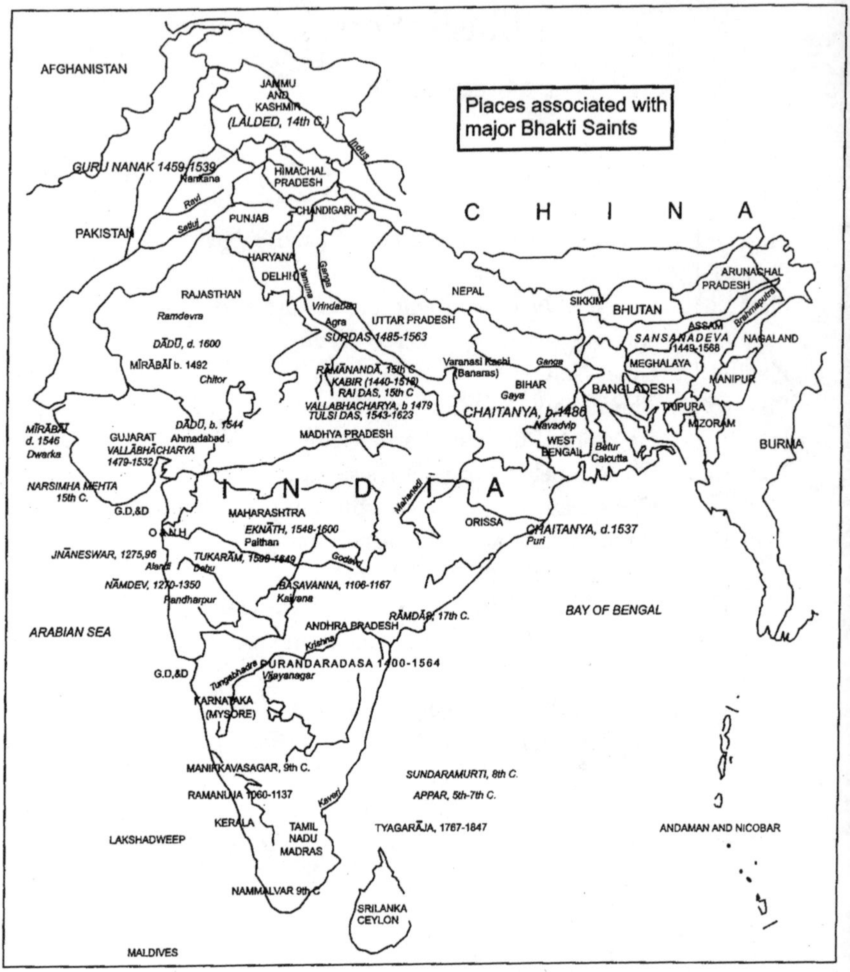

Prepared for *Hinduism: New Essays in the History of Religions*, edited by Bardwell L. Smith (Leiden: E.J. Brill, 1976). Note that Nandanar, Tiruppan Alvar and Chokhamela and his family are not considered 'major'. Tiruppan Alvar should be placed with Ramanuja at Srirangam. Nandanar was transformed into a Brahmin at Chidambaram, marked under Manikkavasagar in the map. Chokhamela should be located at Pandharpur and his sister Nirmala at Mehunpuri, a village in Maharashtra north of Paithan. The map was prepared to illustrate Eleanor Zelliot's article, 'The Medieval Bhakti Movement in History: An Essay on the Literature in English' in the above volume. Thanks are due to Joseph and Philip Schwartzberg.

Introduction

ELEANOR ZELLIOT
ROHINI MOKASHI-PUNEKAR

This volume has a long history, beginning with my discovery of the historical importance of the Marathi Untouchable saint of the fourteenth century, Chokhamela, some forty years ago when I was doing research on Dr B.R. Ambedkar and the Untouchable movement. Several seminars at Carleton College on the literature and culture of India, in which some students wrote papers on bhakti, allowed me to see how fascinating a comparative study of the various *bhaktas* would be. This volume began to take shape some ten years ago when Joseph Schaller, Vasudha Narayanan, Karen Pechilis Prentiss, and I participated in a panel on bhakti at the Association for Asian Studies. David Lorenzen moderated that panel, and has consistently encouraged and produced studies on bhakti. Through the years I have added to the file a number of articles that dealt with any of the four basic Untouchable saints, or commented on bhakti and untouchability. I had been in touch with Rohini Mokashi-Punekar in connection with her translations of Chokhamela's poetry, which I considered excellent work. I invited her to collaborate with me in editing the material I had, and to write some additional essays on those Untouchable saints who also had to be included in this book. In December 2002, Rohini Mokashi-Punekar came to Pune (where I had gone for my annual visit) from Guwahati on the other side of India, and we had several days of solid dawn-to-midnight conferencing trying to make a book out of the material we had collected. We have since worked together on the book with the help of the electronic medium. Her grasp of Marathi and Hindi, and her poetic sense, were invaluable not only in producing articles on Chokhamela,[1] Banka, and Kaımamela, but also in the editing process. The result is the volume we offer to you in appreciation of the lives of the *bhaktas* and the meaning they hold for the history of that important group called the Untouchables, or now more often the Dalits (the oppressed), in India. While this introduction is 'told' by Eleanor Zelliot, we have both contributed to it conceptually. To refer to ourselves in the third person, as some joint editors do in their introductions, did not appeal to us. The following framework of the field of study is therefore outlined by both of us.

* * * * *

The presence of poet-saints from all walks of life is one of the hallmarks of the bhakti (devotional religion) movement, which began in south India in the seventh century and left an imprint in the following centuries on most language areas in the subcontinent. Brahmins and low castes, farmers and cobblers, potters and tailors, drummers and even Muslims, joined in the passionate singing of religious experience. In at least three language areas, Tamil, Marathi, and Hindi, saint-poets from Untouchable castes are counted among those remembered in legend and song. Each of these saints who hail from the lowest of castes is surrounded by stories that give one an intense sense of real persons. All but one have left songs and poems that tell of devotion, but also at times are a revelation of the experience of being an Untouchable. Chokhamela and his family and Ravidas sang of their place in society, sometimes sorrowfully, and sang joyfully of their fellow *bhaktas*. Although time and the oral tradition have undoubtedly changed their songs, one still has a sense that these are the first authentic voices of Untouchables, those outside the four-fold varna system, and the only voices until the nineteenth century. In the south, there are no such voices. All that has survived from Tiruppan Alvar and Nandanar is one ecstatic song of praise to Vishnu. One wonders why this is so, especially since the legends about both the saints are so rich and poignant.

In the Tamil-speaking area in about the eighth or ninth century, the Untouchable Panar,[2] Tiruppan is heralded as a devotee of Vishnu among the twelve Alvars, and the Untouchable Pulai or Pulayan, Nandanar (or Nantanar), sometimes referred to as a Paraiyan,[3] is counted one of the sixty-three Nayanars, devotees of Shiva. In the fourteenth century, the Untouchable Mahar[4] Chokhamela, and his entire family—wife, son, sister, and brother-in-law—became honoured members of the Marathi-speaking pantheon of poet-saints. A century later, Ravidas or Raidas, a Chamar[5] from Varanasi, became one of the most well-known saints of the Hindi tradition. The work of these saints and the legends about them constitute an intriguing part of hierarchical Hinduism. What do those who are seen as polluting, as being beneath association or respect in society, have to say, to teach, to sing about the divine? How do the legends about them reconcile their low place in society with the high regard in which they are held as religious figures?

The presence of these Untouchable saints represents the belief that emerged in the bhakti movement that a human being from any caste, man or woman, could be beloved of God, or, if God was considered to be formless (*nirgun*), filled with the knowledge of the divine. In many of the legends about these saints, God shows special favour, even works a miracle, for those who were not allowed to enter the temple. Tiruppan Alvar was carried into the temple on the back of a Brahmin instructed to do so by God. The stone image of Shiva's bull, Nandi, was commanded by the Lord to move to one side so that Nandanar could see the image of God, even though he had to remain outside the temple. The statue of Vitthal at Pandharpur was found to have a swollen cheek after an indignant Brahmin struck Chokhamela. The image of Hari leapt into Ravidas's arms and the stone block on which he repaired shoes floated on the water when the aniconic symbols of the Brahmins did not. The legends claim that God accepted the devotion of these *bhaktas*, even when their contemporaries did not. And in Maharashtra and the north, Chokhamela and Ravidas were accepted by their fellow *bhaktas*, although not by the orthodox until, in the case of Ravidas, God worked a miracle indicating his divine favour.

The differences in the poetry of the Untouchable saints are in some ways more apparent than the similarity in the legends about them. While Tiruppan Alvar has left a long paean to Vishnu, we have no song at all from Nandanar. Tiruppan Alvar does not mention his caste in that song, but the legends about both make it clear that they are from the Untouchable strata of society. Chokhamela and his family, on the other hand, frequently use the caste name Mahar and mourn their low-caste status. An enormous volume of Marathi songs is attributed to this family: one hundred and ninety-two to Chokhamela, sixty-two to his wife, twenty-four to Chokhamela's sister, thirty-nine to his brother-in-law, and twenty-seven to his often angry son. These songs have survived in the canon of Marathi saint literature, together with a hundred and fifty-seven added to a later collection.[6] Ravidas is somewhere in between, stating the fact that his caste was leather-working but not dwelling on his hardships. In addition to the poetry that we have, later authors in all three language areas have gathered stories and legends in such quantity that we actually have a sense of the lives of these saints, their sufferings and their triumphs. We have chosen some of this older material especially to facilitate comparisons of the saints and the culture of the areas in which they flourished.

Terms and Practices Used

A few definitions and explanations are in order at the very beginning of this volume. We use the word *saint* advisedly. The Hindi/Marathi term *sant* is used for a holy man, a mendicant of pious behaviour, and in recent bhakti studies for *nirgun* bhakti practitioners, those devoted to the Formless One, the divine without qualities. The pioneering volume edited by Karine Schomer and W.H. McLeod, *The Sants* (1987), rejects the use of the word 'saint'. But the book by John Stratton Hawley and Mark Juergensmeyer published the next year is entitled *Songs of the Saints of India. Sant* is not used in most Tamil writing, and a 1988 study by Vidya Dehejia is entitled *Slaves of the Lord: The Path of the Tamil Saints.* Molesworth's classic 1831 Marathi dictionary defines *sant* as 'saint'. 'Saint' seems appropriate not only because it is becoming freely used in translations and studies, but also because 'saint' indicates a person of godly temperament, one whose behaviour is beyond question and who is genuinely 'good'. In contrast to the ideal 'guru', a master who can enlighten a disciple regardless of his or her own personal characteristics, the bhakti saint behaves in a pious way, and certainly these untouchable saints are models of saintly demeanour.

Some of our spellings are popular rather than scholarly in nature. We have chosen to write Chokhamela rather than Cokhamela, Chamar rather than Camar, also Chandal instead of Candal, in order to facilitate pronunciation. We have also used the spelling *brahmin* for the ritually highest caste in order to avoid confusion with the word for the inherent divine substance *brahman.* While Nandanar is also pronounced as Nantanar, we have retained the former spelling for the titles. Ravidas is also known as Raidas in the north; he is known as Rohidas in the Marathi-speaking area, and our articles use all three versions. The bibliography at the end of the volume is for all sources in the Indian languages as well as in English. We have also tried to keep away from theoretical discussions in our endeavour to present the Untouchable saints to a wider readership. The intention has been to narrate and to analyse, in non-theoretical jargon, the lives and literature of these saints and the implications of these on social structures. There is also some inevitable repetition in this volume, but it seemed necessary to us to make sure each article stood on its own.

'The bhakti (devotional religion) movement', the phrase in the opening sentence of this introduction, requires a longer explanation.[7] While bhakti in the sense of sharing with God, yoked to God, devotion to God, is an important concept at least as old in texts such as the *Bhagavad Gita* and probably a religious concept of much greater antiquity, the word 'movement' implies a historic context. Shaiva bhakti, devotion to Shiva, 'moves' from the Tamil region in the seventh to ninth centuries to its neighbouring Kannada-speaking region in the eleventh, although one can trace no direct links. Marathi bhakti emerges in the late thirteenth century with a centre in a town also holy to Kannada speakers, although the Marathi poets pay no tribute to either the Shaiva or Vaishnava Kannada traditions, and devotees from Karnataka do not join in the yearly *varkari* pilgrimage. In contrast, one can find many traces of a Marathi–Hindi connection. A Namdev who many think is the same as the Marathi-speaking Namdev travelled to the north to emerge as a voice in the collected songs of the Sikhs along with another Marathi saint, Trilochan. By the eighteenth century, the Brahmin biographer of all the Marathi-speaking saints, Mahipati, could include many Hindi-speaking saints in his collection of hundreds of stories, among them Tulsidas, Mirabai, Kabir, and Rohidas (Marathi usage for Ravidas, who is also known as Raidas in the north); he included the Gujarati Narsi Mehta as well. In the last *khanda* of the *Padma Purana*, Bhakti speaks: 'I was born in the Dravida country, matured in Karnataka, spent my youth wandering in Maharashtra, attained old age in Gujarat.'[8]

The Common Features of the Bhakti Movement

While the links between the regions are not always clear, there are 'benchmarks' or commonalities in the bhakti literature of the various language areas that mark the bhakti movement as a historical phenomenon in a way which, for example, the concept of *advaita vedanta* (non-dualistic) philosophy does not. These common features are:

- Acceptance of all castes and women into the fold of the saints; in some areas, the songs of Muslim saints are also included in the stories and the canon.
- The importance of the authors of the songs with legends about each author. In most cases, the saint 'signs' his poem with his or her own name, although the Tamil song of Tiruppan Alvar is an exception. The legends of the saints were collected a century, even centuries, later after their lives, in all three traditions–Tamil, Marathi and Hindi–showing how closely linked were the lives of the saints with their songs. The authors of much other religious literature are not known or, as in the cases of the epic authors, Vyas and Valmiki, are mythical.
- In the three traditions represented here–Tamil, Marathi, and Hindi--knowledge of a circle of saints, a companionship or a fellowship, is expressed often in the songs themselves, or is seen at least in the later collections of the saints' lives.
- A critical attitude towards orthodox religion, expressed harshly at times, in most *bhaktas*' songs, although this is not true of the Tamil Untouchables. There are no recorded songs of Nandanar and only one of Tiruppan and that is not at all critical, but since anti-orthodoxy is generally true of other bhakti saints, the silence seems significant. Some modern writers have detected 'rebellion' among the Tamil saints by virtue of the legends about them.
- Usually some sort of ongoing institution: a pilgrimage in Maharashtra; a new sect, the Virashaivas, in Karnataka; a new religion, Sikhism, in the Punjab; a host of groups owing devotion to one or another of the Hindi-area saints such as the Kabirpanthis or Dadupanthis; bhajan sessions in the Tamil country as well as in Maharashtra and the Hindi area; the presence of rows of statues of the Nayanars in or just outside Tamil temples, etc.
- The vernacular as the medium used by the *bhaktas*. In Marathi and Hindi, the songs are among the first vernacular literature of the area.
- Personal experience as the basis for the *bhaktas*' songs. This is perhaps the most telling of all the benchmarks. Often the occupation of the saint provides metaphors for the association

with the divine, but in any case, the bond between the saint and the divine is intensely personal.

THE TAMIL SAINTS: TIRUPPAN ALVAR AND NANDANAR

Bhakti in its medieval form of identifiable saint-poets singing of God in the tongue of their area emerged in the Tamil country in the seventh–ninth centuries CE. The Tamil Shaiva saints, called the Nayanars, numbered sixty-three and included court aristocrats, Brahmins, peasants, an Untouchable, and a woman. The circle of Vaishnava saint-poets of the same period, the twelve Alvars, although far fewer in number, also included a range of classes and castes. Tamil was already an established literary language by the time the saint-poets appeared, but the content of that literature was generally didactic, romantic, or heroic, with some songs dedicated to the god Murugan. The saint-poets added a vast quantity of more specifically religious poetry dedicated to the worship of Shiva or Vishnu.

Tiruppan Alvar (eighth–ninth century CE) was perhaps the earliest Untouchable poet within the Hindu tradition to be thought of as a saint. His poem in praise of the Vishnu image of Ranganatha at Srirangam was introduced into temple and home worship by the eleventh century and is still recited in all Srivaishnava temples as part of the daily liturgy. Vasudha Narayanan has given us a beautiful translation of the poem in her essay, written specifically for this volume. Steven Hopkins has set the poem in the tradition of the Song of Solomon as well as given us a reference to Tiruppan in the work of a much later poet. Hopkins's article, which is somewhat shortened in this volume, gives a most unusual reading of this poem, very different from a comment on caste or untouchability.

In contrast to some other Alvars, Tiruppan does not leave a signature name. His long poem is a straightforward panegyric, praising Ranganatha as the manifestation of Vishnu in the Srirangam temple. There is no reference to caste in Tiruppan's lyric, although it is possible that 'slave of slaves', the term used by Hopkins, refers to his status. Note that Narayanan in her article uses the term 'servant', not slave in her translation. Hopkins's initial stanza reads:

I

Pure primordial lord,
    radiant god who has made me a slave

of slaves; flawless
    overlord of angels
who lives in Venkata of fragrant groves;
    sinless dweller
in righteous heaven–
    our dear father,
here in Arangam of long high rampart walls:

It seems as if his lovely lotus feet
    have come and entered
my eyes!

Tiruppan Alvar begins with a description of the feet of the sleeping Vishnu. According to legend, the moment that Tiruppan Alvar finished his poem by describing the mouth of Vishnu, he disappeared into the feet of the Lord of Srirangam.

Hopkins translates the final verse this way:

As the cowherd boy
his mouth ate the sweet butter:

the Lord the colour of a rain cloud
    entered me,
ravished my heart.

Ruler of all worlds,
    Jewel of Arangam
These eyes, seeing him,
    My nectar
Will never see anything else.

Disappearing into the feet is an appropriate way for an Untouchable to be absorbed into the Lord, but it does not necessarily refer to his caste status since humility before the Lord is a *bhakta*'s characteristic mood.

Tiruppan Alvar's name reveals his identity, although the given name of the poet has not been retained. *Tiru* is an honorary term of respect. *Pan* means song and *panar* or *panan* indicates a bard or singer.[9] *Alvar*, the title given by the Srivaishnavas to the twelve poet-saints, means those deeply immersed in the love of God. The name reveals that

Tiruppan Alvar is the poet-saint, worshipper of Vishnu, who belonged to the class of Untouchable bards. Tiruppan is the only Alvar whose name tells us his clan or caste.[10]

A biography of Tiruppan Alvar appears in each of the five collections of the lives of the Alvars written between the twelfth and the fifteenth centuries.[11] The stories in these collections are traditional hagiographies, a combination of fact and myth. According to most, Tiruppan Alvar was born near Srirangam, just across the river from the temple town. He was an incarnation of the mole on Vishnu's chest, born in a class lower than the four varnas or, in some legends, was found in a rice field by a man of the Panar caste. His singing, a gift traditionally associated with the Panars, was exceptionally sweet, but he was not able to go to Srirangam to see the Lord about whom he sang. The goddess Lakshmi asked the Lord to bring Tiruppan into the inner temple, but Tiruppan refused because of his impurity and refused a second time because of his sins. But the Lord then instructed a Brahmin, Loka Saranga Muni, to put the Panar on his shoulders and bring him into the inner sanctum of Srirangam. So, riding on the shoulders of a Brahmin, Tiruppan was brought into the temple. In this way the devotee was rewarded with the sight of the Lord but did not set foot on temple ground. It is not stated, but it is clear that this unusual act of a Brahmin also performed the function of preventing the pollution of the temple floor. As he gazed at the Lord, here called Ranganatha, he sang the ten songs of the experience of looking at the Lord from foot to head. This poem of Tiruppan Alvar is often sung in Tamil bhajan sessions and in temple services.

In a corollary story, crucial in the twentieth century but not found in the medieval biographies, a muni went to the river to fetch water for the bathing of the Lord, found Tiruppan there immersed in song, and asked him to move away. Tiruppan did not hear him, and the muni threw a stone at Tiruppan, who bled profusely. When the muni carried the water into the temple, he found the forehead of the image of the Lord covered in blood. In the contemporary *Amar Chitra Katha* comic book retelling of the story, the priest hit Tiruppan on the head with his stick. The comic book also gives a north Indian character to the story by relating that the child was abandoned by his parents and raised not by bards but by a 'sweeper', a change which reflects a north Indian stereotype of Untouchables as sweepers, bhangi, or leather workers, not as bards.

Narayanan describes an Untouchable community in Bangalore which is devoutly Srivaishnava. The first temple in their area was to 'their' *bhakta*, Tiruppan Alvar, but the chief worship and the main temple is for the high-caste Nammalvar, the most beloved of the Alvars. It is quite possible that the community consists of descendants of Untouchables converted to Srivaishnavism by the eleventh-century philosopher Ramanuja and were given special privileges by him of temple entry, which are today not used. A poem by Nammalvar would indicate acceptance of Untouchable saints as equals, or even 'masters':

The four castes
    uphold all clans;
go down, far down
    to the lowliest outcastes
    of outcastes:

if they are the intimate henchmen
    of our lord
    with the wheel in his right hand,
    his body dark as blue sapphire,
then even the slaves of their slaves
    are our masters.[12]

The Srivaishnava community hailed Tiruppan as the paradigmatic devotee. As an exemplary devotee, Tiruppan Alvar, like the woman devotee Antal, was considered to be an exception to the normal social order, not someone who disturbed it.

* * * * *

In Tamil Shaiva bhakti, the list of saints, the Nayanars, is much longer—sixty-three in number—and in contrast to other circles of saint-poets, many of the saints were not composers of hymns. The Untouchable Nandanar (also transliterated as Nantanar) is among the Shaiva saints who are remembered by deeds, not songs. The hagiographic work that is basic to Tamil Shaiva bhakti is the twelfth-century collection of Cekkilar, whose *Periya Puranam* tells of the character and deeds of each saint. So interesting is Cekkilar's life of Nandanar that we have included it here in Karen Pechilis Prentiss's article and have also referred to various editions of the *Periya Puranam* in English in the Bibliography.

Nandanar was born in a Pulai (or Pulaiyan) community just outside the town of Atanur on the Coleroom river, in the Pulaippadi, the living quarters of the Pulaiyas. It is described by Cekkilar in evocative terms: dark-skinned children with bracelets of black iron, a labourer sending her baby to sleep on a sheet of leather, drums hanging from mango trees, crows crowing before dawn to call the Pulaiyan to their day's work, the women staggering in intoxication in a dance after husking paddy (Manickam 1990: 20–1). The hamlet was 'thick with kith and kin, the thatched huts connected by green gourd creepers spreading across their roofs'. Nandanar was a village servant, a watchman, a town crier who beat the drum and provided skin coverings for the drums in the temples of the Lord, and worked in the fields as well. From birth he was 'endowed both with prior knowledge of Shiva and with a character that was suited to his hereditary station in life . . . he excelled at the traditional agricultural duties', writes Prentiss, and another legend tells us that he was assigned work in the fields too onerous for any one man, and God helped him to finish the task.

Nandanar not only made musical instruments out of leather, such as the drum and strings for the vina, but he would also sing and dance outside the Shaiva temple. One day he set out on a pilgrimage to see Shiva at Tiruppunkur. He could only stand at the entrance to the temple and his view of Shiva was obstructed by the image of Shiva's bull, Nandi. Shiva granted Nandanar darshan (a sight of the Lord) by moving the bull to one side. It is said that for this reason the bull is still off centre at the temple. Nandanar was in ecstasy, and began to visit many temples. For him, Chidambaram was the most sacred place in Tamil country, but because of his polluting status, he put off the trip, saying, 'I will go tomorrow', a phrase which has become one of his alternative names: Nalaippovar, 'he who will go tomorrow'.

Eventually, Nandanar went to Chidambaram and circled the temple night and day, longing to see Shiva Nataraj. Then, hearing Shiva's voice in a dream, he entered a fire that was built at the temple entrance, emerged as a Brahmin on the other side, entered the temple, and merged with the image of the dancing Shiva. The reaction of some Untouchables to the idea that Nandanar had to burn himself alive in order to change his caste is described later in this essay.

The story of Nandanar continued to be told. In the nineteenth century, Gopalakrishna Bharati wrote the *Nantanar Charittira Kirtanai* (the kirtan of the story of Nandanar) to celebrate the life of the saint, which was first told in the twelfth-century *Periya Puranam.* His retelling became the standard version of the hagiography, immensely popular among urban Tamils and giving rise to at least eight additional versions. His purpose was perhaps to convert the Pulaiyas to Shaiva bhakti as a way of uplifting them. Some years later, Gopalakrishna Bharati wrote the *Nantanar Charitram* (The Story of Nantanar), a dramatic rendering of Cekkilar's classic, but with emphasis on the social disabilities endured by Nandanar's caste. Bharati used the term 'May I come'? as the first words of his drama as well as a refrain, a reference to the legend that Nandanar had to yell this request at the entrance of each street as a warning to high-caste people. In spite of, or perhaps because, of its social message Paul Younger (1995: 226) reports: 'One of the most beloved of Tamil operas is the *Nantanar Charitram* of Gopalakrishna Bharati, which elaborates on the story of the watchman who could never get to see the Dancing Image until he was found one day in the sacrificial fire of the priests.'

There have also been more contemporary adaptations of the story. Manickam (1990: 14–17) reports that K.B. Sundarambal staged the story several times; a Tamil film on Nandanar starred Dandapani Desigar; N.S. Krishnan popularized the Nandanar story through a narrative art form; and A. Padmanabhan published *Saint Nandanar*, a small booklet for schoolchildren. Manickam adds information on Bharati's drama, noting that Bharati's Nantanar was a rebel and that Bharati added a Brahmin landlord to the story to represent conflicting social orders. Manickam concludes that while the medieval biography was a justification of the status quo, Bharati's purpose was to 'mitigate the tyranny of caste through awareness-building'.

Karen Pechilis Prentiss reports that a tank (a pond of water) in Chidambaram is considered holy because it is believed to be the spot where Nandanar emerged from the fire. There is also a small temple, recently built, to Nandanar in the south-west corner of the town, which means that 'Nandanar has become the temple'.

Lynn Vincentnathan's fieldwork in a community near Chidambaram offers more information on the meaning of Nandanar today (Vincentnathan 1993: 164–72). She interviewed both Paraiyas and caste Hindus and discovered striking differences in their versions of the stories. Caste Hindu legends of Nandanar often make him out to be an anomaly as an Untouchable; he is in their versions a Brahmin, or perhaps even God himself, somehow encased in an Untouchable's body, coming to his proper and real being through fire. Other legends told by caste Hindus stress Nandanar's acceptance of caste rules, his obedience to his master, and his unwillingness to try to enter the temple. Untouchables, however, have no problem in believing the Untouchable Nandanar's piety as an Untouchable. His troubles are all caused by Brahmins; God is always on his side. 'For Untouchables, their versions of the Nandanar legend fit in with what they know about themselves– that they are capable of religiosity comparable or superior to that of caste Hindus' (Vincentnathan: 174).

The film version of Nandanar's life shows him becoming absorbed into God's thigh; however, these Untouchable devotees prefer to think of him 'swallowed by God'. A touching image in the mind of one informant interprets the sashes floating on either side of the image of Shiva Nataraj at Chidambaram as the legs of Nandanar, symbolizing the merging of the saint with the God (Vincentnathan, 172). It should be added that for the younger Untouchables today, Nandanar is not much of a hero. They have other heroes, such as Dr B.R. Ambedkar,[13] and either do not know much about or are not interested in the obedient Nandanar. The criticism of at least the way Nandanar is portrayed as becoming a Brahmin by immolating himself goes back many decades. There are reports that there were objections to the portrayal of Nandanar in the Tamil film among workers in the Kolar gold fields in the 1920s.

Chokhamela, His Family, and the Marathi Tradition

As is customary in the Marathi tradition, Chokhamela was a householder, and the fact that his wife, son, sister, and brother-in-law were also saints and poets is also not unusual for the many saint-poets in the Marathi-speaking area.[14] But the very volume of their poetry, and their extraordinary consciousness of their caste status, gives us considerable insight into the ethos of the time as well as their own devotion to the God Vitthal or Vithoba of Pandharpur. Although the manuscript findings for Marathi are not nearly as full or authentic as those found in Rajasthan for the Hindi-area sants, and there are no manuscripts at all for Chokhamela, we are fortunate in having a compendium of all the saints' poetry, appropriately entitled *Sri-sakalsantgatha* (1923) (All the Holy Sants' Works), and English translations of much of the hagiographic material that tells their legends (Mahipati: 1933).

Rohini Mokashi-Punekar's work on Chokhamela reveals an unusual poetic sensibility even as it gives a compelling narrative of Chokhamela's life. The material on Banka and Karmamela is probably the first to appear in English and portrays the very unusual situation of an entire family devoted to Vithoba and to song-poems. Banka is Chokhamela's brother-in-law and probably Soyrabai's brother. Whether or not Karmamela is the rebel of the family is a question—many *abhangas* indicate extreme discomfort, even anger, with his place in life.

The life of Chokhamela includes miracles but none are as dramatic as those of the Tamil country. Legend does give him and his son miraculous births, but aside from this there is no attempt to relate his existence to any other realm than that of the Untouchables. In other words, he has not been brahminized, although the birth legends contain possibilities. According to a popular story, his birth involves his parents' carrying mangoes to Pandharpur (some say Bidar, which would make more sense if Chokhamela lived in Pandharpur) on the orders of the village headman, a duty expected of the Mahar village servant. On their journey, the god Vitthal, worshipped as the central figure in the Marathi bhakti tradition, disguised as a Brahmin, begged a fruit from Chokhamela's mother. The Brahmin tasted it, found it sour, and returned it to her. She tucked it into the folds of her sari and delivered the other mangoes to the priests at Pandharpur. The fruit was counted, the number found to be short, and so she pulled the bitten mango from her sari—and it had taken the form of a lovely child, Chokhamela.[15] It seems to us that the Brahmin here is simply a characteristic kind of beggar to whom alms would naturally be given, or whose requests met, and his appearance probably does not signify the brahminization of the Chokhamela story.

According to Mahipati[16] in a kirtan so vivid we have reproduced most of it later in this volume, Chokhamela's home was Pandharpur, the destination of the pilgrimage of the Vaishnava saints of Maharashtra. He would bathe in the Bhima, circumambulate the whole city, and then prostrate himself in front of the main door of the great Pandharpur temple of Vitthal. He could not go into the temple. However, one night the Lord of Pandharpur himself took Chokhamela by the hand and 'lovingly led him into the innermost shrine'. A Brahmin priest heard Chokhamela talking to the god, and thought, selfishly, according to Mahipati, 'If a man of low caste can touch the god on whom are garments and ornaments, then our duties as Brahmins will cease.' The

Brahmin told Chokhamela to go to the other side of the Chandrabhaga river (the name for the Bhima as it runs past Pandharpur) lest the Lord keep bringing him into the temple. Chokhamela protested that the Ganga is not polluted by low castes, nor is the holy earth defiled, but he left the temple domains and worshipped from afar. God came to him there and dined with him. His wife spilled some food on God and a nearby Brahmin who heard Chokhamela talking to God about the accident came near and slapped Chokhamela on the face. But when the Brahmin went into the temple, he found food on the clothes of god's image, and the cheek of the idol was swollen. And so the Brahmin repented and took Chokhamela by the hand into the temple.

One wonders where Mahipati got his story. The samadhi (memorial place) of Chokhamela is at the foot of the great door of the temple in Pandharpur and until the independence of India in 1947, no Untouchable could go beyond that spot. A Brahmin reformer, Sane Guruji, fasted for days in front of the great door, fighting for the rights of the Untouchables. (See V.L. Manjul's eyewitness account in 'God in a Copper Pot' in this volume.)

Chokhamela himself was both a devout and often joyous singer of songs of devotion and a man anguished by his status in life. His poem on purity is the strongest of any of the saint-poets:

> The only impurity is in the five elements;
>   the same impurity pervades the whole world.
> Then who is pure and who is impure?
> The cause of pollution is the creation of the body.
> In the beginning, at the end,
>   there is nothing but pollution.
> No one knows anyone who was born pure.
> Chokha says, in wonder, who is pure?
>
> (*Abhanga* 84)[17]

He is also capable of an almost amusing sense of a God for those pure and those impure:

> [They say] in the company of the lowly, God is polluted.
>   Bathing him in water makes him pure.
> But he is pure from the beginning; where can he be impure?
>   He is the see-er and the act of seeing.
>   He is pure in the place of the pure;

why should he not be impure in the place of the impure?
Chokhā says, God is different for both; I have filled my eyes
only with him. (*Abhanga* 85)

And Chokhamela sang one angry *abhanga* which ridicules the very idea of pollution:

The Vedas are polluted; the Shastras are polluted;
the Puranas are full of pollution.
The soul is polluted; the oversoul is polluted;
the body is full of pollution
Brahma is polluted, Vishnu is polluted
Shankar is full of pollution
Birth is polluted; death is polluted.
Chokha says: there is pollution at the beginning and at the end.
(*Abhanga* 86)

The song of Chokhamela, which is sung by pilgrims on the path to Pandharpur, could be interpreted as a reference to his low caste, but not necessarily:

Cane is crooked, but its juice isn't crooked.
Why be fooled by outward appearance?
The bow is curved, but the arrow is straight.
Why be fooled by outward appearance?
The river is twisting, but its water isn't twisted.
Why be fooled by outward appearance?
Chokha is ugly, but his feelings aren't ugly.
Why be fooled by outward appearance?
(*Abhanga* 125)

This translation is chiefly by Maxine Berntsen, who encourages her students in her school in Phaltan (a town on the pilgrimage route to Pandharpur) to create their own versions of Chokhamela's songs. R.D. Ranade (1961: 161) is more caste conscious; his final line reads: 'Chokha may be Untouchable but his heart is not Untouchable.' The word for the qualities of the cane, the bow, the river, and Chokha himself is the same, the Kannada word *donga*, which has a multiplicity of meanings. In his poem in this essay, Sadanand More twists the well-known line of Chokhamela to make an ironic comment on the current state of bhakti.

Many of the other saint-poets of Maharashtra sang of Chokhamela. Namdev the tailor told a long story of the birth of Chokhamela's son. It seems that Chokhamela was distressed at the idea of the messiness of the coming birth, and left his pregnant wife to visit his sister. When her time came, the God himself in the guise of Chokhamela's sister came to help her with the birth and the rituals of birthing. Chokhamela returned in time to greet his healthy new son, and his ever-forgiving wife said, 'You just missed seeing your sister.' Then Chokhamela said, 'That was the God Vithoba Himself.' The story is told with great realism, and with no credit at all to the saint. (See Zelliot on Nirmala and Soyrabai in this volume.) Namdev, in a well known story, went to Mangalvedhe after Chokhamela's death which occurred when he was repairing the wall of the city and found his bones to bring to the samadhi in Pandharpur. He recognized the bones of the saint because they emitted the sound of the name of God, 'Vitthal, Vitthal'.

Jani or Janabai, the serving maid of Namdev and a well-known and very imaginative *bhakta* (Sellergren, 1996), a contemporary of Chokhamela, sings:

> Low-caste Chokhamela yearned for bhakti
> God became his servant, sheltered always in his house
> God ate in his house because of his true devotion
> People say he polluted God, but Jani sings a song. [18]

Jani also creates a picture which is reproduced on posters at various sites enroute the Pandharpur pilgrimage; the various *bhaktas* of her fourteenth-century world are included in this description:

> My Vitthal has many children
>   with him is a merry crowd.
> Nivritti rides on his shoulder
>   he holds Sopan by the hand.
> Dnyaneshwar walks in front
>   beautiful Mukta close behind
> Gora the potter rides his hip
> Chokha is in his very heart
> Vunka [Banka?] clings to his waist
> Nama holds his smallest finger
> Jani says, Oh Gopala,
>   it is a festival of your dear ones.

Eknath, a radical Brahmin,[19] sang in the sixteenth century:

> What bhakti was Chokha's bhakti! God loved him because of his love.
> God dragged the dead carcasses into His house; He did the low dirty work Himself.
> Janardan [Eknath's Guru, here God] Himself was midwife to his wife.
> Look! What love for the devotee! God was drawn to his joy.
> He did not mind his low caste. Look! Ekajanardan longs for Chokha.

Tukaram in the seventeenth century has some strong comments to make about caste, including this poem specifically about Mahars, Chokhamela's own caste:

> He's not a Brahmin who abhors
> The touch of a Mahar.
> What retribution can he pay?
> He won't throw his life away!
>
> A Chandala drives him wild,
> It's his heart that is defiled.
> Tuka says, his caste is defined
> By what fills his mind.
>
> (translated by Gail Omvedt and Bharat Patankar)

Tukaram has also praised Chokhamela in an *abhanga* which does not refer to his caste, only his character.[20]

> Out of a thousand of the King's soldiers,
> You will get twelve good ones.
> There is one commander among hundreds of thousands of men.
> For a rupee and a quarter you get five 'pearls',
> But one real pearl goes for thousands.
> The cowries in a rupee will fill a gunny sack,
> But a gold coin can be tied in the end of a scarf.
> Listen, among hundreds of people there is one virtuous person.
> Tuka says, He is Chokha from Pandhari.[21]

Tukaram as well as Jani, Namdev, and Eknath have songs which indicate the importance of bhakti in the Marathi-speaking area as a close and continuing tradition of saints, a *panth* or *sampradaya*. Tukaram's *abhanga* in part reads:

> Who is purified by pride
> of varna, tell me if you know!
> Untouchables are saved by hymns to Hari . . .
>
> Tuladhar Vaishya, the potmaker Gora,
> the leatherworker Rohidas,
> the momin Kabir, Latif the Muslim,
> the barber Sena are servants of Vishnu.
>
> Kanhopatra, Khodu, cotton-carder Dadu . . .
> Banka, Chokhamela, by caste Mahar,
> all have united with the Lord . . .
>
> Vishnu's servants have no caste![22]

Chokhamela, however, does not sing of other saints, except in *Abhanga* 64, which adds Kabir and 'Rohidas Chambhar' to the list of the Marathi saints, and another one not in the canon of *Srisakalsantgatha* which asks for a daughter like Mira (Chokhamela 1950). These songs are clearly, at least in part, additions to the earlier songs, since none of the north Indian saints lived in Chokhamela's time, but they also indicate a strong sense of a tradition with links past and present. It is also interesting that Chokhamela does not sing of his work, not of removing cows from the village nor obeying the orders of the village headman, even though other songs tell of God's helping Chokhamela to drag out the dead cattle from the village. And by legend Chokhamela was killed when the wall of Mangalvedhe, a town near Pandharpur, caved in on him as he was mending it, which seems to have been Mahar work.

Chokhamela's wife Soyrabai[23] often calls herself 'Chokha's Mahari', and refers quite frequently to her low status. She is also conscious of being very poor, and her most famous line concerns the simple food she gives the God:

> I'll place a leaf before You and I will serve you family food.
> O God, it's not fit for You, but imagine it sweet and accept it.

And then Soyrabai refers to Puranic stories, and stories from the *Mahabharata* and *Ramayana* that indicate her poverty:

> Vidur served watered broken rice, O mother and father, O Lord.
> O Narayana, Draupadi's one leaf smeared with leftover food satisfied You.
> It's just like that here, says the Mahari of Chokha.
>
> (*Abhanga* 1)

There are references to her low caste and that of her husband here and there in her poetry: 'O God, I am lowly.' 'The great river flowed, but my body is still not pure.' 'The Brahmins of Pandhari harassed Chokha.' She also uses the images of sitting at the great door of the temple at Pandharpur (but going no farther) and of receiving gladly the God's leftover food, both of which are Mahar references. In two poems, however, she is specifically and keenly aware of pollution and equally adamant that purity is a state of mind, not of the body. In a powerful poem, she cries:

> Not a creature in the world has a place of origin anywhere other than in gore.
> This is the glory of God; defilement exists within.
> The body is polluted from within. Be sure of it, says the Mahari of Chokha.
>
> (*Abhanga* 6)

The basic tone of Soyrabai's poetry, in spite of many references to low status, is a delightful intimacy with God, a scolding, loving, very close relationship. 'I sit shouting at Your door,' she tells God. She threatens him: 'Now, if You discard me, who will call You great? 'I sit alone and talk to You. I embrace Your feet.' 'Our conditions are different; who will take us to their bosoms? Who will care for us? Except You? Now You understand. Now do whatever You feel proper. That's all I have to say.' 'What a tease You are; why do You say no to me? Now I don't have any respect for You, but I have no other love. How much should I say, Lord? Now, don't be angry with me.'

Soyrabai also glories in the festival of Pandharpur with all its noise and music and colour. And she delights in her sister-in-law Nirmala, whom she sees as merging in Chokhamela to form the divine. And she revels in the Name, which is the only antidote to the worldly life that she despises because it keeps her from God.

Nirmala, Chokhamela's sister, speaks of her low caste only once in her twenty-four poems. Chiefly she regrets the limitations of this worldly married life, samsar, and delights in the God of Pandharpur who is 'an ocean of bliss, a storehouse of beauty'. One poem does stress in an interesting way her belief, shared among almost all saint-poets, in the efficacy of chanting the name of God, although its meaning is ambivalent; must one go through innumerable births or will chanting the Name free one?:

> The name of Hari is on the lips only of the one
> who has merit tied in his garments throughout innumerable births.
> The name of Hari is on the lips only of the one
> who carries in his purse the good deeds of innumerable births.
> The chanting of Narayan's name is only for the one
> who has practised discipline throughout innumerable births.
> The sweetness of Hari's name is only for the one
> who has left worldly attachments throughout innumerable births.
> Nirmala says, the sin of innumerable births disappears as you chant the Name.
>
> (*Abhanga* 9)

Although Soyrabai speaks of her husband, Nirmala never mentions her husband. Her final *abhanga* concludes:

> At the great door, Chokha and his sister prostrate themselves.

But she gives no hint that neither of them can go beyond the great door of the Pandharpur temple to actually see the God Vithoba.

The songs of Karmamela, the son of Chokhamela and Soyrabai, are rather unusual in that he accuses God of forgetting him, making him low caste, creating a miserable life for him, indeed behaving very badly. An example of this is *Abhanga* 4:

> Are we happy when we're with You? O Cloud-dark one, You don't know!

The low place is our lot, the low place is our lot, the low place is our lot.
We never get good sweet food. It's a shameful life for us here.
It's a festival of bliss for You, but misery is written on our faces.
Chokha's Karmamela asks, O God, why is this our fate?

But then in another mood, in *Abhanga* 17, he accepts his lot in life:

Which joys and sorrows are tied in our garments, that was decided long long ago.
Now what use is it to call it bad? We will endure our daily lives.
You are all-pervading, different from all else;
we will endure the fruit of our karma.
Karmamela says, according to Your promise,
we have come to know our inner selves.

This philosophical acceptance is so unlike the majority of Karmamela's songs that one wonders if it is authentic. If one wants proof that an Untouchable saint-poet feels deeply the curse of his birth, Karmamela offers the most evidence.

Banka, the husband of Nirmala and possibly the brother of Chokhamela's wife, Soyrabai, speaks of many different subjects, most of them quite the usual happy and peaceful observation of the beautiful god of Pandharpur. He does occasionally speak of birth in a low caste, but the more usual poem is praise of the god Vitthal, who is not known in the Sanskrit texts:

The *Agamas* and the *Nigamas* don't know God in this form;
Shruti and *Shastra* don't know His greatness.
That God, *Srihari* [i.e.Vishnu], fills our eyes and hearts,
stands as Vitthal on the bank of the Bhima.
Ocean of happiness, protector of bhaktas
That One's fame resounds among the moving and the unmoving.
Banka says, He is such a Great God,
and He comes so easily to those who love Him.
(*Abhanga* 37)

Banka refers to a dozen other saint-poets in his verses, including a reference to Mirabai which must have been inserted later since the

Rajasthani princess lived at least a hundred years after Banka. He also refers to Puranic stories, again a common theme among Marathi saint-poets of all castes. At times, his story-telling ability enters the verse; this is seen in the following *abhanga* about the potter-saint Gora, who was a contemporary of Chokhamela and his family:

Look, what a wonder! At Gora's place
God himself has become a potter.
He's left aside all his wealth,
His vehicle [the eagle] that roams the three worlds has become a donkey.
He fills the gunny sack [with clay], brings it in Himself;
His wife helps Him.
Banka says: about this fondness of God towards His bhaktas,
the Vedas don't say a word!

(*Abhanga* 31)

Banka also tells stories about his own family, describing the birth of Karmamela in this way: God knew about the wish of Chokhamela's wife Soyrabai for a child, and so he came to her door in the guise of an old Brahmin beggar asking for food. She protested that she was a low-caste Mahar and couldn't think of doing such a wrong thing as giving him something to eat, that people would censure her, beat her, thrash her, if she did. But he persisted and told her that would have a child if she gave him a morsel. So she gave him a bowl of rice and curd. When Chokhamela came home, he was extremely angry with his wife for her action! And Banka does not tell us if he was ever reconciled, ending cryptically with another reference to God's coming to the 'broken hut' of Chokhamela and staying there.

There is still another Mahar, a woman, who enters the contemporary bhakti canon. Nothing is known about Bhagu and she is not considered a part of Chokhamela's family, but she is identified as 'Bhagu Maharin' in the *Srisakalsantgatha*. One of her poems is reminiscent of the south Indian story of Tiruppan Alvar's being carried into the temple:

We have come for Your darshan ; please meet us.
All the saints are inside the temple.
I am alone outside, pining.
Oh Mother Vithu, listen to my plea.

I am a poor girl, please meet me.
God came outside and took me in on Her shoulder.
Says Bhaga, I met God and my fears disappeared.
(*Abhanga* 1)

Many of the saints refer to God (and to the most important of the saints) as Mother, but no other poem that I am aware of in the Marathi tradition tells of God as either male or female carrying in an Untouchable saint on his/her shoulder into the temple.

Among the Dalits of Maharashtra, Chokhamela is now only of minimal interest. There is some attention given to him by scholars and there is a certain pride in the fact that a Mahar was creative six centuries ago, but there is no *dindi* to Pandharpur and only the traditional pujaris pay attention to the shrine of Chokhamela at the foot of the great door. Chokha was part of the Hindu tradition which has been rejected by most former Mahars in favour of egalitarian Buddhism; Chokha also accepted that his status was because of his previous sins, a belief no longer acceptable to present-day former Mahars.

But Chokhamela does inspire some creativity. A very unusual example is a poem by Daya Pawar from the Marathi journal *Sadhana* (November 1991), which casts blame on the God himself. The reference to the river Indrayani brings to mind the story of Tukaram, who was made to throw his book of songs into the river by the orthodox; the songs were miraculously restored to him. The late Daya Pawar was one of the most influential of the Dalit literary group as an autobiographer, a poet, and a consultant on film:

O Lord of Pandhari, why is Chokha outside your temple?
You are really the false one, you're the one who showed him his
place.

Your devotees came to the door of the temple.
But you created a wall, you with your hands on your hips,
And now you are afraid, you hide in the inner sanctum.

When Chokha comes forward, they throw stones at him,
they smash his bones.
This Indrayani is a river of blood.

That step he stepped on moans in heat and rain.
You are inside, dressed in brocade, underneath the decorated parasol.
Your silver eyes have become blind white stone.

Another response is from Sadanand More, a professor at the University of Pune and himself a descendant of the bhakti poet Tukaram. His ironic poem refers to a campaign by the reformer Baba Adhav to get villages to commit to One Village, One Well. One senses that the village is Tukaram's own home place, Dehu, and the new version of the slogan, 'One Village, One Hooch House', may be based on reality. 'Atpat' is the way traditional folk tales begin, 'once upon a time'.

Ek Gaon Ek Hatbhatti (One Village One Hooch House)

One day an urgent order came from above to the police patil of atpat village.
If in one week there is not 'one village, one well', then your
rationing supply will be stopped.

The patil, the sarpanch, the gramsevak all were astonished.
'Oh my, our village river is of historic importance:
Brahmin ghat, Kunbi ghat, and, below all others, Mahar ghat.
Let us protect these historical remains.'
(Near the lands of the police patil are the Mahar *watan*
lands grabbed by the *inamdars.*)

Do you want to test our egalitarianism?
Why do you want to wait a week?
Come any time within a week.
Let it be a surprise visit.
Come in your uniform or come in ordinary clothes.
Its okay if it's the Sunday holiday.
At our place, its
one village, one illicit still!

Next to the gate is a Chokhamela temple.
Going on the road around the village,
our ancestors used to do *namaskar* to that temple.

They never went inside.
'Chokha may be ugly but his spirit is not ugly'?
they used to sing that *abhanga*, but from outside!

Compared to our ancestors, we are very advanced.
We are educated, we are cultured,
Even more, we are reformers.
We are aware of the twentieth century.

Folk outside the temple converted
and since then we have taken care of the temple.

Before the conversion, Bhiva Mahar
used to light the lamp in the evening
in that temple.

For that, he got *inam* land
but Chandbhai's Amin eyed it
and one day got possession of that land.
Where was Kashi, where was Gaya, where, where
was the Kabah?
(Selfishness steps in and men quickly forget religion, brother.)

Bhiva became unemployed. He took the form of Chokhoba.
We couldn't stand his unemployment.
We had to help him.

Down with unemployment, save Bhiva!
Everyday the prices of things went higher and higher.

For him we started a small-scale industry
right there in the temple.
The capital was ours, the advertising was ours.
The whole enterprise was ours.

From then on the temple became
a socially useful building.
If there is a raid, we are totally ready.
Come any time, come any way,
we always get some warning!

As a rule, every evening
if any guest turns up–
at proper or improper times–
we all come together there:
untouchable–touchable, caste–non caste;
Hindu, Muslim, Christian, Buddhist;
Brahmin, Kshatriya, Vaishya, Shudra
everyone has equal rights there.

Sitting hip to hip and touching our glasses,
we drown all the differences,
we wash away all the inequalities.
Everyday we have a drink of the Ganga of equality.
There, no one has pride
about anything.

'Chokha may be ugly, but liquor is not ugly.'

Why should our village need any other new measure of progress?
At our place we have
one village, one liquor still.[24]

Ravidas: Best Known of the Untouchable Saint-Poets

Of all the Untouchable saint-poets, the fifteenth-sixteenth century Ravidas or Raidas is by far the most important today. Groups of Chamars use Ravidasi or Raidasi instead of their caste name. Temples to him are still being built, including one by Ravidasi Sikhs (former Untouchable converts from the Chamar caste) and an impressive one by the late Jagjivan Ram, both in Varanasi. Books in Hindi abound; there are more in English by Indian scholars than about any other low-caste *bhakta*; and a critical edition of Ravidas's *vani* has been completed by Winand Callewaert. He is important in Uttar Pradesh, Bihar and Rajasthan and also among the Chambhars in Maharashtra.[25] More non-Indian scholars have worked on Ravidas than on other Untouchable saints. Ravidas is included in Hawley and Juergensmeyer's *Songs of the Saints of India* (1988); an article by Joseph Schaller appears in Lorenzen's *Bhakti Religion in North India* (1995) and another one in this volume; and Callewaert and Friedlander's book (1992) contains the life, the teachings, and translations of all the Ravidas poetry they find authentic, as well as the critical edition of the *vani.* Callewaert and Friedlander (1992: 9) state the basic truth that Ravidas's 'message was simple and clear, without arrogance and self-interest. Raidas still is, at the beginning of the twenty-first century, a catalyst for all who yearn after the "Uplifter of the fallen, the Master of the meek". Humble is his origin, humble is human existence and the voice of Raidas sounds for all, then and now, who identify with that status.'

There are many historic references to the life of Ravidas. Callewaert and Friedlander (1992: 11–21) list twenty. The Sikh *Adi Granth* not only contains songs by Ravidas but also four verses by two of the Sikh Gurus which praise him. Peter G. Friedlander in 'The Core of the Vani of Raidas'[26] discusses the development of the study of Raidas, including nineteenth-century and twentieth-century studies and the many manuscripts available. Scholars of the bhakti saints of Maharashtra can only envy the plethora of north Indian sources and mourn the lack of similar archives for the saints of Maharashtra.

Medieval sources which are biographical rather than tributes in verse are Nabhadas's *Bhaktamal*, composed around 1600, the same time that the *Adi Granth* appeared; Priyadas's *Bhaktirasabodhini*, a commentary on Nabhadas from a hundred years later; and Anantdas's *Raidas Parchai*, from the late sixteenth century. Lochtefeld (1992) has commented on the biographies, noting that Nabhadas does not mention Ravidas's caste, only that he had pride in his lineage, and that Nabhadas claims that Ravidas's verses were not opposed to the Vedas or the shastras. Anantdas and Priyadas's accounts are much longer and filled with miracles. These two biographies cast Ravidas as either a Brahmin who ate meat and so was reborn a Chamar or as a disciple of Ramananda who took food offerings that had been ritually polluted by contact with low-caste people and so was cursed by Ramananda to be reborn an Untouchable. These two and some other sources tell of Ravidas's ripping open his chest to show a sacred thread inside.

There is, of course, disagreement about Ravidas's brahminical status. Darshan Singh tells us that 'Ravidasa nowhere claims that he was a brahmana in his previous life',[27] and it is doubtful if all Chamars believe in the previous incarnation of Ravidas as a Brahmin. Just as Vincentnathan found the high caste and Untouchable accounts of Nandanar opposed to each other, so Khare (1984: 40–50) has found that caste Hindu and Chamar beliefs about Ravidas differ from each other. He tells us that the Chamars of Lucknow believe that Ravidas 'did not obey the Hindu Vedic and scriptural constraints . . . he revealed his real spiritual identity as a Chamar without any camouflage or pretext, and he encountered resistance and opposition from the Brahmans (and the caste Hindu)–householders and ascetics–throughout his life and overcame them like a true Chamar'.[28]

Darshan Singh (1981) also notes that Ravidas' own verses do not mention Ramananda as his guru. Although it is often said that both Ravidas and his contemporary Kabir were disciples of the great south Indian Brahmin exponent of Ramanuja's bhakti, Ramananda most probably lived a hundred years earlier. And while he may be credited with bringing Vaishnava devotion to the north, he may not have had a direct connection with Varanasi's two low-caste saint-poets.

Callewaert and Friedlander (1992: 17 and 34) cast doubt on the authenticity of references to Ravidas by the two most famous saints of the north Indian tradition, Mirabai (who in some sources claims Ravidas as her guru) and Kabir, who supposedly had a long debate with Ravidas over the *nirgun* (formless) or *sagun* (with qualities) nature of God.[29] Callewaert does note that the hagiographic sources tell that Ravidas initiated a woman from the royal family of Chittorgarh as a disciple and that this is such a rare note that it probably is true, although Mirabai is probably not that woman.

Whatever his previous birth, there is no question but that Ravidas the saint-poet lived as a Chamar. He calls himself a Chamar, states that his trade is low, his labour is degrading, his caste not honoured. More than any other saint, he sings about his traditional work: 'My trade is dressing and cutting leather and daily removing dead cattle round about Banarasa'.[30]

> I keep my hands engaged,
> with the Cobbler's tool and the Leather cutter.
> Honest work is my righteous duty.
> This will ferry me across the world, sayeth Ravidas.[31]

Friedlander illustrates a core belief of Raidas–that the lowly can be uplifted through devotion–with this verse:

> O mind awake! Awake! Why are you unaware?
> Look at Valmiki!

None has ever reached such a state through caste,
but only through special devotion to Ram.[32]

Ravidas or Raidas probably was born in Varanasi, holiest city in India. His most probable dates are the latter half of the fifteenth century and the first quarter of the sixteenth. He mentions Namdev, Kabir, Trilochan, Dadu, Sadhna, and Saina (the author of the Kabir–Ravidas debate) in his songs. He speaks of the high-born coming to him in recognition of his worth, and this is repeated in several ways so that one wonders if perhaps it is true. Much of the rest of his story is clearly myth.

Perhaps the best way to understand the power of the oral tradition is to read the story of Ravidas as it was recorded in pre-modern times. We have included a translation of a Hindi version of his life and also of a Marathi version which appeared in the eighteenth-century hagiography of Mahipati, the *Bhaktavijaya* (Victory of the *Bhaktas*)[33] in this volume. In it Ravidas bests a Brahmin in a debate about the holiness of leather (and the skin which covers all beings) and in the end rips open his chest to show his brahminical sacred thread.

A miracle left out of the Marathi story is told by Priyadas. In a dispute with the Brahmins of Benares in the royal court, the king put them all to a test. The Brahmins' chanting of Sanskrit mantras left the image of the God unmoved, but it leapt into the arms of Ravidas at the sound of a single verse. And in another story, Ravidas visited Jhali, the queen of Chittor. Although he was the queen's guru, the Brahmins refused to eat with him and he left the room. But as the Brahmins sat to dine, they found an image of Ravidas appearing at the side of each of them (Lochtefeld, 1992). In still another myth, Ravidas's stone *saligram* floats in a pool of water.

Lochtefeld also reports that the *Amar Chitra Katha* comic book on Ravidas published in 1986 illustrates the social discrimination suffered by Ravidas and other Chamars. And in a new twist, Ravidas liberates Mira from slavery to a statue of Krishna by saying that they are already one (which is the argument of Ravidas in the text of the Kabir–Ravidas dispute over the *nirgun* and *sagun* nature of the divine). The comic book teaches the ideals of equality, compassion, and brotherhood.

In his poetry, Ravidas, like Chokhamela, challenges the very concept of purity and pollution, but in a different idiom. As Anne Murphy has given us in a new translation, Ravidas questions it in this way:

The baby calf makes the cow's udder unclean,
the bee spoils the flower and the fish, the sea.

Oh mother! What can I bring to offer in worship to Govind?
There is no perfect flower to be found!

In another song from the *Adi Granth*, Ravidas shows that anyone who is devout and pure rises above caste:

In whatever family a good Vaishnav is found,
whether they be high caste or outcaste, lord or pauper,
the world will know the one by its flawless fragrance.

Judging the effect of Ravidas's life and teachings on Untouchables today is difficult. At the very least he is a source of great pride and dignity. Since 1967, the people of an enclave of Untouchables near the Banaras Hindu University have worked on the temple for Ravidas founded by the All India Adi Dharm Mandal, which is a Hindu Scheduled Castes organization. The current devotees, Ramdasi Sikhs, have gilded its cupola with gold through donations from Ravidasis who have emigrated to the United States.[34] These devotees take out a procession through Varanasi each year to celebrate the birth of Ravidas. Hawley (1988: 16) reports that 'a group of Ravidasis . . . not long ago travelled to far-off Rajasthan to visit the temple of Mirabai in her natal village of Merta, only to be denied entrance once they arrived'.[35] The other Ravidas temple in Varanasi is at the far end of the river Ganga's ghats, the last great project of the long-time Congress political leader, Jagjivan Ram. The pictures of Kabir and Surdas are in the temple, and there is a shrine to Mirabai. Sayings from Ravidas in gold, chosen by the Hindi scholar Sukhdev Singh, line the walls.[36] Spires on each corner commemorate Hinduism, Buddhism, Christianity, and Islam, while the great spire in the middle is a tribute to Ravidas. Hawley notes that the Ravidas temple says many things: 'First and foremost, of course, it says that Ravidas belongs on the high lands along the Ganga as much as any other Hindu god or saint' (Hawley 1988: 21). But one should note that the Ganga flows past all other ghats before arriving at the ghat for Ravidas.

One wonders at the fate of Ravidas as Dr B.R. Ambedkar (and the Buddhist conversion that he felt was the way out of untouchability) becomes ever more popular in the north, but it seems that Ravidas is reinterpreted and even more influential. Schaller (1992) reports that the devotees he interviewed described themselves as following *nirgun* devotion just like Guru Ravidas, but most were devoted to Dr Ambedkar as well as Ravidas. Ravidas does not seem to have met the fate of Chokhamela as someone inextricably tied to the Hindu theory of karma or an ongoing religious pilgrimage which still exhibits some caste prejudices (Karve 1988: 142–72). He is still a genuine voice for Untouchable piety, courage, and pride. And he is not discarded when there is an interest in Buddhism, as Lochtefeld indicates in his lengthy report on the thought of Jijnasu. Posters have been seen in Kanpur, in the home of a Kabirpanthi, in which Raidas is depicted as the founding father of a Dalit lineage with his son Buddha and his grandson Dr Ambedkar.[37] We have included two very contemporary notes, one emphazing Ravidas's importance and the other claiming a Buddhist influence on his thought. At times in the Buddhist Circle e-mail, Ravidas is called 'Bodhisattva Ravidas'.

Ravidas is not only important in the north, but he is also celebrated as their saint by the Chambhars or Charmakars of Maharashtra as Rohidas. A *dindi* to Rohidas is part of the great *palkhi* procession that leaves Alandi for Pandharpur for the pilgrimage to the god Vithoba. A lawsuit several years ago won the right for the Rohidas *dindi* to be right behind the riderless horse that represents the great saint of Alandi, Dnyaneshwar, rather than in front of the saint. The position of the Rohidas *dindi* as the first, with the Brahmin *dindi* for Dnyaneshwar at the very end of the *palkhi* procession, does not dim the enthusiasm of the Charmakars for the pilgrimage. Some eight hundred *bhaktas* walk the many miles from Alandi to Pandharpur with the *paduka*s (sandals) of Rohidas. It is reported that women dance in the *dindi* procession, a most unusual happening, and also that the Charmakars are building a new four-storey building in Alandi to serve as a dharmashala.[38]

In Pandharpur itself, there are two Charmakar dharmashalas in the name of Rohidas. A Charmakar woman, Shantabai, is also honoured with a samadhi in the main dharmashala. Her story concerns her unstoppable devotion to Vithoba of Pandharpur in spite of family opposition. Locked in the house at night, she was still able to spend the night in adoration of Vithoba in Pandharpur, and when this miracle was recognized, she became free of family pressure and is acknowledged as a saint.

Ravidas has also joined the migration to the West. Sikh devotees in Vancouver, British Columbia, Canada, have erected a temple to him, and recently, in April 2003, the Ravidasi Sikhs there hosted a conference on Dalit problems and progress. There are also temples in New York and California.

Similarities and Differences

When one looks at the lives in legend of all these Untouchable saints, some striking parallels and even more striking differences are clear. The inability of the saints to enter the temple because it was feared that they would pollute the god is a given in all the stories of the saints, although it is not an important feature of the legends of Ravidas. This prohibition on temple entry was the most fundamental characteristic of the restrictions on the Untouchables. When the list of 'Scheduled Castes' was formulated in the 1930s, temple entry prohibition was one of the features which indicated that an Untouchable caste should be placed on a schedule to receive social and political benefits. In some rural areas, the prohibition prevails for Untouchables even today.

The purity of the temple is preserved in different ways but with similar goals in Tamil Nadu and Maharashtra. In Tamil Nadu, Tiruppan Alvar was carried into the temple on the shoulders of a Brahmin, a fact so important that one title for the saint is 'The Untouchable Who Rode Piggy-Back on the Brahmin', according to Hardy (1991). The temple remained unpolluted by the feet of an Untouchable but the Brahmin was certainly subject to pollution. One wonders if he underwent purification or if the command of the god removed the problem of pollution. The other Tamil saint, Nandanar, became a Brahmin through immolation in a fire and then entered the temple, merging with the god.

In Maharashtra, the temple at Pandharpur was closed to the Untouchables until the fasting of Sane Guruji at its great door in 1947, and then the essence of the image of Vithoba was removed to a copper pot in a Brahmin home. V.L. Manjul, a young boy at the time, has described this in 'God in a Copper Pot' in this volume. Manjul has also told me that one of the chief *bhaktas* among the Brahmins will still not enter the temple, although this fact does not seem to be widely known. It should be noted that few of the temple priests are *varkaris* and they do not worship the bhakti way. Participating in the pilgrimage to Pandharpur, and entering the temple to Vithoba there, is of increasing importance to the Charmakars. If the other important Untouchable caste of Maharashtra, the Mangs, had a suitable saint of their own, they might also, as they become more politicized and organized, find a way to participate in this all important religious practice.

Although there was a massive effort made for temple entry at Pune in 1929, a less lengthy effort at Amravati, and a five-year-long satyagraha in Nasik from 1930 to 1935, temple entry was never an important issue to the chief Untouchable leader, Dr B.R. Ambedkar. In 1954, almost twenty years after he declared his vow to renounce Hinduism, he persuaded a group at Dehu Road to dedicate the temple they had built to the Buddha rather than to Chokhamela. The Mahars, important though Chokhamela and the *varkari* pilgrimage was to them, made no recorded attempt to enter the Pandharpur temple.

One set of comparisons is that of the ways in which the gods respond to their Untouchable devotees. The god of Srirangam comes to a Brahmin in a dream and tells the muni he must carry Tiruppan Alvar into the temple. In another story, a Brahmin throws a stone at Tiruppan Alvar, and when the muni goes into the temple, he finds the forehead of the image covered in blood. Shiva's bull moves himself, stone though he is, so that Nandanar could see past him into the temple. Vithoba comes to dine with Chokhamela, and the proof of this visit is that his image in the temple is stained with the curd that Soyrabai inadvertently spilled on him. Ravidas performs miracles with leather and stone, proof that he is one of God's devotees, formless though that God is. This seems to be one of the hallmarks of bhakti: God loves his devotees, no matter how low their caste, and wants them near him. There is little that is radical about this, however. The devotees are not necessarily beloved of other human beings, or even treated as worthy humans by them.

One of the most interesting differences is in the legends that tell of the origin of the Untouchable saints. Tiruppan Alvar was the avatar of a mole on Vishnu's chest, born into an Untouchable caste for inexplicable reasons. Nandanar seems to have no divine origin. Chokhamela is clearly a Mahar, but his birth was enabled by the god begging fruit from his mother as an old Brahmin. Ravidas has the clearest identity as a Brahmin in a previous life, brought down by any number of legendary reasons to his Chamar status. Brahmins figure in all the stories, and Nandanar even sacrifices himself to become a Brahmin, but in the stories of Chokhamela, it is simply the god of Pandharpur disguising himself as a Brahmin. And in the Chokhamela stories, there is no help at all from the Brahmins, as there is with Tiruppan Alvar and Ravidas.

The Importance of the Untouchable Saints in Contemporary Times

Both Shaiva and Vaishnava bhakti movements in Tamil Nadu were legitimized (or perhaps engulfed would be a better word) by larger schools of religious identity: the Alvars into the Srivaishnavas, the Nayanars into the Shaiva Siddhanta. The hymns of the saint-poets and the legends about them were canonized by various hagiographies and collections several centuries after the saints lived. All sixty-three Nayanars are acknowledged with statues in the courtyards of Shaiva temples.[39] It seems no separate non-conformist strain of bhakti remains in the south, but even so the lives of the Untouchable saints, Tiruppan Alvar of the Vaishnavas and Nandanar of the Shaivas, have considerable social importance in the twentieth century as well as the nineteenth.

Although the Tamil saint Tiruppan Alvar does not refer to untouchability in his song and we have no song at all from Nandanar, both saints have become part of a reform movement either among the Untouchables themselves or among caste Hindus. Nandanar has received the most attention. A number of dramas have brought his story to the attention of millions. And in the Untouchable world, as noted by Vincentnathan (1993), Nandanar was the subject of pride and admiration before the recent change to a more secular and more political stance adopted by the young under the influence of Ambedkar's life and thought. Nandanar's representation in the statues of the dancing Shiva—as the scarf that floats from his waist (or his thighs)—is a touching reminder of the earlier need of the Untouchables to adopt higher-caste Hindu practices.

In Maharashtra, Chokhamela received the attention of the radical young filmmakers of Prabhat Studio in the 1930s (see Sapkal's article), but his chief importance was for the Mahar movement itself. In the first third of the twentieth century, Chokhamela was a very important source of pride for the Mahars attempting to better their lives and to find pride in their own history and community. Hostels were named after him, some Mahars called themselves Chokhamela, poems were written urging militancy in the name of Chokhamela. Chokhamela, however, in just a few songs tells of sin in a previous life as the reason for his low caste, and this made him unacceptable to the Ambedkar movement, which swept through Maharashtra.[40] Chokhamela is the subject of scholarly study now, among a few of the descendants of those who were once Chokhamela's followers, but there is almost no worship of him, and only a handful of pilgrims stay at the Chokhamela dharmashala in Pandharpur. There is no attention paid to his very interesting family, except by one devout Ambedkar follower and dramatist, B.S. Shinde, who finds in Karmamela (Chokhamela's son) a radical voice from the past; there is also a tribute paid to Chokhamela by the well-known Dalit writer, the late Shankarrao Karat.[41]

The most important figure by far today is Ravidas, both in India and among the Ravidasi Sikh migrants to Britain and the US. The temples in Varanasi attest to his importance both to Ravidasi Sikhs and such Chamar leaders as the late Jagjivan Ram. The homage paid to Ravidas overseas is even more striking.

Recently there have been efforts made by those in the Ambedkar movement, chiefly Buddhists, to cooperate with the followers of Ravidas. Notes in the Buddhist Circle e-mail communications, sent mostly by young Dalits in technological jobs, have referred to 'Bodhisattva Ravidas', claiming him as one of their own. This is a development probably not acceptable to Ravidasis, however. Even more telling, several Ravidasi occasions have been also occasions to celebrate Ambedkar's life. In 2001, the Sri Guru Ravidas Sabha of New York commemorated the 110th birth anniversary of Dr Ambedkar with the Indian Ambassador, three Buddhists, and an American scholar as guest speakers. In 2003, a very ambitious conference was sponsored by the Ravidasis and planned by the Dalits in Vancouver and Seattle in cooperation with local Ravidasi Sikhs. Several hundred interested Dalits and others from Canada, the United States, Europe, India, and Nepal attended, and a Vancouver Declaration, a 'Dalit Vision for the Twenty-first Century', was issued. The conference saw itself as a successor to the International Dalit Conference in Malaysia in 1988, the Dalit participation in the Durban World Conference on Racism in 2001, and the Bhopal (Madhya Pradesh) Conference of 2002 which also issued a declaration. It should be added that the Ravidasi Sikhs in the Vancouver area maintain their separate gurdwara, noting that they are not allowed leadership positions in the larger Sikh gurdwara in spite of their high educational and economic achievements.

There is also the appearance of new Untouchable saints. Shyamlal, author of several books on the Bhangis (many of whom prefer to be called Valmikis), has also written an article entitled 'Maharishi Naval: A Bhangi Saint-Reformer of Rajasthan' (Shyamlal: 1991). Naval Maharaj (1840–1965), in the time-honoured manner of the saints, was a pious child and a practitioner of meditation as an adult. His preaching annoyed the Brahmins of the area, and he fled to Jodhpur where he established his own sect in order to reform his own community. It is claimed that Naval performed miracles, raising the dead, both human and bovine. There are no translations of his songs or poems, but Shyamlal comments that he taught *nirgun* philosophy similar to Kabir's and left behind many followers.

The Bhakti Movement and Untouchability

It must also be said that the condemnation of religious difference and discrimination by many of the saints is the strongest we have until the modern period. Some scholars (see Lele: 1981) have attempted to show the relevance of bhakti to reform, but there seems to be little momentum for social change within the movements themselves. Dadu (1544–1600) of Rajasthan, a Jat guru with Untouchable disciples, sang:

> God belongs to the caste of love,
> Love is dear to him,
> Love is his body,
> And love alone is his colour
>
> (Nayak in *Poet-Saints of India* 1996: 94)

The sixteenth-century Kanakadasa of Karnataka was low caste, although not Untouchable. He was not allowed to enter the temple at Udupi and so, according to legend similar to that told of Chokhamela, he went behind the temple to pray and the image of Krishna turned to face him, remaining 'in this position even to this day. There is a little window through which people get the *darshan* of Lord Krishna . . . known as Kanakana khindi, Kanaka's window' (Shastri in *Poet-Saints of India*, 1996: 183). Not surprisingly, Kanaka had strong words about caste and lineage (*kula*):

What is the caste of God Narayana?
And Siva?
What is the caste of Atman?
And of Jiva?
Why talk of *kula*
When God has blessed you.

(Shastri, ibid.: 184)

Another little-known *bhakta*, the woman Virashaiva Kalavve, tells us, in Ramaswamy's words, using somewhat curious logic in a powerful anti-brahminical verse:

Those who eat cock, fish and parrot
Are regarded as high caste.
But those Madigas who eat beef of that
Cow whose milk is offered
By Brahmins to Shiva,
Why are they alone polluting?
The darbha grass Brahmins eat
Is licked by dogs while the cow
Madigas eat, is worshipped by Brahmins.
The Madiga is superior to the Brahmin.

(Hiremath, quoted in Ramaswamy 1996: 56)

The Madigas are an Untouchable caste centred in Andhra Pradesh, but found all over the south, whose traditional work is with leather.

The strongest voice, however, was that of the twelfth-century Basava or Basavanna of Karnataka, founder of the movement which became Virashaivism, or the caste of the Lingayats. His followers did not retain his egalitarian attitude, and the Lingayats today function more or less as a non-Brahmin high caste, but there is some acknowledgement of his radical attitude in other aspects of Indian culture. Girish Karnad's play, *Tale Dande* (1993), is a powerful re-enactment of the story of Kalyan society. Basavanna encouraged an inter-caste marriage between the daughter of a Brahmin and the son of an Untouchable. Such an uproar followed that the king of Kalyan was forced to have the parents of the couple executed and Basava driven from the city.

Shiri (1992: 22) has described Basava's firm commitment: 'Basava's simple yet very strong belief was that a true devotee of God will never practise casteism. In other words, according to him, casteism was a contradiction to Shivabhakti. No one is high-born simply because he is born into a high caste and no one is low-born for the crime or accident of birth into a low caste.' Basava believed that there was neither high nor low among humankind and therefore all are equal. What makes one high is love of God and what makes one low is lack of faith in God. What makes one high is good conduct and what makes one low is bad conduct. 'What matters if one is lowly born? Only a Shivabhakta is well-born,' he affirmed:

> Vyasa is a fisherman's son, Markandeye of an outcaste born
> Mandodari, the daughter of a frog!
> O, look not for caste; in caste what were you in the past?
> Indeed, Agastya was a fowler; Durvasa, a maker of shoes;
>   Kasyapa, a blacksmith.
> The sage Kaundinya by name was, as the three worlds know, a
>   barber . . .
> Mark ye all the words of our Kudala Sangama
> What matters if one is lowly born?
> Only a Shivabhakta is well-born.

In addition to these Puranic references (very common among the Untouchable saint-poets' songs in Maharashtra and among Dalit writers today), Basava 'held Shivabhaktas of Dalit origin in the highest esteem. In several *vachanas* he had profusely acknowledged and thanked many Shivabhaktas of Dalit origin for all that he received from them. He claimed that the cobbler Chennayya was his spiritual guru, who had washed off his dirt, the taint of caste. . . . He had acknowledged how several devotees of Dalit origin constantly helped him to grow to spiritual maturity' (Shiri, ibid.: 21).

Kabir's is the best-known voice for equality of castes and religions, condemning caste and religious divisions in poetic, picturesque, fiercely strong terms. Linda Hess's elegant translations include this one, which contains references commonly used in bhakti to the making of pots as a metaphor for the making of the human body and to the traditional eighty-four lakh lives that every human being must live before returning to the eternal *Brahman*.

> Pandit, look in your heart for knowledge.
> Tell me where untouchability

Came from, since you believe in it.
Mix red juice, white juice and air.
A body bakes in a body.
As soon as the eight lotuses
Are ready, it comes into the world. Then what's
Untouchable?
Eighty-four hundred thousand vessels
decay into dust, while the potter
keeps slapping clay
on the wheel, and with a touch
cuts each one off.
We eat by touching, we wash
By touching, from a touch
The world was born.
So who's untouched? Asks Kabir.
Only he
Who has no hint of Maya.

(Kabir, 1983: 55)

NOTES

1. *On the Threshold: Songs of Chokhamela*, translated from the Marathi by Rohini Mokashi-Punekar, New Delhi: The Book Review Literary Trust, 2002, is the first book of translations to be devoted to the poet. This volume was published in a new world edition, with additional translations, by the International Sacred Literature Trust in cooperation with the Alta Mira Press, New York in April 2005.
2. Panar or Panan is an Untouchable caste chiefly concerned with agricultural labour, but they are also known as traditional bards. Caste names are capitalized. Diacriticals may be found in the Glossary.
3. The Pulai were agricultural labour, drummers, and singers. Our English word 'pariah' is a reflection of the importance as well as the low status of the Paraiya caste. The name is probably from the Tamil word for drum, and the caste duties of drumming were important for many village occasions.
4. The large caste of Mahars in the Marathi-speaking area were, in British parlance, 'inferior village servants', with some duties, such as dragging out dead cattle from the village, which were polluting but others which simply involved service to the village. As with all Untouchable castes, they could not use the village well nor enter the temple.
5. The Chamar (*Camar*) castes extend throughout the north, with a Chambhar or Charmakar component in Maharashtra. Leather working has been their time-honoured traditional occupation.
6. *Srisakalsantgatha* (A Collection of All the Saints' Songs) is as near a canon of Marathi sant literature as we have. There are no medieval manuscripts for

Chokhamela that one finds in Rajasthan for Ravidas's work. The Marathi collection was made by Srinanamaharaj Sakhre and edited by Kashinath Anant Joshi, and published in Pune first in 1923, with a second edition in 1967 containing additional songs by Chokhamela.

7. My essay 'The Medieval Bhakti Movement in History: An Essay on the Literature in English', was an attempt to explain the nature of the historical component of bhakti together with an annotated bibliography of the English sources available in the 1970s. It appeared in *Hinduism: New Essays in the History of Religions*, edited by Bardwell L. Smith in the Human Series of E.J. Brill, Leiden, 1976, which was reprinted in 1982. Also see Lutgendorf 2003.
8. See Vidya Dehejia, *Slaves as the Lord: The Path of the Tamil Saints*, New Delhi: Munshiram Manoharlal, 1988, Dedication.
9. See the work of George L. Hart III for an interesting discussion of the importance of the low-caste bard and the influence of south Indian bardic literature on Deccan poetry: *The Poems of Ancient Tamil: Their Milieu and Their Sanskrit Counterparts*, Berkeley, California: University of California Press, 1975 and *The Relation Between Tamil and Classical Sanskrit Literature* (A History of Indian Literature Series), Wiesbaden: Otto Harrossowitz, 1976.
10. This information and much else about Tiruppan Alvar in this essay comes from the work of Vasudha Narayanan, q.v.
11. See Friedhelm Hardy's 'Tiruppan-Alvar: The Untouchable Who Rode Piggy-Back on the Brahmin', in *Devotion Divine: Bhakti Traditions from the Regions of India: Studies in Honour of Charlotte Vaudeville*, edited by Diana L. Eck and Francoise Mallison, Groningen: Egbert Forsten, and Paris: Ecole Francaise d'Extreme-Orient, 1991, for an analysis of all the Tamil hagiographies and also for an interpretation of the south and north Indian branches of Srivaishnavism in relationship to the Untouchable Alvar.
12. A.K. Ramanujan, *Hymns for the Drowning: Poems for Vishnu by Nammalvar*, Princeton: Princeton University Press, 1981, p. 60.
13. For the importance of Dr Ambedkar, see my *From Untouchable to Dalit: Essays on the Ambedkar Movement*, New Delhi: Manohar, 2001 (1992). It is interesting that Ambedkar dedicated his book, *The Untouchables* (New Delhi: Amrit Book Company, 1948), which puts forward the idea that the Untouchables were former Buddhists, to the memory of 'Nandanar, Ravidas, Chokhamela—Three renowned saints who were born among the Untouchables and who by their piety and virtue won the esteem of all.'
14. My article 'The Householder Saints of Maharashtra' appeared in *Studies in Early Modern Indo-Aryan Languages, Literature and Culture*, edited by Alan W. Entwistle, et al., New Delhi: Manohar, 1999, pp. 417–26.
15. This version is taken from *Chokhamela abhang gatha* (Collection of Chokhamela's Songs), Bombay: Balkrishna Lakshman Pathak, 1950, pp. 1–2.
16. *Stories of Indian Saints: An English Translation of Mahipati's Marathi Bhaktavijaya*, vol. I, no. 9 in the Poet Saints of Maharashtra series, translated by Justin E. Abbott and Narhar R. Godbole, Pune: Office of the Poet Saints of Maharashtra, 1933. Chokhamela's story, although not the birth story, is on pp. 377–84.
7. All references are to the *Srisakalsantgatha*. Translations were made with the invaluable help of Vijaya Deo, S.G. Tulpule and Jayant Karve, although the final

versions are my decision on wording. See Rohini Mokashi-Punekar for other translations. *Abhanga* is the Marathi word for the flexible form and meter of the saints' songs. Its meaning is 'unbroken'.

18. The collection of Chokhamela's songs and stories in *Srisant Chokhamela Maharaj yanche charitra va abhang gatha*, edited by S.B. Kadam, Bombay: Mandakini S. Kadam, 1969, contains the songs about Chokhamela of Jani, Namdev and Eknath.
19. See my 'Chokhamela and Eknath: Two Bhakti Modes of Legitimacy for Modern Change', in the *Journal of Asian and African Studies*, vol. XV, nos. 1 and 2, January–April 1980. Reprinted in *Tradition and Modernity in Bhakti Movements*, edited by Jayant Lele, Leiden: E.J. Brill, 1981, pp. 136–56 and to be reprinted in *Subordinate and Marginal Groups in Early India up to 1500 AD*, edited by Aloka Parasher-Sen for Oxford University Press, New Delhi. Eknath also wrote forty songs as if he were a Mahar in a remarkable sixteenth-century display of empathy. Some of these have been translated in my 'Eknath's *Bharuds*: The *Sant* as a Link between Culture', in *The Sants: Studies in a Devotional Tradition of India*, edited by Karine Schomer and W.H. Mcleod, Berkeley: Religious Studies Series, New Delhi: Motilal Banarsidass (1987: 91–110).
20. This *abhanga* was a recent discovery made by V.L. Manjul in an old book of *abhangas* which was given to him by Prakash Ghatpande of Pune. The *abhanga* is not found in any other collection.
21. The news and the poem appeared in *Sakal* for 2 July 2002. Translation is chiefly by Sucheta Paranjpye, who found the *abhanga* to be 'very fine poetry'.
22. Translated by Gail Omvedt and Bharat Patankar. This is a draft form, not yet published. The reference is *Abhanga* 4299 in *Tukaram Gatha*, published by the Government of Maharashtra.
23. I have discussed 'The Untouchable Women Saint-Poets of Maharashtra, in *The Banyan Tree: Essays on Early Literature in New Indo-Aryan Languages*, edited by Mariola Offredi, New Delhi: Manohar, 2000, pp. 273–82, and a version of that paper is included in this volume with permission.
24. This poem was given to Eleanor Zelliot by Dr Sadanand More, and translated by Sucheta Paranjpe and Zelliot from the Marathi.
25. There is a *dindi* (a group of devotees usually from one caste or village who are part of a larger *palkhi* going to Pandharpur on pilgrimage) in the name of Rohidas in the Maharashtrian bhakti tradition. There is also a Rohidas *math* (teaching centre) and dharmashala (place for pilgrims to stay) in Pandharpur. However, no Marathi translations of Ravidas have been made.
26. Peter G. Friedhander, 'The Core of the Vani of Raidas', in *Studies in South Asian Devotional Literature*, edited by Alan W. Entwistle and Francoise Mallison, New Delhi: Manohar and Paris: Ecole Francaise d'Extreme-Orient, 1994, pp. 455–79.
27. Darshan Singh, *A Study of Bhakta Ravidas*, Patiala: Publication Bureau, Punjabi University, Foreword by L.M. Joshi, 1981, p. xli.
28. Khare, R.S., *The Untouchable as Himself: Ideology, Identity, and Pragmatism among the Lucknow Chamars*, Cambridge: Cambridge University Press, 1984, p. 46.
29. David Lorenzen (ed.), *Bhakti Religion in North India*, New Delhi: Manohar, 1996, pp. 169–81, tells us that although the debate may be legendary, there are at least nine unpublished manuscripts of the text. His translation allows us to see the radical implications of Kabir's *nirgun* God, since 'perfect Brahman pervades all

bodies, how can we distinguish between a Brahmin and a Shudra?' But as Raidas and Kabir argue about avatars, various gods join in the debate. Raidas acknowledges Kabir as his master, but Vishnu appears at the end, declaring Kabir the possessor of the truth and Raidas to be blessed.

30. Darshan Singh, *A Study of Bhakta Ravidas*, p. 35.
31. K.N. Upadhyaya, *Guru Ravidas, Life and Teachings*, Beas: Radha Soami Satsang, 1982, p. 15.
32. Peter G. Friedlander, 'The Core of the Vani of Raidas', in *Studies in South Asian Devotional Literature*, edited by Alan W. Entwistle and Francoise Mallison, New Delhi: Manohar and Paris: Ecole Francaise d'Extreme-Orient, 1994, pp. 455–79, p. 471.
33. Translated by Justin E. Abbott and Narhar R. Godbole in the *Stories of the Indian Saints* series, the story of 'Rohidas' is one of some fifty about *bhaktas*, many of them from the Hindi-speaking area. See Mahipati, 1933: 401–5.
34. Conversation with devotees in Govardhanpur in December 1996.
35. I found a small temple to Ravidas containing his *paduka* (footprints) opposite the Mirabai temple in the Chittor fort. Both temples were open to all, and a woman was presiding over the donations at the Mira temple.
36. Conversation with Sukhdev Singh at the Ravidasi temple in 1996, when it was under construction. Singh credits Jagjivan Ram with the Ravidas revival and popularization in Uttar Pradesh.
37. Maren Bellwinkel-Schempp, 'Kabir Panthis in Kanpur: From Sampradaya to Dalit Identity', unpublished manuscript.
38. Conversation with V.L. Manjul in Pune in December 2002. Manjul also reports that the Untouchable Mang caste had a *dindi* in the name of Ajamila, a Brahmin who abandoned his wife for a Mang woman, whom some sources claim he married. Recently they have rejected this association, but do not know how to join the pilgrimage with their own saint.
39. I was prevented from entering the outskirts of a Shaiva temple in Chennai to photograph the statue of Nandanar even though it was explained to the guard that he was an Untouchable and so should have been in a place open to me!
40. See my 'Chokhamela: Piety and Protest', in *Bhakti Religion in North India: Community, Identity and Political Action*, edited by David N. Lorenzen, Albany: State University of New York Press, 1995, pp. 212–20.
41. See Eleanor Zelliot and V.L. Manjul, eds., *Sant Chokhamela Vividh Darshan*, Pune: Sugawa Prakashan, 2002.

I

THE TAMIL SAINTS: TIRUPPAN ALVAR AND NANDANAR

1

The Life and Lyrics of Tiruppan Alvar

VASUDHA NARAYANAN

Tiruppan Alvar (eighth–ninth century CE) was perhaps the earliest Untouchable poet within the Hindu tradition to be thought of as a saint. There is only one poem by him that survives today. This poem was introduced into temple and home worship by the eleventh century and is still recited in all Srivaishnava temples as part of the daily liturgy. The poem itself is brief (eleven verses) and is a vivid description of the Lord Ranganatha (Vishnu) at Srirangam. In contrast to the compositions of the later Untouchable saints of northern India, we notice a startling absence of any protest, bitterness, or rancour in Tiruppan's lyrics; the poem is almost a generic panegyric.

Although the Srivaishnava community hailed him as the paradigmatic devotee, it did not allow other Untouchables to enter the temples. Tiruppan Alvar, like Antal the woman devotee, was considered to be an exception to the normal social order. Thus, while Tiruppan was installed in Srivaishnava temples and worshipped, Untouchables were not allowed into these temples to worship Lord Vishnu or Tiruppan, and this study considers some of the tensions between Srivaishnava theology and practice. It also focuses on the hagiographic tradition and the transformation of Tiruppan Alvar into a divine incarnation, and how in this process, his human birth into an outcaste family is marginalized and his divine status reaffirmed. The final section of the essay discusses the ways in which Tiruppan is venerated in brahminical temples and in the shrines of Untouchable Srivaishnavas today.

* * * * *

Tiruppan Alvar is the name given to a Tamil-speaking poet who lived around the eighth century CE. There is only one poem by him that survives today. This poem was included as part of a compendium of devotional hymns that came to be known as *Nalayira Divya Prabandham* (*The Sacred Collect of Four Thousand Verses*). All poems in this collection were addressed to Vishnu, especially his incarnations in a worshippable form (*archavatara*) in the temples of south India. These poems were introduced into the liturgy and recited alongside the Sanskrit Vedas in many Srivaishnava temples; we know this from inscriptions dating from the eleventh century CE.

We do not know the real name of Tiruppan Alvar; the title 'alvar' was given by the Srivaishnavas to the twelve poet-saints whose works form the *The Sacred Collect of Four Thousand Verses*. The Tamil word *al* literally means 'deep'; *alvar* refers to those 'who are deeply immersed in the love of Vishnu, *Tiru* is the Tamil equivalent of the Sanskrit sri, and *pan* refers to the Untouchable community to which the poet belonged. *Pan* means song, vocal music, or melody; *panan* or *panar* referred to an ancient class of Tamil bards and minstrels.[1] Thus, 'Tiruppan Alvar' meant the 'poet-saint who belonged to the *panar* or singing class of society'. It is significant that the collective memory of the community has not retained the given name of this poet; it is only the clan name that has remained, although it is followed by the honorific 'alvar'. Occasionally he is referred to in commentaries as 'he who had the holy man as his vehicle' (*muni vahana*), but this is generally not the name by which he is known or recognized. Even in the Sanskrit biography, *Divya Suri Charitam*, his name is *Pan natha suri*, and the word 'pan' is remembered. He is the only Alvar to be remembered by the name of the class[2] of society to which he belonged; many of the other Alvars are referred to by their Sanskrit and Tamil names. *Vishnu chitta* (one whose thoughts are on Vishnu) is known as Periya Alvar (great Alvar) in Tamil; the woman Goda is called Antal (she who came to rule); Vipranarayana's Tamil name is *Tontar ati poti* alvar (the Alvar who is dust on the feet of the devotees), and so on;[3] but Tiruppan is known by his caste.

Unlike the other Alvars, he does not leave a signature name in the last verse (*phala sruti*) of his poem. For this, we do find a few parallels in other Alvar poetry, but it is generally rare not to find a name. The connection between the poet Tiruppan Alvar and the poem which is known by its first three words, *amalan ati piran* or 'the pure primordial lord', is made in three different kinds of works. These works, all of which glorify the poet and the poem, can be grouped under the following categories: (a) laudatory verses (*tanian*) that are prefixed to his poem; (b) biographical literature that began to be recorded around the twelfth century CE; and (c) the commentatorial tradition on the poem that began around the thirteenth century CE. The laudatory verses were perhaps composed (we have no definite proof of this and can rely on oral tradition for lack of better records) by two teachers of Ramanuja. The Sanskrit verse which glorifies the poet was composed by Periya Nampi (better known as Mahapurna) and the Tamil one which summarizes the theme of the poem was composed by Tirumalai Nampi (Srisailapurna, an uncle of Ramanuja). The biographies provide several details about the poet's life, and we shall look at these before we consider the poem itself.

Life of Tiruppan Alvar

There are about five famous biographies of the Alvars and the early teachers (acharyas), written between the twelfth and the late fourteenth/early fifteenth centuries CE. The earliest one, *Divya Suri Charitam*[4] (*The Life*) is in Sanskrit; two later ones, both entitled *Guruparampara-prabhavam* (The Splendour of Succession of Teachers; hereafter referred to as *The Splendour-1* and *The Splendour-2*), were written by different sub-sects in the Srivaishnava community around the thirteenth and fifteenth centuries CE. In the fifteenth century, or possibly a little later, there also appeared a biography of all the Alvars in Tamil verse; the *Alvarkal Vaibhavam* (*The Glory*) was written by Vativalakiya Nampi Tacar and contained not only the life stories of the Alvars, but also a summary of their poems. The *Periya Tirumudi Ataivu* was possibly composed in the sixteenth century and is almost like a short 'who's who' entry on each Alvar and acharya, giving astrological details of their birth, the names of their works, their teachers, their main students, and a short laudatory verse.

While the differences in style and emphases in these biographies merit a more sustained study to bring out the different agendas of the writers, I shall confine myself here to summarizing the common themes and minor variations found in all of them. I shall note one important incident which appears in just one biography, an incident which may be an interpolation. It is interesting that the one possible interpolation is the incident that becomes central in the retelling of Tiruppan's story in *all* the twentieth-century biographies in Tamil and English.

According to traditional hagiographies, the child who came to be known as Tiruppan Alvar was born in the city of Uraiyur, near Srirangam. Srirangam is an island in the Kaveri River and Uraiyur was on the southern bank of the river, separated from Srirangam by the waters. According to almost all biographies, he was the incarnation of Srivatsa, the mole on Vishnu's chest; he was born in the month of Kartikai (November/December according to the Hindu calendar), when the moon was near the star Rohini. He was born into a class that is 'lower than the four castes which make up the caste system, that is the fifth *varna*';[5] some call his birth an avatar into the 'sacred clan' (*tiru kulam*; *The Glory*, vv. 5-6). Other biographies reject this *physical birth* into a clan of Panars and instead say he was born miraculously (*ayonija*; *The Splendour-2*) and was found by a man of the Panar class. In this clan he grew up in a special way; he was like a 'fruit that is hidden by the leaves', i.e. his divine nature was hidden by the surroundings (*The Glory*, vv. 7). From the time he emerged from his mother and fell on this earth, the Lord's glance was on him and even as a baby he never wept (*The Life*, ch. 7, v. 18); most important in the Hindu context, he was given 'clean food' (*shuddha aharam*), even though he was raised by Untouchable foster parents (*The Splendour-2*). It is very significant that in all these ways the 'higher'-caste authors of these biographies tend to insulate and protect the poet from his Untouchable birth. The poet is seen to be a divine incarnation, a recipient of Lord Ranganatha's grace, not tainted by impure food or surroundings.

Tiruppan Alvar grows up to be eighteen, and is like the celestial musician Narada, so sweet are the melodies he plays on his lute (vina, *yal*). However, he can never go to Srirangam to see the Lord. The goddess Lakshmi (known as Ranganayaki in Srirangam) asks Lord Ranganatha to bring Tiruppan into the inner chambers. The Lord instructs his guards to fetch the devotee; the Alvar, only too aware of his impurity, refuses vehemently, saying that he is of low birth (*The Glory*, vv. 12-13); the Lord then sends forth a command, asking Tiruppan to come again and this time instructs the temple priests to say that according to the Vedas, the oldest and highest clan of all is the clan of devotees. Tiruppan again refuses, saying that he, a sinner, cannot set foot in the place where the Lord, light of all lights, abides (*The Glory*, vv. 15 and 18). Notice that the argument has shifted now

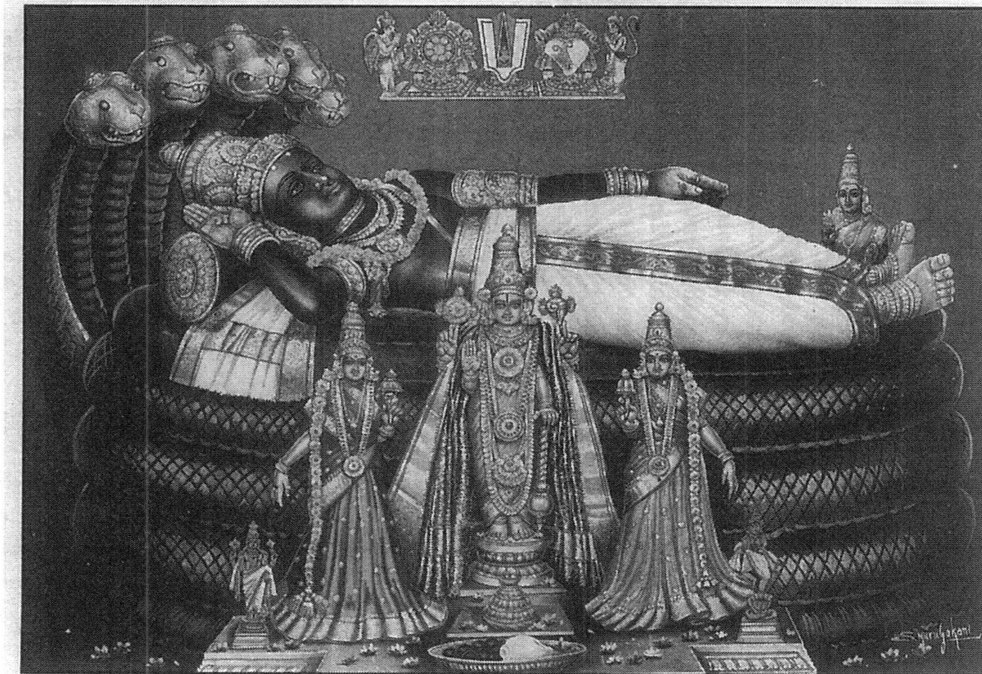

Plate 1.1: Lord Ranganatha at Srirangam, the image described in Tiruppan Alvar's poem. A direct photograph of the image is not allowed. This print is from the temple.

from lowliness through birth to lowliness because of sin. The Lord then instructs (directly in some biographies and in a dream in others) a holy man, a Brahmin, called Loka Saranga Muni to go and fetch Tiruppan Alvar on his shoulders. Loka Saranga Muni is described as one 'who does not know the pride of high birth, learning or wealth' (*The Glory*, v. 29); he approaches Tiruppan, falls at his feet, and begs him to come to Srirangam. The poet refuses again; the muni and some others literally 'kidnap' the poet, forcibly lift him up, put him on Loka Saranga Muni's shoulders, and take him to the holy island of Srirangam. Notice that the community (and the biographer) still maintains the tenuous sanctity of the land of Srirangam; after all, the temple is sacred not just to the Srivaishnava community, but also to the larger Hindu communities, to many *sampradayas* and to many castes which may not share the 'equality' issues of the radical Srivaishnavas. The *smartha* (Shaivite) Brahmins, the Kshatriya royalty, and the Vellalars who are not Srivaishnavas, were all patrons of the temple; for them, an 'Untouchable' setting foot on the island would mean that the land had become defiled. So, Tiruppan Alvar's not setting foot in the temple, but riding on the shoulders of a Brahmin safeguards the 'purity of the land' and, at the same time, does reverse the caste hierarchy within the bhakti context.

An incident that is crucial in the retelling–both oral and written–of Tiruppan Alvar's life in the twentieth century is, interestingly enough, not found in the medieval biographies. In *The Splendour-1*, the incident does appear, but in parentheses, and the editor adds that that section is not found in some manuscripts, and is replaced with a conversation between Lakshmi and Ranganatha. The story goes that Loka Saranga Muni went to the Kaveri River to fetch a pitcher of water for the Lord's ritual bath. There he saw Tiruppan immersed in song. Recognizing him to be of low caste, he asked the poet to move away. Tiruppan was so deeply engrossed in his song that he did not hear the muni. The muni then, in frustration, threw a stone at Tiruppan. The stone hit him on the forehead; he bled profusely and, at the same time, was upset that he had proved to be an obstacle to someone engaged in the Lord's service. Loka Saranga Muni went to the temple with the pitcher of water; there, according to one account, he saw the Lord's forehead bleeding, and, according to another version, saw the temple doors locked shut. The Lord's voice told him about his sin in hurting a *bhakta*, and he was then commanded to bring Tiruppan on his shoulders into the temple.

The fact that this story is not included in the medieval accounts except for some manuscripts of *The Splendour-1* is curious. The story reflects a deep antagonism against the Panar clan and emphasizes the arrogance of the Brahmin muni. What is interesting is that this holy man is specifically mentioned in at least one biography as 'not having the pride of high birth, learning or wealth', a description that contradicts the story of his hurling a stone at Tiruppan. It seems clear that this story is an interpolation from a later century when prejudices were even stronger. Since even the sixteenth-century biographies do not contain a record of this incident, it is probably not more than three hundred years old, but its centrality in all modern versions is significant. Thus, four twentieth-century versions[6] repeat the story in some detail, including the 'clot of blood over the idol'.[7] It is possible that if we check the biographical literature in Telugu and in Kannada between the seventeenth to the twentieth centuries, or oral narratives from the many Srivaishnava caste groups, we may find some clues as to when the interpolation took place. There is a possibility that this incident may have been known in the Tamil oral tradition for a very long time and was just never recorded in writing. This alternative sounds less plausible, because it is highly improbable that all biographies should fail to refer to the incident.

The questions that we may ask if we accept the story to be an interpolation are: who inserted it and why was it inserted? It is highly unlikely that the Panars could insert it in a few manuscripts of *The Splendour-1*, because they did not have access to these manuscripts that were traditionally in the hands of the Brahmin community. It may be possible that some high-caste persons inserted the story to convince the non-Srivaishnava Brahmins that Loka Saranga Muni did after all have a 'politically correct' attitude towards the 'Untouchable', at least until commanded otherwise by the Lord. Srivaishnava theology is full of statements upholding the importance of low-caste devotees, and the community had laid itself wide open to criticism, especially from the non-Srivaishnava Brahmins on their so-called lax attitude towards caste. The story of Loka Saranga Muni throwing the stone at Tiruppan may well have been some orthodox Srivaishnava's defence against such criticism. This again seems rather unlikely since there is very little evidence that non-Srivaishnavas were interested in the life stories of the Alvars and acharyas. (This story also has some parallels to the one about Adi Shankara throwing a stone at an Untouchable to get him to move; it may quite possibly be a variation of this formulaic story.)[8] It is difficult to interpret the story in view of the insufficient understanding of the social and cultural contexts from which this incident has evolved. In all probability it is an interpolation/addition portraying a more realistic touch than the story depicted in the biographies.

Even more interesting is the *Amar Chitra Katha's* creative retelling of the story, which clearly reflects the late twentieth-century preoccupations with and attitudes towards the horrors of untouchability. The story says the child was abandoned by the parents and raised by a sweeper. This is incorrect since the Panars are singers and not sweepers, and this attribution of occupation may be the projection of a north Indian stereotype.[9] The Panars were singers in the early body of Tamil literature, which consisted of secular poems of love and war. Entire collections of poems are credited to the Panars. Even in the eighth and ninth centuries, the Panars were musicians with the traditional *yal*; the Tamil Shaivite poet Sambandar was usually accompanied by a Pan musician called Nilakantan.[10] This musician, whose full name was Tirunilakanta Pal Panar, apparently set Sambandar's hymns to music. So we do know that Tiruppan Alvar was raised by a group whose occupation was singing, not sweeping.

The comic book also portrays Tiruppan going to the temple precincts and being thrown out by the brahminical priests. He is shown sometimes to be full of anger and sorrow: 'The priests have made my Lord a prisoner; he can't see those whom he wants to see.' At times he is philosophical, at least as far as a comic book will allow him to be: 'I wish I were dead, Lord. With death, the questions of birth and impurity cease to exist. No one can separate us then.' The comic book is obviously different from all the medieval biographies in depicting Tiruppan as smouldering with anger, humiliation, and some rebellion. Some aspects of the story differ too. Tiruppan is sleeping when the muni approaches him, not singing; even in the interpolation in *The Splendour-1*, Loka Saranga Muni throws only one stone at Tiruppan; in the comic book, the 'priest hit Tiruppan on the head with his stick . . . still smouldering with anger the priest showered a volley of stones on poor Tiruppan . . . at last the priest turned to the task for which he had come'. The comic portrays senseless violence heaped upon the 'Untouchable', perhaps echoing the social conditions of the twentieth century in this biography. This, however, is not to contend that these atrocities did not happen in the eighth century, but only that these details do not appear in any of the biographies. The comic goes on to more innovative features, but they need not detain us here. The author has a clear agenda; he introduces the story in stern tones:

> Even as early as the time of the Buddha, Hinduism was already vitiated by the hierarchy of the caste system. . . . The caste system is still a blot on Hindu society despite the relentless campaigns carried on against it by enlightened social reformers and thinkers through the ages. . . . [11]

We see a creative retelling of Tiruppan's life with the twentieth-century agenda of social reform, and in a sense this adapting of the story to the times is typical of *all* the biographies we have discussed.

One last incident remains to be discussed before we move on to look at what Tiruppan composed. When we last looked at the medieval biographies, Tiruppan had been taken to the temple by the muni. The commentaries on the poem have long discussions on whether they circumambulated the temple, whether Tiruppan began the poem as they were going around or after he went into the *garbha griha*, the inner sanctum, and so on. Once inside the temple, Tiruppan gazes at the form of Ranganatha reclining on his serpent bed, and sings in praise of him, describing him from his feet upwards to his head. According to all the biographies, the end is startlingly miraculous; he unites and disappears into the Lord:

> By the love that was born of the experience [of looking at the Lord], he sang the ten songs even as he underwent the experience. He sang the *prabandha* called 'the pure primordial Lord' (*amalan ati piran*) so that later generations could meditate on it and live . . . as he so stood, the Great Lord [the name of Ranganatha] accepted him with his body (*angikarittu*), just as those people who adorn themselves with certain [fragrant] roots do not mind the mud that comes with it. The alvar, in a manner that everyone could see, gracefully disappeared into the sacred feet of the handsome Ranga.[12]

Other biographies repeat the sentiments; just as a child goes instinctively to the mother's breasts, Tiruppan goes unerringly to the Lord's feet.[13]

The notion of physical assumption into a consecrated deity in the temple is limited to just two Alvars in the Srivaishnava hagiographies. Antal, the woman *bhakta*, and Tiruppan Alvar are the only two Alvars to so disappear, and both incidents take place in the Srirangam temple. Nammalvar is also said to have physically ascended to heaven; he was taken there with his earthly body. The Alvar's connection with his physical body is not severed despite his union with the Lord. In fact, in Srivaishnava theology, the physical body of the Alvar, which he wants to get rid of, is actually 'craved' by the Lord:

> Even though the alvar took refuge in the Lord and requested the Lord to sever his connection with his material body, the Lord did not do so, because he covets (the Alvar's) auspicious body and because it is his will to use (the Alvar) to complete the Tiruvaymoli. . . .[14]

The sense-organs and the body, which are seen as impediments to the union with the Lord in many Hindu traditions, are actually preserved and enjoyed by him. While this may seem unusual, it must be pointed out that in Srivaishnava theology, the universe is an expression of the Lord's glory; and while a human being from ignorance may think of the body as vile and defiling, from the point of view of liberation, the whole universe, both matter and spirit, is the body of the Lord. The saint's physical body is precious, for it is the vessel of the saint's soul; and both are precious to the Lord. The later biography, *The Glory*, while discussing the issue of physical assumption says:

> Maran (Nammalvar) told [the Lord], 'Please destroy the five elements, the motor organs which grasp at material substances and this deceiving body.' The Lord replied, 'What did you say? Would those who live on this earth and wish to anoint themselves with fragrant sandalwood paste, break the perfume container and then anoint themselves? . . . This is your body which has contained you who have clear [wisdom]. . . .[15]

Thus, even the physical body of the saint becomes precious to the Lord; the biographer's analogy is that just as a perfume bottle is not broken in order to enjoy the perfume, the Lord does not wish to destroy the Alvar's body to enjoy his soul. This emphasis on the delectable nature of the physical body is also seen in the stories of Antal and Tiruppan Alvar, who are said to have merged with their physical bodies into the Lord at Srirangam.

The earliest biography of Tiruppan Alvar was probably composed at least four hundred years after his life. The later biographies preserve a core story, but as we see in the *Amar Chitra Katha* version, the social context of the times influences the retelling. What is most significant in these biographies is the isolation of Tiruppan Alvar from the human/ Untouchable context and the process of divinizing him. Some biographies portray him as being born into the Untouchable group but somehow being different; he does not cry, the glance of the Lord falls on him, he eats 'clean' food, and so on. Other biographies simply talk of him as not born of a human womb (*ayonija*); this last removes the problem of his Untouchable birth. He is also an avatar, an incarnation of a part of Vishnu; he is not just another human being. Thus, he is simply an Untouchable by force of circumstances. In other words, there is a desire in these life stories to explain away, and *not* come to terms with his Untouchable status. Given the fact that by the time the biographies were written, Tiruppan was already seen to be an elevated Alvar and was in some cases even venerated in temples, there seems to be a need to demonstrate that this was a unique 'Untouchable', that he is not really a model for other Panars to emulate. One may make similar arguments about the lifestories of the woman saint Antal, too; there is a need to reassure the audience that she was special and was removed from humanity. Antal refused to get married to a human being and insisted that she be wedded to the Lord himself; biographies make her a divine incarnation of the Goddess Earth, thus implying clearly that she is not necessarily a social model for young girls. Rather than being a paradigmatic woman, she is portrayed as one whose devotion is to be selectively emulated by all human beings; her refusal to accept the dharma and the shastric role for women is played down by portraying her as a divine being. Tiruppan Alvar, the Untouchable saint, is similarly portrayed as a unique case; just because his lyrics are a part of temple liturgy, it did not mean that all Panars were allowed into the shrine in later years. According to at least one temple history, Ramanuja made special provisions for a group of Untouchables, whom he renamed *tiru kulattar* (sacred clan), to enter the Melukote temple for one day of the year. This issue will be discussed shortly. But before we look at the larger issue of Srivaishnava Untouchables, let us consider the poem that the community regards as Tiruppan Alvar's.

The Song

Tiruppan Alvar's poem is a *stotra*, a straightforward panegyric, praising Ranganatha as the manifestation of Vishnu in the Srirangam temple. He describes Ranganatha from feet to head, and says how entranced he is by the beauty of his Lord. It is a description of a particular, specific, and local manifestation, whom he identifies with the Vishnu manifestation in the sacred hill of Tiruvenkatam (present-day Tirumala–Tirupati, the Balaji shrine in Andhra Pradesh) and with the generic Vishnu of the Puranas.

I

Pure lord
Primordial lord
faultless one
who made me a servant
of his servants.

King of the celestials
Lord of Venkatam
    hill filled with gardens
    lush and fragrant.

Holy one, pure one
righteous lord of the sky
Lord of Arankam
    city with lofty walls
his sacred lotus feet
    come and enter my eyes.

II

With exalted heart
he measured the worlds
and rose in height
tearing off
the top of the sky
Lord with long hair.

The other day, Kakuttha
with fiery arrow
conquered the demons
who confronted him.

Lord of Arankam
    city of fragrant groves
my thoughts
are on the red cloth
wrapped around his waist.

III

He stands
on the great Venkatam hill
here monkeys leap
and the celestial ones
come to worship him.

he reclines
on the serpent bed
in Arankam

garments coloured
like twilight.
Above this
he created Ayan
on his navel.

O sweet life of me
    your servant!

IV

He shot the fiery arrow
that scattered the ten heads
of the king of Lanka
    city surrounded by mighty walls
Lord, the colour of the sea
Lord of Arankam
    where large bees
    drunk on nectar, sing
    and graceful peacocks dance

your waist belt
    binding the belly
    enters into
    and moves my heart!

V

Destroying the bonds
of my ancient sins
he made me his own, his love

keeping me so,
the other day
he entered inside me.
I don't know
what penance
long and harsh
I ever did.

Lord of Arankam
O! his sacred chest
resplendent with Sri
has made me its slave.

VI

He ended the grief
of (the god on whose head)
is a sliver
of the silver moon.

Exalted father of Arankam
    city surrounded by gardens
    where bees
    with pretty wings prosper.

O look, the throat
that swallowed the worlds
and all that is outside of it
the spreading lands,
the seven mountains,
time and all else
makes me, his servant, live.

VII

In his hands
conch with graceful swirls
spitfire wheel;
majestic torso
tall as a mountain
hair suffused
with fragrance of the tulsi.

My lord, wondrous one
who hugs his serpent bed

Lord of the jewel Arankam.

His red lips
    capture my thoughts.

VIII

Lord who ripped open
the demon with swollen body.

Primordial lord
Precious one of the immortals
Pure one of Arankam.

Your large eyes
dark on your face
now open like a flower;
    red lines run through them
long eyes,
    their splendour
    makes me wild.

IX

As a baby,
lying on a leaf

of a great banyan tree,
he ate the seven worlds,
he who reclines on the serpent
 in Arankam.

Long chains of glowing gems
heavy ropes of pearls
beauty without end.
Dazzling blue body
 fills my heart!

X

Dark as the stormy cloud
cowherd whose mouth
swallowed butter.
Lord who captured my heart
King of the skylords,
Lord of the jewel, Arankam

my ambrosia.

My eyes which have seen him
cannot see anything more.

The poem makes no mention of the poet's social class; the poet refers to himself only to say that he is captivated by the Lord's beauty. He does not even mention his own name, or the place from which he hails. Certainly, as we saw, there is no rancour, no bitterness, no chafing at the social order. This is particularly interesting as a point of contrast with many of the north Indian poets. In fact, there is nothing in the poem to suggest that a Panar has composed it. What we have are a few hints, little clues, which by themselves may not seem like much, but which seem significant in the light of the poet's background. The emphasis on the concept of 'purity': the words *malan*, *vimalan*, and *ninmalan*, appear in breathless succession within a few lines, and the audience, knowing the poet's 'impure' social status, can certainly wonder why these words rather than any others were used to describe the Lord.

The verses do continue, in the style of bhakti poetry, the kind of poems that Panars composed in honour of kings between the third and the fifth centuries CE. This is, of course, generic praise, and people other than Panars have done it in the Indian subcontinent. There were four kinds of minstrels in the Tamil lands; the Panars are the peripatetic variety. The Panars in ancient Tamil poetry praised kings, frequently using standard formulaic phrases,[16] and two of the oldest Tamil collections are called *Perum pan arruppatai* and *Cirup pan arrupatai.* One set was possibly meant for people with small *yals* and the other set for those musicians with large ones. These Panars generally praised the king's righteous rule:

> Even as the right-whorled conch is white and flawless,
> The rule of King Ilanthirayan is faultless and noble . . .

In another place, this king is said to dispense justice and to give gifts to those who need them.[17] The king's justice and righteousness were affirmed, and it is interesting to note that Tiruppan Alvar does this in the very first verse itself:

> Holy one, Pure one
> Righteous lord of the sky . . .

Unlike some of the other Alvars, Tiruppan Alvar does not proclaim his lowliness, either moral or social. Consider the following verses of Tirumankai Alvar:

> I desired the pleasures
>   of women with beautiful breasts,
>   women with delicate foreheads, wide shoulders,
> and smiles radiant like the glowing moon;
> and now,
>   knowing the error of my ways,
>   ignorant and unable
>   to end the misery of repeated births,
> I think and fret.
> Ashamed of my copulation with young girls,
> I have come and reached your sacred feet,
>   my lord at Naimicharanyam.

Without any feeling and with cruel mind,
    with actions filled with rage.
Wandering with packs of dogs,
    rejoicing in sport,
I ran and roamed, destroying several lives.
The world of Yama has to be refashioned
    to fit my crimes.[18]
O Supreme One! O you on the Sea of Milk!
Searching,
    I have come and reached your sacred feet,
    My lord at Naimicharanyam.

(*Periya Tirumoli* 1.6.1 and 6)

There is no ranting about his wicked past; the closest we come to the acknowledgement of 'sin' in the poem is seen in Tiruppan Alvar's gratitude that the Lord has cut his bonds of ancient sins:

Destroying the bonds
of my ancient sins,
he made me his own, his love,
keeping me so.
The other day
he entered inside me.
I don't know
what penance
long and harsh
I ever did.

(verse 5)

Even here, the words are generic, without any specificity. Nor is there in the poem any fervent desire expressed about wanting to serve other devotees of the Lord, however low they may be. Nammalvar, who is generally considered to be the most important Alvar, declares that the devotees of the Lord are his masters, even if they are Chandalas, Untouchables:

Even if they have fallen below the four castes
    that hold this society together
and are outcastes of the outcastes
    who have no trace of virtue;

if they are the servants
of those servants
who have mingled with
the Lord who bears the discus in his right hand,
the gem-coloured one,
they are my masters.

They are my masters:
those who are the servants
of the servants
of the servants
of the servants
of the servants
of the servants
of the servants
of my father, my Lord
who eats the worlds that he paced
and lies on a banyan leaf,
like an innocent babe.

(*Tiruvaymoli* 3.7.9 and 10)

There is no similar statement about caste, as in the poem above, in Tiruppan Alvar's poem. He, like other Tamil poets, does identify the Lord in one sacred city to be the same as his manifestation elsewhere; thus, in two places, he talks of the Lord in Arankam being the same as the Lord in Venkatam. The iconic image of the Lord dominates any of the avatar references; in practically every verse, there is a reference to Arankam and a description of Ranganatha. A few well-known Vishnu myths are cited; there is one reference to the Trivikram avatar, two to Rama, one to Vishnu rescuing Shiva, one to the killing of a 'huge demon', which commentators take to be Hiranya, two references to Vishnu's swallowing of the worlds, and one to Krishna. Like the other Alvars, Tiruppan assumes the primacy of Vishnu, especially in his temple manifestation, and identifies this Lord with all the other avatars.

Legacy

Although the Srivaishnava community hailed Tiruppan Alvar as the paradigmatic devotee, it did not allow other Untouchables to enter the temples. Tiruppan Alvar, like Antal the woman devotee, was considered to be an exception to the normal social order. Thus, while Tiruppan was installed in Srivaishnava temples and worshipped, the Untouchables were not allowed into these temples to worship either the Lord or Tiruppan. This section will focus on the Untouchable Srivaishnavas of the twentieth century who live in Bangalore in the south Indian state of Karnataka. These Srivaishnavas articulate an assertive and positive reinterpretation of the meaning of the Vedas and the epithet 'twice-born'. Further, their pride in their ancestry, of having descended from a clan of Vishnu and Alvar devotees, comes through very strongly in their sense of identity. Before we meet these twentieth-century Srivaishnava *bhaktas*, let us briefly look at some medieval (post-Tiruppan Alvar) discussions on Untouchability within the Srivaishnava community.

There are many isolated incidents to show that at least in spirit, if not in actual practice, the Srivaishnava community tried to uphold the notion of the equality of devotees over caste hierarchy. But when it came to communal issues like temple worship, where more than one religious tradition was involved, and where a strong brahminical resistance was encountered, traditional views of caste purity and impurity won over. These isolated incidents in hagiographical literature and oral tradition demand a detailed study that is beyond the scope of this discussion. Nevertheless, the tenor of these stories, which depict the tensions with which the community was struggling, may be noted:

> A corpse was found floating down a river and it seemed obvious that it was that of an outcaste [it is never made clear how this was determined]. A Srivaishnava Brahmin sees the marks of the conch and discus on the body and realizes that this is the body of a Srivaishnava Untouchable. He performs the last rites for the body and is ostracized by the orthodox segment of the society. The Lord's voice vindicates the Brahmin; the divine voice proclaims: *urukku pollan; enakku nallan* (He is unacceptable for the people of this town, but good for me). From that time, the Brahmin's descendants are called *nallam chakravarti*, the good Brahmins.

This is the kind of incident that is frequently cited by the Srivaishnava tradition to prove the active interest in reform amongst the Srivaishnava teachers. Certainly, theological treatises speak of the greatness of bhakti and the supremacy of all devotees. Some teachers like Pillai Lokacharya say in the *Sri Vachana Bhusanam* that Tiruppan Alvar is higher than all other devotees. A curious reason is given for this; the author says that every Srivaishnava should know that he is the *sesa*, the servant, the slave, one owned by the Lord, and a high-caste devotee has to assume this lowly role, which may not be natural to him. But Tiruppan's lowliness was 'natural'; he did not have to assume it and he knew more easily than the others what it was like to be a humble slave. A similar argument is made by a different theologian about the superiority of Antal's love for the Lord; she spoke naturally from a woman's place, but the men had to assume this attitude. These are, at best, back handed compliments and reinforce the assumptions of the audience regarding the lowliness of the lower castes and women.

The community also 'converted' people into the Srivaishnava fold by the sacrament of *pancha samskara* and for nearly a thousand years now, people of several castes as well as outcastes claim to be part of this religious tradition.

Perhaps the incident that is best known by Srivaishnavas, and which is quoted as evidence to show their relative openness to the Untouchables, is the one that is associated with Ramanuja. Ramanuja spent several years in exile in the Hoysala kingdom in Karnataka when he was persecuted by the Shaiva Chola king. Some information about his travels is retained in biographical literature, temple *mahatmayas,* and temple inscriptions. Apparently, once while Ramanuja and his retinue were lost in the wilderness, some Untouchables gave them shelter and showed them the way to their destination. Ramanuja is said to have called this group *tiru kulattar* (the sacred clan or the clan that belongs to the Goddess Lakshmi) in gratitude. Some say that he allowed them to enter the Melukote temple on certain days of the year. These privileges are still exercised by the members of the *tiru kulattar* community.[19] What is important to note is that while the outcastes may have been held high in theory, in practice they were not allowed into the temples. Many of them formed their own groups for worship, learnt *The Sacred Collect of Four Thousand Verses*, venerated the Alvars and the acharyas, but never set foot into a Srivaishnava temple. The term *tiru kulattar* remained a euphemism.

Many members of the *tiru kulattar* now live in Bangalore.[20] Although they are allowed into the temples, they prefer to worship in their community shrines. It is possible, though not known for sure, that these Srivaishnava outcastes, who speak Tamil and know some Sanskrit, came originally from Mysore and are the descendants of a community converted to Srivaishnavism by the acharya Ramanuja in the eleventh century CE.

Several groups live clustered around shrines dedicated to the various Alvars, and the people whom I got to know well were members of the Sri Nammalvar Sabha, a congregation formed in 1881 under the leadership of Sri Parasurama Dasar. They live around a shrine called the Sri Nammalvar *cannati* (*sannidhi* in Sanskrit).[21] Sri Vipranarayana (note that he bears the name of a Brahmin Alvar, Tontar *ati poti*, one who wanted to be like the dust on the feet of devotees) directs, supervises, and conducts the main recitation in a manner conforming to the traditional way in which he believes it to have been performed by his ancestors. He takes pride in continuing an unbroken chain of ritual and recitation that was carried on by his forefathers since the inception of the *cannati* in 1881, when the land was obtained from the British and the shrine was built by the devotees in the evenings and during the nights. Parasurama Dasar, who built the *cannati*, was a bartender at the army mess close by; in fact, even now, many of the devotees who worship at the shrine and who live within a radius of a mile in Gowthamapuram work at the army workshop. Sri Vipranarayana, the grandson of Sri Parasurama Dasar, worked at the army mechanical workshop till 1985; he now has a little shop outside his house.

Sri Vipranarayana believes that the traditional recitation was carried on by his ancestors even before the shrine was built in the nineteenth century. Parasurama Dasar, who was a disciple of a person called Tiruvaymoli Acharya of Mysore, established contact with a number of Srivaishnava Untouchable communities and organized their recitation rituals by encouraging the formation of congregations that could recite the *Divya Prabandham*.[22]

The first shrine to be built was, naturally enough, in honour of Tiruppan Alvar. It is known today as the Pan Perumal *cannati* and is located near the Ulsoor lake in Bangalore Cantonment. Sri Nammalvar *cannati* was built not long after that. Twelve such shrines were built at the time. In addition to the shrine for Tiruppan Alvar, there are also shrines dedicated to the Alvars Tirumankai, Kulashekara, and Tontar *ati poti*; some are dedicated to the acharya, the teachers Ramanuja (known as Utaiyavar *cannati*) and Manavala Mamuni. Other shrines are dedicated to the manifestations of Vishnu. Of the twelve shrines in Bangalore, eight are dedicated to Alvars or acharya, and only four to the Lord Vishnu.[23]

A significant, and perhaps, an unparalleled feature of the Untouchables in these shrines in Bangalore is that many of the members wear a sacred thread like the 'twice-born' communities. This custom apparently flows from the belief that the *Tiruvaymoli*, the composition of Nammalvar, and the other works of the *The Sacred Collect of Four Thousand Verses* are the Tamil Veda, equivalent in every way to the Sanskrit Vedas.

When asked about it, the explanation came from Sri Govinda Ramanuja Dasar, their spiritual advisor who was visiting from Ganeshapuram, Chennai. He first quoted from the *Tolkappiyam*, the Tamil text. A Brahmin was known by a thread, a water carrier, three staffs, subdued senses, and detachment.[24] The Alvars, he said, spoke about detachment in their poems and everyone in his community was striving towards that goal. Sri Govinda Ramanuja Dasar also emphasized several times that *The Sacred Collect* was Veda and that this congregation was being prepared to study the most sacred of all revelations. The Tamil Veda dealt with the knowledge of Vishnu, the supreme Brahman (*Brahma vidya*), and since one could not study the word of God without the right preparation, they were given the [sacred] thread; the wearing of it was, however, optional. Sri Vipranarayana said that the ceremony had been conducted for him in 1945, when he was thirteen. He had stopped wearing it, but his younger brother had it on throughout the rituals.

With the authority to wear the sacred thread came the authority to study the most essential segments of the Sanskrit Vedas pertinent to daily ritual: the chanting of the *Purusa sukta* and some sections of the *Taittriya Upanishad.* The significance of this recitation has to be noted; in all classical Sanskrit texts only male members of the higher castes had the authority to recite from the Vedas. In the daily ritual at the *cannati*, Sri Vipranarayana chanted the *Purusa, Sri,* and *Nila suktams* as well as the *Taittriya Upanishad* (*samno mitra sam varunah*, etc.) along with verses from the *Tiruvaymoli.* Sri Vipranarayana also pointed out that one of the meanings of the Tamil word *vaymoli* was, in fact, Veda. The point made repeatedly by Sri Govinda Ramanuja Dasar as well as Sri Vipranarayana was the *superiority* of the Tamil Veda, the four thousand verses of the Alvars; and if they had the authority to recite *that*, then surely the authority to chant the Sanskrit Veda could be assumed. They described the *Tiruvaymoli* as containing knowledge of Vishnu, the supreme Brahman, and therefore, this knowledge (*vidya*) was like *Brahma vidya.*

It was in this connection that I was given the pamphlet called

Apasudradhikaranam, written by Sri Govinda Ramanuja Dasar. The name of the pamphlet is the same as a section in the *Sribhasya* of Ramanuja, in which he takes up the question of the authority of the shudras to receive *Brahma vidya.* While Ramanuja states clearly in the *Sribhasya* that shudras cannot study the Veda, he does admit the possibility of their being wise (like Vidura in the Mahabharata), because of the lingering effects of previous good deeds. He also clarifies some incidents from the *Chandogya Upanishad* where it may be superficially assumed that the people enlightened by *Brahma vidya* are shudras. In discussing these incidents,[25] Ramanuja points out the origin of the word 'shudra'; he derives it from the root *suk*, to grieve.[26] With some interesting exegesis, Sri Govinda Ramanuja Dasar shows how an instructor of *Brahma vidya* in the story of Janasruti, one Raikva, is actually a person without an ashrama (an identifiable station in life recognized by the Sanskrit law manuals) and is therefore a shudra. Thus, in the self-image of the community we find the conviction that the teacher Ramanuja had believed them to have the authority to obtain the knowledge of Brahman, or what we would call salvific knowledge. Members of the Sri Nammalvar Sabha believe that this salvific knowledge is obtained by the recitation of the Tamil Veda, that which was graciously vouchsafed to them by the Alvars.

Sri Vipranarayana said several times that for twenty-four generations prior to Sri Parasurama Dasar their family had been Srivaishnavas.[27] What is to be noted is the expression of pride in ancestry, akin to that exhibited by some Brahmins. To belong to a family of devotees and have a place in this line was important to the identity of Sri Vipranarayana. The recitation was important in itself, but he was also very conscious of carrying on an unbroken tradition that had lasted several centuries. This spiritual heritage and biological ancestry coincided; he came from a long line of Srivaishnavas who were presumably devoted to the Alvars. He quoted verses from *The Sacred Collect* to illustrate his points; a few translations follow. In the first few lines of the following verse, Tirumankai Alvar says with pride that he hails from a long line of Vishnu devotees:

> My father, and his father
>   and further seven times more,
> were old servants of yours;
>   you have entered my heart

and I shall not let you go.
My dear Life! My king!
My lord who without pausing
granted me grace!
O perfect lord of Naraiyur!

(*Periya Tirumoli* 7.2.6)

Similarly, says Sri Vipranarayana, he comes from a family where twenty-four generations were Srivaishnavas and servants of Vishnu and the Alvars. This in itself is reason for prosperity and good fortune, as Nammalvar himself proclaimed:

Keshava's followers
for seven generations before
and seven generations to come
have the great fortune and prosper along with us,
through [the grace] of the lord, my dark gem, my adored one,
the lord of the celestials, my god, my Narayana.

(*Tiruvaymoli* 2.7.1)

Anyone even remotely connected with a devotee of Vishnu would have good fortune because of the Lord's grace. The best way that he could describe himself and the members of the congregation who venerated the Alvars, said Sri Vipranarayana, was that they were the servants of the servant of God.

For the members of the congregation, the utterances of the Alvars seem to have salvific value, and the recitation of the verses guarantees salvation no matter what the qualification of the devotee. On a different level, they say, the recitation is already indicative of the salvation achieved. Nammalvar, ultimately, is a saviour, and the members of the congregation believe that it is because of their relationship to him that they were saved. The congregation's recitation honouring the Alvars may be understood as their celebration of the poets and their procuring salvation to the devotees. Salvation is *contagious* and a relationship to one who is saved, whether it is biological or spiritual, guarantees the highest state. Sri Vipranarayana quoted an incident from the biography, *The Splendour-1*: when Ramanuja was asked about the certainty of salvation, he replied that there was an unbroken *chain* of devotees going from those bound on earth to the Lord. The links began with Sri

(Lakshmi), the consort of Vishnu, and the first human link was Nammalvar. Nammalvar represents all the Alvars, all of whom got salvation. So all the teachers who were connected with him obtained salvation. When the gardener watered an areca tree, all the banana trees close by got the water as well. Ramanuja concluded that just as he, by his connection with his teachers culminating in Nammalvar, was sure of salvation, everyone else connected with him should be assured of it because of their relationship with him. For Sri Vipranarayana, there is a biological chain of Srivaishnava devotees, on the one hand, and a direct link to the Alvars, on the other. Because the congregation was linked with the Alvars, they were also saved. The community may be called 'Untouchable', but it is because of *touch*, because of their biological link with the other devotees and their link with the Alvars, that they will receive salvation. For them, bhakti transcends all dharmic prescriptions; bhakti transcends Manu and his cohorts. Tiruppan Alvar, Antal, and the other Alvars would agree; however, a thousand years of Srivaishnava devotees have agreed in theory, but not in practice.

NOTES

1. *Tolkappiyam*, Porulatikaram, 91. Meanings for all Tamil words are taken from the *Tamil Lexicon*, vols. 1–6, unless otherwise noted.
2. I have used the word 'class' to refer to the Tamil word *kula*, which is used to indicate class, caste, clan, family, or lineage. I use the word 'community' to refer to the Srivaishnavas; this 'community' or 'tradition' (*sampradaya*) includes devotees, from all jatis and the Untouchables.
3. Some like Poykai (tank) Alvar get their names from the place where they are said to have miraculously been born. Pey (possessed or spirit) is said to have been like one possessed by devotion; but they do have alternative Sanskrit names.
4. While traditionally the *Divya Suri Charitam* is dated around the time of Ramanuja (1017–1137), some scholars think it may belong to the fifteenth century. Since the dates of these biographies do not affect my discussion in this essay, I shall simply give some prevalent views so that the reader may get an approximate time frame to contextualize the information.
5. *The Splendour-1*, p. 64.
6. K.C. Varadachari, *Alvars of South India*, Alkondaville Govindachari, *Life of the Alvars*, Amar Chitra Katha's *Tiruppan and Kanakadasa* and Prof. K.R.R. Sastry's *Sublime Biographies: Tamil Mysticism*, all recount the story in some detail.
7. Sastry, *Sublime Biographies*, p. 42.
8. This is just one of the 'formula' stories shared by the Srivaishnava and *advaitin* traditions. I have been struck by the similarity in the stories of how the '*kanakadhara stotra*' (attributed to Shankara by Hindus and refuted by Western scholars) and

the '*Sri Stuti*' of Vedanta Desika came to be composed. In both cases, the acharyas, showing their compassion to poor housewives, pray to the Goddess Lakshmi and a shower of gold coins falls on their doorsteps. A thorough study of these comparative stories in different traditions needs to be done.

9. There is a possibility that the narrative is confused between a group of people called Tiruppani ceyvar and Tiruppan Alvar. This group was apparently chosen by Ramanuja for the purposes of cleaning streets. *Pani* is not connected to *pan* but means 'to serve', 'to do humble work'. They swept, sprinkled water, and made sure that the streets were free of litter. These people were not Untouchables. In fact, they lead processions and gathered the offerings made by people. There is a story that a king spit out betel leaf and a member of the Tiruppani ceyvar immediately cleaned it from the street. Impressed with their attitude and their eagerness to perform a lowly job well, the king apparently appointed his own servants to take over the work of the Tiruppani ceyvar. *Koil Olugu*, translated by Hari Rao, pp. 69–71.
10. Indira Peterson, *Poems to Siva: The Hymns of the Tamil Saints*, Princeton: Princeton University Press, 1989, p. 20 and also the Saivaite saint Cuntarar's lines (p. 336):
    Of the Panan musician Tirunilakantan
    I am the servant.
11. Introduction to *Tiruppan and Kanakadasa*, Amar Chitra Katha, no. 186.
12. *The Splendour-1*, p. 68.
13. *The Splendour-1*, p. 68 and *The Splendour-2*, p. 37.
14. Pillian, in the Introduction to *The Six Thousand Commentary* on the *Tiruvaymoli*, 7.1.
15. *The Glory*, vv. 1043–4, pp. 262–3.
16. On the role of panars in ancient Tamil society, see Hart, *The Poems of Ancient Tamil: Their Milicu and Sanskrit Counterparts*, Berkelay, California: University of California Press, 1975.
17. *Perumpanarrupadai*, 11, 35–43 and 441–47. The first quotation is from *The Golden Anthology of Ancient Tamil Literature*, trans. Mudoliyar, Tinnevelly: Shaiva Siddhanta Publishing Society, 1959–60, vol. II, p. 6.
18. This is a loose translation of the sentence, implying that the standard punishment in the realm of Yama, the god of death, is not adequate for the extensive sins committed by the Alvar.
19. See Alkondaville Govindacharya, *The Life of Ramanuja*, Madras, 1906. Govindacharya does not report the sources for this discussion. He follows the thirteenth-century hagiography, *The Splendour-1*, fairly closely, but this incident is not found in it. He does have an interesting footnote reporting an article from *The Hindu*, dated 5 February 1906. In the midst of its discussion of Ramanuja's liberal attitude towards the *tirukulattar*, the article also mentions the special canopy erected by the *tirukulattar* of Bangalore to 'greet Their Royal Highnesses' when they visited India in 1906. K. Gnanambal in her article 'Srivaishnavas and their Religious Institutions', in *Bulletin of the Anthropological Survey of India*, vol. 20, no. 3, 1977, p. 125, also reports Ramanuja's conversion of the Untouchables to the *tirukulattar*. See also G. Lakshamma, *The Impact of Ramanuja's Teaching on Life and Conditions in Society*, Delhi: Sundeep Prakashan, 1990, pp. 129–31 and 144.

20. The material for this section is drawn from observation and participation in the rituals of the Sabha in 1983 and 1985, and from discussions with two of its leaders. Sri Vipranarayana (whose ancestors founded the shrine) and Sri Govinda Ramanuja Dasar, their adviser and ritual superviser from Ganeshapuram, Chennai, graciously spent several hours recalling the history of their shrine and sharing details of their recitation rituals and textual authorities. Sri Gopalkrishna Ekangi Swami, a 'non-brahmin' sannyasi from Srirangan, was present during some of these conversations.
21. The Sanskrit word *sannidhi* means 'appearance, receptacle, presence'. Srivaishnavas use the word to indicate the sanctum of a temple or a shrine. The word is translated in this essay as 'shrine' or a place in which the divine presence is perceived.
22. K. Gnanambal in 'Srivaishnavas and their Religious Institutions' briefly mentions the establishment of the shrine. She reports a conversation with Sri V.T. Tirunarayana Iyengar of Melukote, who is said to belong to the Tiruvaymoli Acharya family (pp. 164–5). This family was one of seventy-four families appointed by Ramanuja as an '*acharya purusa*'. The *acharya purusas* were spiritual and ritual leaders of the Srivaishnava community and could administer the sacrament of surrender to their own family and to others as well. Gnanambal says that Iyengar's father urged the *tirukulattar* to form religious associations known as Ramanuja Kootam. These are parallel to the congregational halls among the Christians. It seems probable that she is referring to the community under discussion in this essay.
23. K. Gnanambal in 'Srivaishnavas and their Religious Institutions' gives a slightly different list of the shrines. She orders the shrines in the following manner: Pan Perumal Sabha, Andal Sabha, Tiruvengadamudaiyan Sabha, Manavala Mamuni Sabha, Kannan Sabha, and Alvar Sabha. The last one is presumably Nammalvar Sabha. Of these, she claims that the first two are formed by the *tirukulattar*.
24. I have identified the quotation as *Tolkappiyam, porul atikaram*, 9: 71. The exact quotation is, *nule karakam, mukkol, manaiye/ayum kalai, antanarukky uriye.*
25. These incidents are those of Janasruti (*Chandogya* 4.2–3) and Jabala (*Chandogya* 4.3–4).
26. *Sribhasya* 1.3.33. The actual etymology of the word is unknown, according to the Monier-Williams dictionary.
27. He also said that there was a controversy about the question of when the twenty-four generations had actually begun. Sri Vipranarayana's father was one Sri Sarangapani Ramanuja Dasar, and he believed that he was the twenty-fourth generation Srivaishnava from Natamuni, the very first acharya of the Srivaishnava community (tenth century CE); others thought that the count began with the time of Sri Manavala Mamuni in the fifteenth century. In question were five hundred years of Srivaishnavahood for the ancestors, and apparently the difference of opinion on this matter was deep enough to cause a rift between some people in his father's generation. The number twenty-four, however, was believed to be correct.

2

In Love with the Body of God: Eros and the Praise of Icons in South Indian Devotion*

STEVEN P. HOPKINS

The forms of the world appear-
    lightning
from your dark icon

(*Mummanikkovai*, 10)

O lord true to your servants
your body is like dark kohl
a deep blue kaya blossom.

    O munificent king
who showers grace like torrents
    from a monsoon cloud
    over Serpent Town-

those who do not forget your beautiful body
    will not be born again!

(*Navamanimalai*, 6)[1]

This essay focuses on a distinctive genre of devotional poetry in the Srivaishnava tradition, . . . [whose] many themes include the uses of the erotic to speak about the relationship between the human and the divine; the use of divine images in ritual and religious poetry; and the sometimes uneasy relationship between poetry and commentary (or, more broadly put, between philosophy and literary art). But before I begin an analysis of two Indian poems, I want, for reasons of comparison, to draw attention to a persistent and compelling motif in the Hebrew *Song of Songs*.

A World Away: The Body of the Beloved in the Ancient Near East

'Your two cheeks are an orchard of pomegranates, an orchard full of choice fruits. . . .' Many of us have read these curious lines with delight and not a little amazement. The lovers in the Hebrew *Song of Songs* describe the body of their beloved from foot to head or head to foot in hyperbole that at times seems to border on the comic and grotesque. The innovative metaphors and similes of the lovers leap across chasms of association in what Robert Alter has called a poetics of 'flaunted figurations'.[2] Yet in spite of its strangeness, their language is charged with feeling; it expresses an alluring, even disarming, erotic energy. . . .

Since the nineteenth century, when similarities between the *Song* and modern Arabic poetry were first noticed, critics and Biblical scholars have referred to this genre of poetic description by the Arabic word *wasf* (pl. *awasaf*). *Wasf* literally means 'description', a poetic passage that describes in sequence, and by means of a series of exaggerated, sometimes artificial images, the parts of the human body.[3]

The purpose of the *wasf*, as Richard Soulen observed some years ago, is 'presentational rather than representational'. 'Its purpose,' Soulen suggested, 'is not to provide a parallel to visual appearance' or 'primarily to describe feminine or masculine qualities metaphorically'.[4] Rather, the images want to evoke feeling; they 'seek to create emotion, not critical or dispassionate comprehension; their goal is a total response, not simply a cognitive one'.[5] The lovers' metaphorical hyperbole is, in Soulen's words, 'the language of joy' which seeks to 'overwhelm and delight the hearer'.[6] We are invited, even gently coerced, to share a lover's awe, joy, and erotic delight in the physical beauty of the beloved. The visual exaggeration of the *wasf* is related to other rhetorical extravagances of the text, which include tactile images of entering, eating, tasting, and feasting on the beloved, and the olfactory eroticism of flowers, fruits, spices, perfumes, and the many aromas of the Lebanon mountains. And the *Song* not only engages the senses one at a time, but it also often mingles them in a vivid synaesthesia, as in one of its first images, where the beloved's name is said to be a 'spreading perfume'.

AN ICON IN THE GARDEN OF METAPHOR

There are interesting analogues to the *wasf* in Sanskrit literary art (*kavya*) from its earliest strata of development around the first centuries CE. In Indian *kavya* elaborately figured descriptions of beautiful women from head to toe and toe to head are a common conceit. In such poetry, according to one of the early theorists of Indian poetics, Bhamaha (fourth–fifth or seventh centuries CE–his dates are uncertain), hyperbole or exaggeration (*atisayokti*) is quite acceptable, even inevitable, given a suitable poetic pretext (*nimitta*). It would not, strictly speaking, be seen as 'flaunted' at all, but appropriate to the aesthetic enjoyment of the erotic. Moreover, again according to Bhamaha, elaborate figuration (*vakrokti*) is one of the defining characteristics of ornamentation in poetry.[7]

I want to focus here, however, on an analogue to the *wasf* in a much later Indian tradition in the southern region of Tamil Nadu. And this is not a tradition of secular love, but one of devotion to the god Vishnu in the poems of Hindu saints (Alvars: those immersed in God) who flourished in the deep south from the sixth to the ninth centuries CE. I will discuss two poems in this tradition: one in Tamil by Tiruppanalvar, an Untouchable Vaishnava singer-saint who lived in Tamil Nadu around the seventh–eighth centuries; and another in Sanskrit by Vedantadesika in the fourteenth century. And in the case of Tiruppanalvar and Vedantadesika, it is not a male or female *human* lover who is the object of limb-by-limb description, but the male body of the various temple images of Ranganatha (a form of Vishnu) at the great temple in Srirangam.

These Hindu devotional poems follow earlier patterns of Buddhist *kavya* in adapting the conventions of secular love for religious purposes. Our two south Indian poets are heir to a long tradition. As early as the third century CE, in the Buddhist *stotras* or 'hymns' of Matrcheta, we have fully developed examples of the adaptation of this form of sequential description to the body of the Buddha. As A.K. Warder has observed, such descriptions in the Buddhist tradition 'go back to an ancient conventional account of the thirty-two 'characteristics' by which the body of the Buddha or of any 'great man' was supposed to have been distinguished'. Warder speculates that the earliest poetic expression of them in the Buddhist tradition may be found in the Pali *Lakkhanasuttanta* of the *Digha Nikaya* (third century BCE).[8] It is important also to note in this context the ironic use in early and medieval Buddhist literature of idealized descriptions of the female body. . . . The classical language of love is turned on its head and used in the service of a meditation on impermanence.[9] The irony is even more savage in the verses attributed to Bhikkhuni Subha of the Mango Grove, where the young male lover's hyperbolic praise of the beautiful nun's eyes–compared to 'gazelles' enshrined in her face as in the 'calyx of the lotus'–is answered by the nun tearing out her eye in contempt and handing it to the young man. 'Here then,' she says in disgust, 'take your eye!'[10] But women and women's bodies are not always the objects of parody or of religious disgust in Buddhist literature. The important thirteenth-century Sinhala *mahakavya*, the *Kausilumina* contains, for instance, an elaborate foot-to-head description of the beauty of Queen Prabhavati, the wife of a bodhisattva in his birth as King Kusa.[11]

These matters of gender description aside, what the later Hindu religious poems have in common with the early hymns in praise of the Buddha's body is the creative appropriation of a secular poetics whose primary object was praise of the female body, in the sphere of religious devotion to a male divine figure. And as we will see, the Hindu tradition did not discard, as did the Buddhist or even soft-pedal to a great extent, the erotic energies of the secular genre they transformed so deftly. This is precisely why comparison with the *Song of Songs* is both appropriate and relevant.

We find in Tiruppanalvar's Tamil poem and in [Vedanta]Desika's later [fourteenth century] Sanskrit imitation an analogous instance of enraptured description in a tradition remote in time, space, and context from the Hebrew *Song*, but not perhaps from its sensibility and poetics, its use of the senses and of landscape, or its emotional vocabulary. In fact, what we immediately see when we look at the Indian and Hebrew poems side by side is an intriguing reversal in the use of imagery. In the *Song*, imagery appropriate to statuary and icons is at times used to describe a human lover (i.e. the thighs 'like marble pillars on gold sockets', 'belly like an ivory bar' or the golden head). . . . In the Indian case, it is just the opposite: the cultic image is addressed in language appropriate to human love. We see in these Indian poems, unlike in the *Song*, an undeniable cultic locus, yet their exuberance of imagery far exceeds the concrete form of the icon in the temple sanctum. What strikes us when we read the Hebrew *Song* and the Indian devotional descriptions of the beloved God side by side is precisely the ***surplus of metaphoric energies*** in both. Such a comparative reading also foregrounds the rich vocabulary of human love and emotion brought to bear on the temple image by Vaishnavas in south India, and helps to draw our attention more vividly to the radical nature of divine embodiment expressed in this major strand of Hindu devotion.

* * *

The Icon, the Poem, and Its Body Language

The surface texture of the bard's [Tiruppanalvar] song is simple; the emphasis is on direct emotion, what Vedantadesika in his fourteenth-century commentary[12] describes as the 'thick nectar of ecstatic enjoyment' (*anupava kana rasamayirukkiratu*), a miraculous transcription of a unique experience of God. In declaration after declaration, the poet expresses his wonder at the harrowing beauty of God's body. The splendours of each and every limb are enjoyed in ascending order – as one Sanskrit invocatory praise of the bard (*taniyan*) tells us –'from foot to head' (*apadacudamanubhuya*):

> Let us meditate with firm resolve on the singer who rode
> piggy-back on the old priest,
> whose heart's core was filled with deep delight
> at the sight of Hari
> reclining in the middle of the Kaveri's twin streams-
>
> and who,
> after enjoying the Lord from His feet to His head,
> vowed that his eyes would never again
> see anything else!

As Desika says in his gloss on verse 9, one is suffused with a glorious splendour (*sopai*; Skt.: *sobha*) when one 'unites with the splendours of each and every limb' (*charvavayavasopaikal*) of the Lord. And these splendours do not only extend in all directions, permeating the space around the poet, but also enter into the depths of his heart, itself flooded with the glorious splendours of every limb of the Lord.[13]

The terms used here both by the poet and his scholastic commentators for such an ecstatic, limb-by-limb seeing of God's body—roughly equivalent to the Arabic *wasf*—are all cognates of the Sanskrit word *anubhava*: 'experience', 'perception', and, in Srivaishnava theology, 'enjoyment'. Annankaracharya puts it succinctly: this poem is a *padadikesa anubhava*, an 'enjoyment of God, one limb at a time, from the foot to the head'.[14] As K.K.A. Venkatachari has observed in his study of Srivaishnava *manipravala* [literally meaning jewels and coral: a hybrid language made up of Tamil and Sanskrit] prose style, this same term is used for the act of commentary itself. In this tradition, to comment on a text is not so much to strip away its aesthetic skin for the sake of a philosophic or esoteric core, though at times this seems to be the case. Ideally, to Srivaishnavas, the goal of commentary is a kind of 'spiritual enjoyment' that matches the root text's more direct 'enjoyment' of God.[15] And we find the most striking examples of this 'imaginative participation' of the commentator in the object of his commentary, of his aesthetic and religious 'relish' of the primary text, in the treatment of the beauty of God's temple body.

The poets and their scholastic commentators rarely use the usual technical terms to describe the temple images, such as *mula* and *dhruva* (the root, the firm) or *bimba*, *pratibimba* (reflection, copy, imitation). Even the more concrete terms, such as *archa* (what is honoured or worshipped), *vigragha* (what can be held, grasped) or even *murti* (image-embodiment/manifestation) are not as common as those terms which evoke the real presence of a *body*. The icon here is more than a mere image, in English parlance; it is God's body, a material presence, however spiritualized (the icon is thought to be formed from *shuddhasattva*, a rich term denoting 'spiritual matter'). The temple icon dominates as much the imagery of the commentators as it does that of the poet. Annankaracharya, for instance, glosses one of the four Sanskrit synonyms of the first verse, *vimalan* (faultless, pure) by a phrase that alludes to the 'lovely tawny hue' (*cirantapukarai*) of the golden festival image (*utsava murti*) of Ranganatha that stands in front of the god's dark stone image in the temple sanctum, along with those of his two wives.[16] It is these icons that, after being lavishly ornamented, are paraded in the streets in royal palanquins for all to see on festival days. In his prose commentary, the modern *acharya* speaks of *vima-*

lan as referring to the poet's 'enjoyment of a certain extraordinary splendour (*tejassai*; Skt: *tejas*) produced by our Lord's holy body' (*tirumeniyirpiranta*).

One of the most common words used by all the Alvars to describe the temple image is *meni*, meaning 'beautiful or perfect body'. Often an adjective denoting darkness or blue-black is used, as in Tiruppanalvar's *nila meni* in verse 9, which inspires in the mind of the reader-listener an image of the deep blue of monsoon clouds or of the sea, as well as that of the blue-black, *kasturi*-smeared immovable stone icon (the *mulabera*) in the sanctum, shiny and wet from lustrations. Desika glosses verse 4, where the Lord is described as being the 'colour of the sea' (*otavannan*), with an inspired allusion to the *mula* icon in the temple sanctum: 'He has an auspicious holy body (*tirumeni*), glossy blue-black like the sea, that can utterly destroy the burning heat of sins in those who see it!'[17] Annankaracharya also uses the image of Ranganatha as dark as the 'pupil of an eye'.

As in the *Song of Songs*, God's beloved body is continuous with the landscape in which it is placed–in this case not Mount Gilead or Hebron, the rich fragrant paradise gardens or fertile fields, but the shrine and its environs. In the words of the commentator, the poet simply 'exults, seeing before his very eyes Ranganatha who sleeps in the holy city of Srirangam, [his feet] gently massaged by the waves of the golden Kaveri'.[18] In a gloss on 'the colour of a raincloud' (*kontal vannanai*) in verse 10, Desika conjures one of his most vivid word-pictures of a landscape transfigured by the material presence of God: 'He has an auspicious holy body that soothes the weariness of those who see it, like a black cloud come to rest in the very middle of the Kaveri, having drawn into itself all the waters of the sea.'[19]

Thus *meni* evokes images of concentrated energy, alluring beauty, awe, fecundity (it can also mean 'full crop'), and mystery; it gives a sense both of darkness and effulgence. Other common words used for the icons are simply *uru* (Skt. *rupa*) or *vativu* (form, body). The Tamil commentators consistently gloss these neutral terms with the more formal coinage (quoted above) *tirumeni*, 'auspicious, divine beautiful body'.

Only a language of the body, so vivid in a love poem like the Hebrew *Song of Songs*, is able to catch the vividness of this saint-poet's ecstasy, the palpable presence of a transcendent god who yet captured, entered into, devoured the mind, and ravished the eyes of his human 'slave' (Tamil *ati*, 'slave' is synonymous here with 'devotee'). The more neutral language of icons, images, and iconography simply falls short in expressing the devotee's experience. For this radical encounter, the language of human love and human bodies is most appropriate and most powerful.

Ultimately, there is an interesting dialectic at work in Tiruppanalvar and in the other Alvars between metaphors of material body and mental image—God the master, that 'flawless overlord of celestials', standing there (*ninra*) in front of the poet-slave, visible to the 'naked eye' (*kannarakkantu*) as the commentators say, and his image present in the 'sweet core' of the heart. The Alvar here strongly affirms the ontological reality of both the material and the mental 'bodies' of God: the 'lovely lotus feet' that seem to come and enter his eyes as a kind of interior animated image, and the temple icon with its red waist-cloth that *his* eyes in turn capture and take into his mind. Desika, as we cited earlier, speaks of the poet's simultaneous experience, in his ecstasy, of an exterior and interior glory radiating from the limbs of the Lord's body. An exhaustive interpretation of each poem would have to take into account the sometimes subtle interplay of these two symbolic structures.

In other Tamil poets, such as Nammalvar, the mental and material forms of Vishnu are evoked by means of a striking use of alimentary vocabulary, where the poet (in the voice of a girl) himself devours the god, holding in his 'belly for keeps' that great Lord who once swallowed the worlds. A.K. Ramanujan calls this 'drastic' imagery of partaking or merging that of 'mutual cannibalism'. He gives as an example of such mutual devouring a stanza from Nammalvar's *Tiruvaymoli* (9.6.10)

> My dark one
> Stands there as if nothing's changed
>
> after taking entire
> into his maw
> all three worlds
> the gods
> and the good kings
> who hold their lands
> as a mother would
> a child in her womb-

and I
by his leave
have taken him entire

and I have him in my belly
for keeps.[20]

What this passage makes clear—and its immediate context, like that of Tiruppanalvar's poem, is the saint-poet standing before the temple icon—is that God both possesses and is possessed by the devotee. In extraordinary moments of religious ecstasy, the normal hierarchical relation is reversed. As Ramanujan summarizes: 'the reciprocity is carried all the way; the eater is eaten, the container is contained, in a metonomy many times over'.[21]

Tiruppanalvar's rhetoric is more soft-pedalled; there is some ambiguity as to who has 'devoured' whom. Though the poet's senses, 'or better his eyes', as Friedhelm Hardy has observed,[22] 'seem to devour each part of the body and bring them into his soul', and though his 'slave's heart' reaches out to rest on the waist-cloth and the shining navel, the accent seems rather to be on passivity, the poet *having been* entered, filled, ravished, taken captive. God's beautiful body seizes the heart of this Tamil devotional poet above all like a beloved seizes the heart of his lover, inspiring in her a rich 'language of joy' that celebrates union and difference.

And this gender symbolism is not only a literary convention, but also has a resonance in the actual daily practice of image worship among the Hindus. As C.J. Fuller has pointed out in his recent study of forms of 'popular' Hinduism, one might understand the system of exchanges in puja between a worshipper and the temple deity—particularly in regard to food—as conforming to the patterns of a household. By accepting food from a partner of inferior status (the lay person or priest), who then in turn eats the 'leftovers', the deity essentially acts as a husband in relation to his wife in a traditional household. It is thus literally true on the social level that—as the bhakti poets imply, if not outright proclaim—'the worshipper stands in relation to the deity as a wife to her husband'.[23] But here we enter into the real complexities and ambiguities of what Fuller calls 'the hierarchical inequality' between man and woman, deity and worshipper. For in the bhakti poetic tradition, as in puja—along with moments of awe and the overwhelming sense of the gulf that separates the divine and the human—there are vivid moments of union, of interrelationship, even of reversal; hierarchy dissolves for brief ecstatic instants. The moment of union, to use an example from Fuller, is like the moment one touches the camphor flame and, after moving the still-warm fingertips to the eyes, the energies of the divine fire are bodily absorbed through the eyes into the heart.[24] One such instant is wonderfully caught in verse 9 where Tiruppan calls out 'My God! His lovely dark body/of unfading beauty/strung with pearls/and dazzling gems/fills my heart!' The object of worship has filled the worshipper until for a moment they are one composite being.

Yet the 'real presence' of the temple image is never more puzzling and intriguing than when one contemplates the meaning of the final 'marriage' when the lover enters and disappears into the beloved– where God finds one particularly delectable devotee in *his* belly 'for keeps'. The body of the saint, like that of God, is precious in the Srivaishnava tradition. In one hagiographical source, as Vasudha Narayanan has pointed out in a recent paper [included in this volume], it is compared by the Lord himself to a vial of rare perfume. Must one break the bottle to enjoy the perfume? This sense of the delectable bodies of saints is perhaps one of the motifs at work in Tiruppanalvar's nuptial disappearance. He is one of only two saints–the other is a woman, Antal, also a poet of divine love–said to have one day merged into the sanctum icon at Srirangam.

I end here with a Tamil verse by Desika that begins his commentary on Tiruppanalvar's *Amalanatipiran.* It is a verse that elegantly gathers together many of the themes and certainly much of the spirit of our discussion of the bard's enjoyment of God.

> After we see him joined to our hearts
> as our creator,
> standing in his temple, mingling with his loving slave,
> our protector and husband,
> in the ten stanzas sung by the Lord of bards
> that bestow the fruits of the Vedas
> in Tamil song –
>
> we take a hint from the cowgirls who did their kuravai dance
> that day long ago
> for the Lord who became

their cowherd
and king:

we leave behind the loneliness of sinners,
uniting with Him
like the hen with her cock![25]

NOTES

* This essay, as it appears in this volume, is a shorter discussion limiting itself to an analysis of Tiruppanalvar's poem '*Amalanatipiran*' only. The related examination of Vedantadesika's similar fourteenth-century poem has been omitted here by necessity of the theme of the book. The original version may be found in the *Journal of Vaishnava Studies*, vol. 1, no 2, Winter 1993, pp. 17–54.

1. All quotations from Vedantadesika's Tamil poems are taken from *Sritecikappirapantam, uraiyutan* edited, with Tamil commentary by Sriramatecikacaryar, Madras, reprint 1982 (1944). All translations in this study from the Sanskrit, Prakrit, and Tamil are my own, unless otherwise indicated.
2. See his chapter on the *Song*, 'The Garden of Metaphor', in *The Art of Biblical Poetry*, New York Basic Books, 1986, p. 196. Alter distinguishes in this chapter between stock, intensive, and innovative imagery (the latter strikingly apparent in the *Job* and in the *Song*). Cf. also p. 193: 'It should be observed, to begin with, that in the *Song of Songs* the process of figuration is frequently "foregrounded"—which is to say, as the poet takes expressive advantage of representing something through an image that brings out a salient quality it shares with the referent, he calls our attention to his exploitation of similitude, to the artifice of metaphorical representation.'
3. See the section on *awsaf* in Marcia Falk's edition of the *Song, The Song of Songs: A New Translation and Interpretation*, San Francisco: HarperCollins, 1990, pp. 217–35.
4. See Richard Soulen, 'The Wasfs of the Song of Songs and Hermeneutic', *Journal of Biblical Literature*, vol. LXXXVI, part II, June 1967, pp. 183–90.
5. Ibid., p. 188.
6. Ibid., p. 190.
7. For a detailed account of the history of Indian poetics, see A.K. Warder, *Indias Kavya Literature*, vol. 1: *Literary Criticism*, New Delhi: Motilal Banarsidass, 1989 (1972). For passages referred to here on figures of speech in Bhamaha, see pp. 82–89.
8. For a discussion of Matrcheta's, *stotras*, see A.K. Warder, *Indian Kavya Literature, Volume Two: Origins and Formation of the Classical Kavya*, New Delhi: Motilal Banarsidass, 1974, pp. 228–30. Quotation on p. 230.
9. For Ambapali's verses, see *Therigatha*, pp. 252–70, in Oldenberg and Pischel's edition, London: Pali Text Society, 1883, pp. 147–50. For an English translation, see Rhys David, *Psalms of the Early Buddhists*, vol. 1: *Psalms of the Sisters*, London: Pali Text Society, 1909, pp. 120–5.

10. *Therigatha*, pp. 366–99.
11. For one of the few discussions in English of the Kausilumina, see C.E. Godakumbura's seminal study, *Sinhalese Literature*, Colombo: The Colombo Apothecaries Co. Ltd., 1955, pp.148–52.
12. Vedantadesika's manipravala commentary, *Munivahanapokam* (henceforth *MVP*), Madras: Independent Esoteric Treatises, 1974.
13. *MVP*, p. 141.
14. Annankaracharya, *Tivyartta Tipikai* (henceforth *TAT*), Madras: Visisthadwaita Pracharini Sabha, 1966, p. 87.
15. K.K.A.Venkatachari, *The Manipravala Literature of the Srivaisnava Acaryas: 12th to 15th Century A.D.,* Bombay: Ananthacharya Research Institute, 1978, pp. 93–4.
16. *TAT*, p. 88.
17. *MVP*, p. 133.
18. *TAT*, p. 87.
19. *MVP*, p. 143.
20. A.K. Ramanujan, *Hymns for the Drowning: Poems for Visnu by Nammalvar*, Princeton: Princeton University Press, 1981, pp. 150–2.
21. Ibid., p. 151.
22. Friedhelm Hardy, *Viraha-Bhakti: The Early History of Krsna Devotion in South India*, New Delhi: Oxford University Press, 1983, pp. 435–6.
23. C.J. Fuller, *The Camphor Flame: Popular Hinduism and Society in India*, Princeton: Princeton University Press, 1992, pp. 78–9.
24. Ibid., p. 73. I do not entirely go along with the monistic tendencies of Fuller's notion of divine-human identity through the ritual of seeing, smelling, and touching the camphor flame at the end of worship. But I do agree on the importance of this synaesthetic experience for the understanding of the visceral nature of Hindu devotion and its unique mingling of difference and identity.
25. *MVP*, p. 114.

3

The Story of Nandanar: Contesting the Order of Things[1]

KAREN PECHILIS PRENTISS

Nandanar is one of the sixty-three Tamil saints devoted to the god Shiva, selectively known as the *Nayanmar* (sing. *Nayanar*). The first known list of these saints is a hymn that praises them called the *Tiruttontattokai* (Collection of Holy Servants), composed by the Nayanar Cuntarar, probably in the ninth century. Some of the Nayanmar are authors; the Tamil Shaiva canon, called the *Tirumurai*, contains the poetry of the three most famous Nayanmar (the *Muvar*: Campantar, Appar, and Cuntarar) in its first seven books, known as *Tevaram*, and the poetic works of other Nayanmar in its ninth and eleventh books. However, the *Tirumurai's* eighth, tenth, and twelfth books were composed by authors other than the sixty-three Nayanmar.[2] Most of the Nayanmar, then, are not authors. Nandanar is in this group. Instead of being praised for their words, they are remembered by tradition as those who worshipped Shiva with special intensity; their actions in a sense speak louder than words. The stories of all the sixty-three saints are told in the twelfth book of the *Tirumurai*, known as the *Periya Puranam* (Great Story) or the *Tiruttontar Puranam* (Story of the Holy Servants), and composed in the twelfth century. The author of the *Periya Puranam*, Cekkilar, attributes but few words to Nandanar in his portrayal of the saint as an Untouchable man whose religiosity transcends social boundaries.

In the stories of the *Muvar* and Nandanar, the 'foreground' images of Shiva are those of classical iconography in the temples. As with Cekkilar's portrayal of the three most famous Nayanmar authors,

Nandanar also goes on pilgrimages to temples in Tamil Nadu, yearning to see and worship the images of Shiva therein. But if the stories of the three, such as that of Appar, emphasize the imperial aspect of the large medieval temples, the story of Nandanar focuses on the hegemonic group inside the temple, the religious authorities. The central conflict in the story of Nandanar is the temple's inaccessibility to the saint due to his low status as an Untouchable. Cekkilar's story of Nandanar clearly depicts a conflict between the bhakti praxis of seeing Shiva and the *agamic* (ritual texts) praxis of limiting access to the presence of Shiva to those high on its spiritual hierarchy. The temple, at Chidambaram,[3] is where the main and most memorable events in the story take place. It represents the culmination of Nandanar's quest for Shiva, and it is the place of greatest challenge to the traditional conflict, here conceived in bhakti terms, between low-caste status and temple worship. In the *Periya Puranam* story, bhakti is triumphant. Nandanar's body becomes a locus for the reconstituting of religious relationships according to Cekkilar's axiom that Shiva-bhakti is salvation. Cekkilar's narrative betrays a caste consciousness that is absent from the earliest texts on the names and identities of the *bhakta*. Since caste was presupposed in Indian society, it would have been unusual for a detailed description of the *bhaktas* to omit such information, yet it was also a cultural presupposition, illustrated by the *agamic* categorization of people by caste for specific temple duties, that the people who shared a religious path would also share the same caste identity. Cekkilar does not accept this premise in his narrative. Through the details of caste, place, and action, he extends the canon of saints to all known features of life in the Tamil lands. What emerges is an image of a unity in diversity; people whom society would ordinarily view as having nothing in common share the same religious path of participation in Shiva.

The story of Nandanar, whose saint name is Tirunalaippovar (the one who will go tomorrow), is important in this regard. Emphasizing the saint's salvation, Nampi Antar Nampi's *Tiruttontar Tiruvantati* (eleventh century) asserted that Nalaippovar left his Untouchable status (*pulai*) through service to Shiva and the Lord's grace and became a muni (sage) worshipped by the Brahmins of Tillai (today Chidambaram). Salvation was also evoked in Cuntarar's (eighth century) description of the saint as one who 'goes directly to the Lord'. In Cekkilar's[4] narration (twelfth century) of the story, in which he re-emphasizes the pilgrimage context, Nandanar's route to the Lord is not all that direct:

There is a town named Atanur[5] that has an ancient fertility and beauty the world praises. It lies on the western bank of the shining river Kollitam (Coleroon), whose water benefits the wide fields, and whose waves draw out concealed gold and precious gems from the lotus stalks on both its banks.

In this place, where the great light of Shiva's ashes shines, beautiful lotuses flourish, and black crabs that live in the mud walk in the furrows and ridges created by strong ploughshares of yoked oxen, with blades that resemble *varal* fish.

Crowds of trees flourish, stroking the *mandala* of the sun with their dense branches full of fragrant buds. They shake with honeybees and embrace the clouds; rains of water, honey, and flowers shower down without ceasing.

When the flowers have opened and yield fragrance, *valai* fish leap, rising high from the large waterholes, to butt and shake the roots of the coconut trees laden with bunches of green fruits. When the ripe fruits fall, the fish play in their overflowing sweet juices.

Prosperity was everywhere, in both the open fields and cultivated lands. Because of this there was great wealth. Shining houses rose almost without limit up to the clouds, and large families were settled closely together. Indeed, Atanur possesses the closeness of kin.

At the edge of the boundary of cultivated fields lay a *pulai* hamlet. It was densely populated by the kin of agricultural labourers who were devoted to their families, settled in many sturdy huts whose roofs were made of thatched grass, upon which clinging green gourd creepers spread.

A crowd of chicks with soft feet and sharp nails roams about there, while young children wearing black iron bracelets run, seizing puppies. The children have bands made from iron and jewels around their waists, which make gentle sounds that satisfy the puppies.

Everywhere in the *pulai* community these things belong: coconut trees under which puppies rest their heads; *ma* trees from which hang drums made of leather; *kanji* trees whose thin branches shade the large pots on top of which hens incubate their eggs; and *marutam* trees which shade infants that the *pulai* women suspend in leather hammocks.

The rustic songs of the lowly *pulai* women with curly hair are heard everywhere. Under the fragrant shade of the *kanji* tree roosters with red combs call, rousing the strong labourers at daybreak to begin their ploughing.

In all corners of the village tank, water fowl bathe noisily in the cool water. The lowly *pulai* women plant rice in the fields, their legs jostling blue water lilies which open and flow with intoxicating honey. Drums beat harmoniously.

There was an incomparable one who came to stay in this world, named Nandanar. He lived in this agricultural milieu; he came into the world with prior knowledge due to his earnest desire for the feet of Shiva who is truth and love; and he was possessed of the hereditary nature suited to the *pulai* village in that place.

After his birth, his prior knowledge became evident and he undertook the path of service (*tontu*) to the feet of Shiva, as one whose mind was straight due to his exceeding love for the King who wears the moon as his garland, as one who did not possess forgetfulness, and as one of religious virtue who followed the way appropriate to his birth.

Taking for his livelihood the suitable work of servant on pariah lands released to the village, he excelled in his service to Shiva. For every temple of the Lord who holds the sharp three-pronged trident he lovingly (*arvattinutan*) provided skins and straps as covering for drums and other instruments with faces, strings well suited to the lute and vina instruments, and bezoar stone for the worship of the Lord of the gods.

He made all these things to the extent possible in the course of his livelihood. One day while standing outside the entrance to the temple, he became greatly inspired by the exceeding love and truth of the singing and dancing therein, and he meditated on the holy feet of Civalokan, who appears at Tiruppunkur.[6] He experienced a single-minded desire for performing service to Shiva, and set out from Atanur for that place, reaching the edge of town in a state of love.

At the temple entrance, the holy servant who sang distinguished songs thought about his desire to worship the Lord directly. The Lord with the eye in his forehead (Kannutalar), who resides at Punkur, which is surrounded by a wall that rises to the clouds, then gracefully caused the fierce bull (Nandi) to move aside from in front of him, and appeared (directly) to the one who thought thus.

He overcame his birth in this world standing before the entrance to the temple of Civalokan. After he completed his service and worshipped there, he went with the leather straps he used to make instruments shaking on his back (in ecstasy). He saw a small depression in back of the temple, approached it, and began to scoop it out for a tank.

After digging the tank, circumambulating the temple where Peruman resides, performing service, and dancing, he was granted leave by the grace of the Lord whose hair bears golden flower blossoms, and he returned to his own village.

He went to many such places where the Lord full of grace appears for worship, living as a true holy servant, his love (*anpu*) growing more and more. His desire to worship at the court of Tillai (Chidambaram) became overwhelming.

He could not sleep that night. At dawn he thought: 'The nature of that holy place is not suited to my heritage (*kulam*).' And then, reasoning that 'this thought too is a command from our Peruman,' he discontinued his efforts to go there. After this he said: 'I shall go tomorrow,' and his desire grew greater.

Many days passed with him saying 'I shall go tomorrow'[7] in this manner, and his mind was not at rest. Finally, he set out for Tillai, which is surrounded by ripened fruit, flowering betel nut, and fertile fields leaping with fish, as one who would be released from the fetters of his birth.

When he reached the boundary of that holy place, he stood without going further, confronted by the sight of smoke from the great sacrificial fire, and of the brethren of *math* (religious) leaders reciting in their exalted state. He paused, reflecting on the lowness of his heritage.

He stood there, thinking of the greatness attached to that place: 'If one goes through the entrance in the wall surrounding the town there should be three thousand oblations on as many altars, reaching up from each house like mountains.'

Thinking fearfully that 'one must be of that same nature; it is not suitable that I approach,' he remained outside the walls of that place and circumambulated its boundaries with hands clasped and heart melting, while his love increased.

Circumambulating in that manner night and day, while thinking of that rare nature one needs to approach and enter, the servant whose heart swelled thought longingly: 'How can I worship the dance in the hall of the Lord with the black throat?' as he swooned with sleep.

In his sleep he thought: 'This base birth is certainly a hindrance.' But the Lord of the dance in the sacred hall knew of his state, and appeared before him in a dream, smiling gracefully, in order to resolve all his troubles.

The Lord of the sacred hall gracefully told him: 'When you bathe in the fire it will extinguish this birth and you will be as a Brahmin wearing the triple thread on his chest.' The Lord then commanded the appropriate inhabitants of Tillai to light the fire.

All the knowers of the Vedas (*marai*) who heard the command of Peruman came together fearfully before the entrance to the dance hall, and agreed that 'we will observe the command that our Peruman full of grace made known'. The holy servant drew near to that side with his love increasing.

The sages said: 'Aiyare! We have come to you now by the grace of the Lord of the hall, to set the hot fire and give it to you.' The holy servant replied, worshipping with heart melting: 'I am saved,' and the munis who know the Vedas went about discussing how to set the fire.

After the Vedists spoke thus he came through the entrance that rose to touch the moon at the southern wall, and arrived at the pit where they had set the fire. He circumambulated the fire holding the Lord in his mind.

Then, meditating on the dancing feet of the Lord, with hands clasped in prayer, he entered the fire. At that moment his form, which is associated with falsehood due to *maya*, was shed in the fire, and he emerged with a muni's form that is pure, with the three threads shining on his chest, and matted locks.

When he went on that intense fire, he appeared as a Brahmin going over a red flower. Then a heavenly drum sounded in the world, the gods were full of joy, and fresh petals from the heavenly *mantaram* tree showered down.

The inhabitants of holy Tillai clasped their hands and worshipped the praiseworthy servant with joy in their hearts. Tirunalaippovar, the sage of the Vedas, went to worship the feet that dance inside the *ampalam* (sanctum) that contains the rare Vedas.

All the inhabitants of Tillai approached, stopping at the *gopuram* to worship the Lord who holds the deer and the trowel in his hands, then hastily entered inside. But when they reached the place where the dance is performed for the benefit of the world they saw no one.

The Brahmins were amazed, while the rare munis engaged in praise. The Lord of the dance appeared, full of grace, so that the evil karma of the servant who came and joined him would be destroyed, so that there would be continuous worship of his protective lotus-like feet, and so that there would be great bliss instead of spiritual ignorance.

Henceforth, we speak of the honour of the servant who reached the feet of the Lord of the hall as a muni without fault due to his bathing in the fire to remove his impure body; and who conquered the bonds of this world as a servant with the mark of holiness by praising the Lord's shining feet.

Tirunalaippovar Puranam, vv. 1041–77

II

Cekkilar begins the story of Nandanar with a portrait of a Tamil town and landscape morally constituted by Shiva's proximity, which evokes the images and sentiments of the hymns to Shiva composed by the *Muvar*. However, in contrast to the *Muvar*'s hymns, the lay of the land in Cekkilar's narrative is contoured by caste. At the periphery of the social world is the *pulaiyar* community, which has a recognized agricultural function in the larger society, though it is of 'Untouchable' social status. The work of the community also involves the handling of leather and other animal products, which is considered polluting by the townspeople and thus determines the community's 'Untouchable' status and segregation. The hamlet is densely populated, thick with kith and kin, the thatched huts connected by green gourd creepers spreading across their roofs. Nandanar is born in this *pulai* community, endowed both with prior knowledge of Shiva and with a character that is suited to his hereditary station in life. He excels at the traditional agricultural duties, but his special connection to Shiva is evident from his enthusiastic religious service. The kind of religious service he performs is appropriate to his birth; for he makes ritual musical objects out of leather, such as the drum and strings for the vina. Nandanar uses these instruments to sing and dance outside the entrance to the temple.

In this story Cekkilar represents the temple as the powerful social centre of the Shaiva world. Nandanar's pilgrimages to local temples and to Chidambaram represent a journey from the periphery of society to the centre of religious worship. However, despite the virtue of his bhakti, he can only stand at the entrance of the temple because of his Untouchable status. To emphasize the impenetrability of the Tiruppunkur temple, Cekkilar tells us that the walls of the town reached the clouds. Yet when Nandanar meditates on his desire to worship Shiva directly an amazing thing happens: Shiva causes his bull, Nandi, to move aside from Nandanar's path of vision, and the saint can directly see the God. Cekkilar's text speaks of the stone image of Nandi as a boundary for the participation of Shiva *bhaktas* in temple culture, but also shows, in this story, that Shiva knows the plight of his *bhakta* and gracefully has the bull move to one side so that Nandanar can directly see the god. This direct sight of god brings the *bhakta* immense joy, making him behave in a manner that demonstrates his internal devotion (shaking with joy and ecstasy), and his external service to the temple (the making of a well).

In this context, Cekkilar first mentions a theme that dominates the rest of the story: Nandanar's ability to transcend the conditions of his birth. He visits many temples in this manner, and his love for Shiva grows more and more. He begins to think continually about his desire to visit Tillai (Chidambaram), the renowned temple dedicated to the dancing Shiva, Lord Nataraja. The story implies that as his love and desire grew, the only place appropriate to his state was Chidambaram. Thus, a conflict develops as his desire to see Shiva grows. The narrative suggests that Nandanar's love for Shiva grows beyond the bounds of his stipulated caste domain, and beyond the context of local village temples, making it necessary for him to travel to the domain of the prestigious temple at Chidambaram, which is administered by an army of Brahmin priests. Yet worried that his *kulam* is not suited to the holiness of Chidambaram, and thus he will assuredly be denied entry into the temple by the authorities, he puts off his journey, contenting himself with the thought, 'I will go tomorrow' (*nalaippoven*). Because he always thought of going the next day, he became known as 'Nalaippovar'. But his mind is not at rest, and finally he proceeds to Tillai. Cekkilar foreshadows the events at Chidambaram by noting that Tirunalaippovar began his journey as one who would be released from the fetters of his birth.

Nandanar's desire to see Shiva and his joy upon seeing the Lord overflows and thus challenges the efficacy of established boundaries. This is the beginning of his Shiva bhakti bodily transformation, which will culminate in Cekkilar's assertion that Nandanar can transcend the limitations of his birth, by the Nayanar's ritual walk through the purifying fire. The sense of established boundaries includes the prestige of the place to which the *bhakta* pilgrimages. Perhaps more than any other time before, Chidambaram was constituted as a place of religious authority in this medieval context of Cekkilar's narrative. It is known that the kings of the powerful Chola dynasty admired the temple and sought to have a real presence there. But the story portrays the Chidambaram temple not as a Chola stronghold, but as a community of Brahmins of considerable religious power, with overtones of autonomy and hegemony. This was an established way of portraying the temple in Shaiva bhakti literature; for example, Cuntarar begins his *Tiruttontattokai* with praise of the three thousand Brahmins at Tillai.

The awesome religious power of Tillai is reflected in Nalaippovar's emotional turmoil. For him, Tillai is the place of ultimate religious authority and as such is the ultimate test for the force of his own bhakti. At first, he puts the trip off, pushing its genesis into a series of tomorrows that both negotiates the sense of urgency and hesitation and becomes a bhakti name for him. Finally, he initiates his trip, but again his fear takes over as he is confronted with the sight of the large temple walls, the smoke from three thousand oblations, and the priests exalted in their recitation of the sacred Sanskrit texts. At this moment of a seeming impasse, Shiva appears to the *bhakta* to describe a plan for the final resolution of the conflict between his low social status and his desire to see Shiva at the locus of religiously-constituted social power. The resolution is that Nalaippovar will take on a body that society invests with a positive content, and the powerful Brahmins themselves will help to make this possible. The sacrifice of the Untouchable *bhakta* in the fire becomes a Vedic sacrifice, in line with the Vedic logic that does not celebrate the consumption of the sacrificial substance, but instead views the substance as transformed for the preservation of the world. But the change in Nalaippovar does not preserve the known world; his embodiment as a Brahmin gives a radically different content to a known and positive social symbol. Significantly, after he becomes a Brahmin, Nalaippovar does not assume brahminical ritual status or work in the temple with the hereditary Brahmins. Instead, he proceeds directly to Shiva, as captured in Cuntarar's *Tiruttontattokai*, where he is called the one who 'goes straight to the Lord'.

The transformation of Nandanar is one kind of bodily change in the *Periya Puranam*; the stories are full of instances involving the loss of life or limb. One of the most interesting stories for comparison with that of Nandanar is the story of Karaikkal Ammaiyar.[8] This devotee was a young, married, and religious woman who as such represents the pinnacle of proper Tamil society. Her social position was of course very different from that of Nandanar, whose identity is his marginalized position on the periphery. Yet the two stories are similar in that the two saints' participation in Shiva is a result of their overstepping the social boundaries. Karaikkal Ammaiyar appeals to Shiva directly for a mango, which frightens her husband, and Nandanar takes darshan of Shiva at Tiruppunkur, which encourages him to proceed to Chidambaram. In both the stories, there is a narrative thread that holds no threat to the hegemony of the social structure; Karaikkal Ammaiyar does not begin her journey to Shiva's mythical place before her husband releases her from her married duties, and Nandanar does not experience his bodily transformation until the Brahmins of Chidambaram light the ritual fire. But here again the stories diverge; Karaikkal Ammaiyar renounces her social body and takes on the antisocial form of a female ghoul who sits

Plate 3.1: Sketch of Nandanar entering the fire and emerging wearing a sacred thread. From *Periya Puranam* by Sekkizhaar, Sri Ramakrishna Math, Mylapore.

watching Shiva's dance at the cremation ground. In contrast, Nandanar takes on a social body with positive content. In both the stories, however, the saints are saved, being graced with proximity to Shiva forever, which establishes their inclusion among the sixty-three saints.

III

The story is not fashioned as a call to social revolution. Nandanar accepts his *pulai* status and the work appropriate to it. He excels in the duties of his heritage, and even becomes a manager of the cultivated lands set aside for his community by the larger society. Similarly, his participation in Shiva is circumscribed by his caste identity; he handles leather to make instruments for worship. However, the story of Nandanar questions the assumption that heredity is a manifestation of religious capacity. This question was posed by bhakti in medieval Tamil religious culture, and there is evidence that the Srivaishnava community actively explored it with respect to Untouchables and temple worship. A major issue in considering the practice of Untouchables entering temple space was the pollution of the sacrality of the place, which had implications for the community of worshippers beyond the consideration of an individual's capacity for bhakti. It is notable that in the Nandanar story, the sacrality of Chidambaram is preserved by the saint's purification by fire before he entered the sanctum.

There is evidence only from modern times that the story of Nandanar was interpreted in a way that politicized the message of the saint's salvation; for example, in the nineteenth century, the famous scholar-musician Gopalakrishna Bharati[9] emphasized the social disabilities of the protagonist in his dramatic rendering of Cekkilar's classic. His story was told several times on film in the context of the emerging critique of caste hierarchies during the Tamil nationalism movement of the 1930s and 1940s. In contemporary times, as Lynn Vincentnathan has observed, attempts to interpret the story of Nandanar as a call to social action are extremely problematic. According to her research [included in the present volume], Untouchables who today live in the Chidambaram area have internalized the message of Cekkilar's narrative: 'For Untouchables, their versions of the Nandanar legend fit with what they know about themselves—that they are capable of religiosity comparable or superior to that of caste Hindus.'[10] Yet they also acknowledge that this sentiment has not resulted in a change in social status. Ultimately, present-day attempts to view bhakti as a radical social message that serves to change place, rather than define it, have been unsuccessful. Perhaps these interpreters have tried to extrapolate too much from a story such as that of Nandanar, for the story begins to question caste at a very fundamental level. The *pulai* status of Untouchables was characterized by non-human traits; the term connotes vileness and animal food in addition to designating Untouchables. In the context of such degradation, Cekkilar's story defines Nandanar as a human being and argues not only that he has a heart but also that his heart is pure.

Very recently, performing the story of Nandanar has become very popular, especially vocal recitals and dance-dramas that draw primarily on Gopalakrishna Bharati's nineteenth-century rendering of the tale. For example, faculty and students of Madras University's Department of Indian Classical Music performed selections from Bharati's composition in December 1996; V.P. Dhananjayan of Bharata Kalanajali has produced both film and dance-drama renditions of the story (website http://www.bharatakalaanjali.org/productn/solo/nandanrc.html), including performances of the Nandanar story in Benaras and Sri Lanka in 2002–3; Srimati Ramya Ramnarayan and her Nrityanjali dance company in New Jersey performed scenes from the story of Nandanar at Drew University in September 2003; and an English edition of playwright Indira Parthasarathy's 1978 play of Nandan was published a couple of years back (*The Legend of Nandan: Nandan Kathai*, translated by C.T. Indra, New Delhi: Oxford University Press, 2003).

NOTES

1. The arguments made in this paper are discussed in greater detail in my book, *The Embodiment of Bhakti*, New York: Oxford University Press, 1999, pp. 115–33.
2. For a list of the books of the *Tirumurai* and their authors, with a designation of which are *Nayanmar*, see Norman J. Cutler, *Songs of Experience: The Poetics of Tamil Devotion*, Bloomington: Indiana University Press, 1987, pp. 4–5.
3. The history of the Chidambaram temple is complicated, both in terms of the Chola role in its creation and maintenance, and in terms of the nature of the temple's ritual specialists, who distinguish themselves from the Shaiva Siddhanta priests at the majority of temples to Shiva in Tamil Nadu. From the perspective of the story of Nandanar, these differences are de-emphasized within a narrative frame that portrays all temples as inaccessible to the saint.
4. The story is called the 'Tirunalaippovarnayanarpuranam' after the bhakti name of Nandanar, 'Tirunalaippovar', the 'one who will go tomorrow'. He is the eighteenth *bhakta* praised in Cuntarar's *Tiruttontattokai* and his story occurs as chapter eighteen

in the *Periya Puranam.* The edition I have used is C.K. Cuppiramaniya Mutaliyar, translated and edited, *Cekkilar Cuvamikal Ennum Arunmolittevar Aruliya Tiruttontar Puranam*, vol. 2, Coimbatore: Kovait Tamil Cankam, 1968, vv. 1041–77.

5. Many of the towns mentioned in the *Nayanmar's* hymns and in later bhakti literature, such as the *Periya Puranam*, exist even today. Atanur is located approximately 20 km. from the town of Cirkali, which is in turn approximately 12 km. south of Chidambaram.
6. In contemporary times, Tiruppunkur is a quiet rural town located some 8 km. from Cirkali. There is a temple to Shiva there, with the Lord's bull, Nandi, moved to the side of the entrance, as per the events in the story of Nandanar. There is a small temple to Nandanar a short distance from the main temple; the saint stands facing Shiva with his hands clasped over his head in worship. Inside the temple walls there are several images of Nandanar as well.
7. In bhakti hymns and stories, he is often referred to as Tirunalaippovar (the 'Holy one who will go tomorrow'), rather than as Nandanar.
8. For a synopsis of her story, and translations of some of her poetry, see Cutler, *Songs of Experience*, pp. 117–21.
9. The story of Nandanar becomes much more radically socialized in Bharati's dramatic rendering of Cekkilar's classic entitled *Nandanar Charitram.* A major difference between the two stories is Bharati's emphasis on the social disabilities of Nandanar's caste situation. Bharati uses the term *Varukalamao?*, meaning 'May I come?' as the first word of his drama and as a refrain throughout. In his drama, Nandanar had to yell this phrase when he came to the entrance of each street as a warning to high-caste people that they should take cover from his polluting presence. At the other end of the street, he would make another announcement to signify that the coast was clear. It is the degradation of his social condition that makes Nandanar long to visit Tillai. If Cekkilar's version is about temples, Bharati's version is about streets. For discussion of Bharati's story, see G. Vanmikanathan, *Periya Puranam: A Tamil Classic on the Great Saiva Saints of South India by Sekkizharr*, Condensed English Version, Madras: Sri Ramakrishna Math, 1985, pp. 564–7; and B. Natarajan, *The City of the Cosmic Dance: Chidambaram*, New Delhi: Orient Longman, 1974, pp. 101–13. For the words and music see S. Iramanatan, *Kopalkirushna Paratiyar Iyarriya Nandanar Carittirak Kirttanai*, Madurai: Sri Satguru Sangeeta Vidyalayam, 1971. B. Natarajan's condensed telling of the Nandanar story includes an episode that is not in the text of Cekkilar that I have seen, and probably represents one of Bharati's departures from Cekkilar: when Nandanar finally decides to go to Tillai, he needs to get permission from his master, the owner of the land. His master tells him that he must plough all the lands and transplant the rice seedlings before the next morning. This is an impossible task and Nandanar fears he will not be able to go. But overnight Lord Nataraja intervenes and does all the work, freeing Nandanar to go to Chidambaram. On other differences between the two tellings and a discussion of Bharati, see Kamil Zvelebil, *Tamil Literature* in the series *A History of Indian Literature*, edited by Jan Gonda, vol. 10, fasc. 1, Wiesbaden: Otto Harrassowitz, 1974, pp. 227–30.
10. Lynn Vincentnathan, 'Nandanar: Untouchable Saint and Caste Hindu Anomaly', *Ethos*, vol. 21, no. 2, 1993, pp. 154–79, p. 174. Cited in Prentiss, *The Embodiment of Bhakti*, p. 132.

4

Nandanar: Untouchable Saint and Caste Hindu Anomaly*

LYNN VINCENTNATHAN

Cultural beliefs in support of untouchability are still prevalent in India today despite government efforts and new ideologies to combat them. These beliefs, I suggest, cannot be understood solely as a cultural tradition passively carried forward to the present, but are supported as well by psychological and social dynamics. Here, a study of the differing caste versions of a legend about an Untouchable saint helps reveal some of these psychological and social aspects of untouchability beliefs.

In 1984–5 I did fieldwork in Tamil Nadu in a Paraiyar (Untouchable) community near Chidambaram. From interviews with caste Hindus[1] in the vicinity, the sharp insights of some Untouchable informants, and observances of interactions between caste Hindus and Untouchables, I became aware not only of caste Hindus' views of Untouchables–views in accord with the traditional Hindu belief that Untouchables are inherently polluting, immoral, submissive, and lacking in intelligence–but also noted how cognitive manipulations helped maintain these views, even in the face of contradictory information, such as an Untouchable exhibiting positive qualities. These cognitive processes also became evident as I collected stories about Nandanar, an Untouchable saint, and noticed differences between the caste Hindu and the Untouchable versions.

Caste Hindu Versions of the Nandanar Legend

The following is the basic story line found in most caste Hindu and Untouchable versions of the Nandanar legend:

Nandanar, a Paraiyar agrarian labourer, was a great devotee of Shiva. He wanted to go to Chidambaram to worship the dancing form of Shiva, Nataraja. Finally, he went, but from his position outside the temple he could not see Shiva, because an idol of Shiva's vehicle, Nandi the bull, was blocking the view. Nandanar sang of his devotion. Shiva made Nandi move so that Nandanar could see him. Nandanar entered the temple and merged with Shiva.

I collected various caste Hindu versions. The oldest version I found is in Cekkilar's twelfth-century *Periya Puranam.* In Cekkilar's version (Kandaswamy Kavirayar 1978: 124–8, in Tamil and translated here), Nandanar, aware of his low birth, does not enter the temple once he arrives in Chidambaram, until he has a dream:

In his dream Shiva appeared to Nandanar and said, 'Beloved, do not worry. To get rid of your lowly birth, go get submerged into the fire. Then come with the Chidambaram Brahmins before me.' The same way Shiva appeared in the dreams of the Chidambaram Brahmins and said, 'You Brahmins make a fire for Nandanar, who is on the southern side entrance of the temple, so he can enter it. After Nandanar goes through the fire, he will come before me.'

In accordance with Shiva's order, the Brahmins went to the southern entrance of the temple, met Nandanar, and told him of their dream. Nandanar said, 'I am saved,' and he worshipped Shiva in humility. The Brahmins made the fire. Nandanar with his hands pressed together above his head, thinking of the feet of God, rounded the fire, then entered it. Immediately his false image disappeared. Then in the image of a muni who does good deeds, with sacred thread, with the braided tuft of a *munivar* he came out of the fire. The Nandanar who came out of the fire with that new image looked like Brahma, who appeared on the red lotus.

The story then goes on until Nandanar merges with Nataraja. The point to be emphasized here is that Nandanar is not really an Untouchable; the Untouchable form is his false image. When he goes through the fire, this false image disappears, and Nandanar gets rid of his lowly birth, what remains is and his image as a *muni*, with sacred thread and tuft, indicating his true Brahmin form.

There is a film version of Nandanar's life entitled *Nandanar* (Gemini, *c.* 1945). It is composed of songs from the *Nandanar Puranam* and some interesting additional subplots and visual interpretations. For instance, it is not only Nandanar who wants to go to Tirupangudi and Chidambaram to see Nataraja, but also a large group of his Untouchable followers from the hamlet. My upper-caste assistant, familiar with all the other versions, exclaimed this is how it would have been. He liked the film's portrayal of the Brahmin landlord and felt he was being reasonable in not wanting so many of his labourers abandoning their work. In the end, through the use of special effects, Nandanar is shown to merge with Nataraja, in his thigh. My upper-caste assistant pointed this out and explained that Nandanar went back to where he had come from, referring to the *Rigveda* myth (10.90) about the origin of the varnas, supposed to have emerged from various body parts of God. In most of the Untouchable versions, as discussed below, the verb 'swallow' (*muzhungu*) is used, implying that Nandanar merged with Shiva through Nataraja's mouth, from where the Brahmins originally emanated, not his thigh.

A Brahmin professor, age sixty, who lives near Chidambaram, recounted a version that was basically the same as the literary version, including a subplot (not presented above) of Nandanar's dealings with his Brahmin landlord, but here this subplot is enlarged. It includes the subplot of Nandanar's earlier visit to the smaller Nataraja temple in Tirupangudi, which also appears in Cekkilar's version and in many others as well:

> [Nandanar's] landlord was a Brahmin—my caste. Nandanar asked to go to worship Nataraja, but his landlord refused, wondering how a person of such a low caste could be so devoted to Shiva. Nandanar went on worshipping Nataraja in his mind. . . . One day when he was in Tirupangudi he went to the temple there to worship Nataraja, but he could not enter, being a Scheduled Caste man, so he stood outside, but Nandi the bull was there in front of Nataraja and Nandanar couldn't see the god. He went on worshipping there every day. Finally, he prayed to Nataraja that he move the bull so that he could see him. Nataraja moved the large stone statue, and then Nandanar could see. And till today if you go to that temple you will see that it is off centre. Nandanar went back and told his landlord, but his landlord didn't believe him, so he sent some men to find out. They came back and said that it was true, that the statue had indeed been moved.
>
> Nandanar went on praying to Shiva and asking to go to Chidambaram. His landlord refused, saying that forty acres had to be planted with rice seedlings and that Nandanar had to stay and supervise this operation, and that after that he could go to Chidambaram. But Nandanar wanted to go right away because it is only twice a year that they have the *darshan*[2] of Nataraja, when they take him out for all to see, and that day was coming soon, and there was no way the planting could be done. So Nandanar prayed all night and in the morning the whole forty acres had been planted.

The landlord then realized that Nandanar was in fact Nataraja himself, and he bowed down to him, touching his feet, saying, 'I am nothing. You are God.' But Nandanar said, 'No, no. Don't touch me.' In those days there was varna-ashrama-dharma, the four varnas, and the landlord was the highest and Nandanar was the lowest. Then the landlord allowed Nandanar to go to Chidambaram. . . . [and the story continues to the incident where he merges with God]

The realization of Nandanar's true, non-Untouchable form comes earlier in this version and to the Brahmin landlord. Here Nandanar is not a muni, but the god Nataraja himself in the form of an Untouchable. This explanation falls within the framework of Hindu mythological thinking; deities assume the form of mortals. As in Cekkilar's version, Nandanar is not an Untouchable in reality.

One very different version was narrated by a man of the Pattar jeweller caste, who is a welder in Chidambaram. He included the subplot about the southern entrance of the Chidambaram Nataraja temple being sealed up, as it is today, with a large statue of Nandi the bull in front. The welder claimed that he was not very familiar with the Nandanar story, but gave this version:

Nandanar was from a place near Vaithiswaran Kovil, but it is not a grand story for anyone to remember. Nandanar was desirous of seeing Lord Nataraja, so he travelled and came to the Chidambaram temple. He transformed himself into Nandi and said that Nandi and Nandanar are one and the same. He entered through the southern gate of the temple, and was standing in the form of Nandi in front of the entrance to the inner temple. He saw Nataraja from there. He could not enter the temple because he was a Harijan. Lord Nataraja saw him and he said to Nandi, 'You should not enter the temple. You should go away, because it is not the customary practice.' Nandi refused to move away. Then Nataraja could not do anything to move Nandi away, and he said, 'Let this Nandi be there,' and wanted the southern inner entrance to the temple to be closed. Since then the southern entrance has been closed.

Here Nandanar assumes the guise of Nandi the bull so that he can enter the temple, but even in this form he is considered an Untouchable and is not allowed to enter the inner temple and is told by Nataraja to leave the outer grounds as well. Nandanar, as Nandi, refuses to leave, so the southern entrance is closed up. Nandanar is not a hero here, but a scheming nuisance. The legend is discounted even at the very beginning of the narration with the observation, 'It is not a grand story for anyone to remember.' In this version, it is the story line that is changed to discredit the Untouchable character, rather than the Untouchable hero being changed into or discovered to be of a different, higher nature.

A thirty-five-year-old drummer for the Nataraja temple of the Malakarar caste, regarded as a Devadasi (the courtesan caste, non-Untouchable), narrated a version with the usual sequence of events and themes–miraculous paddy planting, Brahmin landlord realizing Nandanar's spiritual power, Nandanar's visit to the Tirupangudi temple and the moving of Nandi the bull, and how Nandanar was made to go through a fire by the Brahmin priests before being allowed to enter the temple. Where it differs from other versions most is in the outcome:

> When he reached the Chidambaram temple, the Brahmins refused to admit Nandanar into the temple, but told him he could enter if he walked through fire. Nandanar went to a nearby area and created a sacrificial fire, and he walked through it. Today there is a tank on this spot known as Omakulam. After that he went and saw Lord Nataraja, and worshipped him with his melodious songs. He lived near the Chidambaram area and died. There is still a temple in Chidambaram for him just at the entrance outside of the city. There is a *samaathi* [grave] for him in the temple area.

There is no mention of Nandanar being other than an Untouchable, except that he is considered to have God's grace and does have to go through fire before he can enter the temple. Here, however, he does not merge with God, but lives and dies near Chidambaram. This version perhaps shows a somewhat more positive view of Untouchables, because the Untouchable saint is not considered a muni or a god, and yet the story has a less spectacular ending. Perhaps the drummer's caste, with its association with courtesans and its low social position, accounts for these differences.

Kannan, a twenty-eight-year-old construction worker of the Vanniyar caste (a low but non-Untouchable caste, mainly engaged in agrarian labour), also offers a more positive story, but he accompanies this account with a lengthy discussion of how bad the condition of Untouchables is today. He lives in a village about three miles from Chidambaram, where they have a large temple, which he proudly claims the Untouchables are not allowed to enter:

> [Nandanar] entered the southern entrance to the sanctum sanctorum in the inner square of the temple. He was stopped by the Brahmins there and was told that he should not enter the temple because he was a member of the

Plate 4.1: Shiva Nataraj. Courtesy of the American Institute of Indian Studies Art and Archeology Center. Note the scarf flowing from his waist. Lynn Vincentnathan tells that some believe when Nandanar entered the image, he became the scarf flowing from the waist or the hip. Photography of the Chidambaram image is not allowed, so the Shiva image from the Tiruvelukudi temple in Tanjore district, now in the Tanjore Art Gallery, is used here.

Paraiyan caste. Nowadays Paraiyans enter the Nataraja temple, but in my village Paraiyans are not allowed in the main temple. . . . After the incident of Nandanar, the southern entrance to the temple was closed and the image of a big Nandi was placed before the closed southern entrance. After Nandanar could not see Nataraja and was asked by the Brahmins to leave, he went away and was absorbed into the heaven.

In this version, propriety according to Kannan's standard is maintained. Nandanar does not enter the temple and goes away. Nandanar is the ideal Untouchable who does not threaten the social order. This, along with Nandanar's piety, is rewarded in Kannan's version with Nandanar being allowed into heaven–not in the temple though, but away from it. The main point in this story is that Nandanar does not violate caste rules and is rightfully turned away from the temple.

A theme that runs through most of the caste Hindu versions of the Nandanar legend is the exemplary Untouchable behaviour of Nandanar, who recognizes his Untouchable position and is obedient to his Brahmin landlord and the Brahmin temple priests, politely following the rules set down for Untouchables. Except in the version where he becomes Nandi, he either voluntarily refrains from entering the temple because of his low birth, or he is turned away by the Brahmins and does not persist in trying to enter. In versions in which he does enter the temple, he willingly submits to being purified or transformed by fire.

Untouchable Versions of the Nandanar Legend

Untouchable versions of the Nandanar legend have some different twists to the themes mentioned above. It should be noted that Nandanar is not much of a hero for today's Untouchable youth, who have other, more progressive heroes, such as Ambedkar, the Untouchable framer of the Indian Constitution and civil rights leader for Untouchables. Most young Untouchables I asked said they did not know the Nandanar story, or they felt uneasy when the topic was brought up, probably because Nandanar was somewhat of an obliging and obedient agrarian worker, and not a role model who could lead them to a different and better life in this world. Furthermore, while Nandanar's piety seems extraordinary and inexplicable to upper-caste Hindus, such piety can be found in the Untouchable community. Many Untouchables are fairly religious, some quite devoted to Shiva. It seems the younger generation does not need a legend to prove the piety of the Untouchables. And some educated Untouchables noted how religion has been used to justify their oppression. This no doubt caused them to have ambivalent feelings towards at least some aspects of Hinduism. Most Untouchable versions of the Nandanar legend I collected are from older people.

Kamachi, age sixty, a retired agrarian labourer now selling milk, offers a version with the following details:

Nandanar was taking care of thousand *kaanis* [about thousand three hundred acres] of land. When he told his landlord he wanted to see Nataraja in Chidambaram, the landlord said, 'What right do you have to go and see Nataraja? You are Paraiyan.' And to discourage him, he added, 'After cultivating the land, raising the crop, and harvesting it, you can go.'

Nandanar prayed to God. God heard his prayers and felt very sorry for Nandanar, and he created enough water and sent elephants and helped him grow the crops in four days. Nandanar then went and told his master that he had finished the work and he should be allowed to go for the *darsanam*. Again his master discouraged him. News about him wanting to go to the festival spread to the Brahmin priests around, and they tried to discipline Nandanar and discourage him from going. However, around nine o'clock in the morning on the day of the festival, Nandanar tried to run away from there and get to Chidambaram. But the Kollidam river was full of water, flooding all over. He jumped in and the Brahmin priests thought he must have died. But he did not die. He got to the other side of the river, where there is a little pavilion built for Nataraja. Again people saw him and saw that he was alive, and they tried to prevent him from going. However, he started running, and when he got to Chidambaram there were some Brahmin priests, and they told him he had to be in Omakulam, which is made of fire. And he had to walk through that before he could get into the temple and see Nataraja. When he got into the temple compound, Nandi the bull entered into that fire and immediately the whole place became water. And due to this there is a tank called Omakulam, still there.

All along people saw that Nandanar had some special powers, and they were perhaps jealous of him. So they tried to chastise and discourage him by saying, 'What right does a Paraiyan have to see Nataraja? God is not welcoming him.' And things of that sort were told to him, and again people tried vehemently to stop him with threats from going into the temple to see his god, Shiva. From the tank he ran to the feet of Nataraja through the southern entrance. . . . He entered through that entrance and before entering sang a song. Nandi the bull moved away because of the grace of God, and Nandanar was able to reach the feet of God. And God in trying to protect him from the people who were chasing him, swallowed [*muzhungu*] him. And everyone shouted, 'He is a Paraiyan. How can God swallow him?' But God replied, 'He belongs to the first jati, and of course they are placed now in a lowly position.' He gave great protection to Nandanar. And whenever he suffered or was made into pieces, he came together into one person because of Nataraja's blessing.

The Brahmins who noticed this closed up the southern entrance to the temple, saying, 'God should not face towards the south.' And they created stories that Nandanar had died and did not come to the temple and said that he had not been swallowed by God and did not get any of God's special blessings or graces.

Here the Brahmins are all trying to stop Nandanar. He does not go through the fire; Nandi turns it into a tank. And Nandanar is still an Untouchable when God swallows him; this is clear in the Brahmin's exclamation: 'He is a Paraiyan. How can God swallow him?' Here the verb is 'swallow', which God would not have done if Nandanar had been polluting. The words used by caste Hindus for the merging do not have the sense of swallowing, but simply 'merging', or 'being absorbed', or 'becoming one with'. As mentioned earlier, the film version shows Nandanar being absorbed into Shiva's raised thigh.

Raman, a fifty-seven-year-old illiterate Untouchable, recounts a similar story, including Nandanar's swim across the river. Again, Nandanar plants and harvests crops in one day with the help of *buuthams* (demons or ghosts) sent by Nataraja, thus frightening the landlord. In Raman's version, Nandanar does enter the fire at the request of the Brahmins; the fire is not meant to purify him but rather to kill him. But Nandanar, miraculously, is not killed. There is no mention of a new or different form after his emergence from the fire. The final episodes of Raman's version are as follows:

At the same time, knowing that he was coming, the Dikshitars [Brahmin priests] stopped him and told him, 'If you have to see Nataraja, we will raise a fire in the temple and you have to pass through the fire in order to see Nataraja.' In the temple they raised a fire and Nandanar entered into it and at the time the Dikshitars threw into the fire a lot of camphor, thinking that they could kill him in this way, but Nandanar by the grace of Nataraja came out of the fire and ran towards the place where Nataraja was and, pressing his hands together, he worshipped him. Immediately Nataraja swallowed Nandanar. The Dikshitars ran behind him, saying, 'He's running, he's running there,' and they followed him to the place where Nataraja was. Hearing the noise of the Dikshitars, Nataraja did not completely swallow him, stopping temporarily. Because of that the legs of Nandanar are still sticking out of Nataraja's side. After this incident, the Dikshitars closed the southern entrance.

The Brahmins are chasing Nandanar even after the fire episode because he is still an Untouchable. The two sash-like things sticking out of Nataraja's side are interpreted here to be Nandanar's legs, making Nataraja a composite of Shiva and Nandanar.

Govindan, a fifty-five-year-old retired foreman from the technology department at Annamalai University, gives a version similar to the Untouchable versions cited above, including the claim that Nandanar's legs are sticking out of Nataraja. The fire episode is more like the Brahmin version, with the claim that the purpose is to change Nandanar's body, except afterwards it is made clear that Nandanar is still an Untouchable: 'At that time Nataraja, holding Nandanar, swallowed him. The Brahmin priest who saw this asked God, 'You swallowed a Harijan. You, our Lord. How can you do that?' Immediately Nataraja burned them [the Brahmin priests].'

Conclusion

The caste Hindu anomalizing of Nandanar or the downplaying of his actions upholds cultural knowledge about higher-caste superiority and Untouchable inferiority. Furthermore, in none of the caste Hindu versions are Nandanar and his deeds threatening to the caste order or the material order, because they deal primarily with the spiritual realm, and Nandanar, except in the version that shows him to be a nuisance, is a 'good,' obedient, and docile Untouchable, ever willing to submit to caste rules. This might have the implication that the rest of the Untouchables fit their low status because of their low nature and not because of external causes, otherwise they would also have achieved the great religious heights that Nandanar achieved. Nandanar may thus serve to emphasize the inherent inferiority of all other Untouchables.

For the Untouchables, their versions of the Nandanar legend fit in with what they know about themselves–that they are capable of religiosity comparable or superior to that of caste Hindus.[3] Nandanar serves as an example that proves the rule, rather than showing other Untouchables by contrast to be inherently inferior. In the framework or background of caste Hindu resistance that Nandanar meets in his attempts to go to see Nataraja, the social structure of caste Hindu domination is also shown for what it is according to Untouchables: unfairly restrictive and oppressive. The external restrictive structure, and not inherent abilities, can then be understood as being the cause for the Untouchables' lowly position. At least in the case of the older Untouchables who narrated the legend, their versions boosted their self-esteem and strengthened their communal identity through identifying with Nandanar, an Untouchable from start to finish who, despite all opposition, achieved his quest, an Untouchable who was more greatly blessed and favoured by God than persons of other castes.

NOTES

* Excerpted with permission from 'Nandanar: Untouchable Saint and Caste Hindu Anomaly', *Ethos*, vol. 21, no. 2, 1993, pp. 154–79.

1. Caste Hindu refers to those upper and lower castes that are above the level of Untouchables and are considered clean castes.
2. Darshan or *darsanam* (in Tamil) refers to a mystical vision or gaining sight of God. In this case, it refers to the biannual festival with an exposition and procession of Nataraja in the streets around the temple in Chidambaram.
3. Anbur Untouchables tend to view themselves as being morally superior to caste Hindus, whom many characterize as selfish and deceitful for oppressing the Untouchables. Most Anbur Untouchables hold beliefs about various deities and participate in public and private devotions, festivals, ecstatic (including self-torture) rituals, and pilgrimages. They believe in heaven and hell (*sorakkam* and *naraham*) and hold that sins such as selfishness (which they attribute mainly to caste Hindus) will cause one to go to hell.

II

THE MARATHI SAINTS: CHOKHAMELA, SOYRABAI, KARMAMELA, NIRMALA, BANKA

5

On the Threshold: The Songs of Chokhamela*

ROHINI MOKASHI-PUNEKAR

Chokhamela was a fourteenth-century Untouchable saint-poet of western India. He belonged to a community of devotees called the *varkaris* whose traditions and forms of worship are still alive in practice today, coming to us in an almost unbroken continuum from the late thirteenth century. This introduction to his life and work and the tradition he represents is divided into three parts. Part one traces the background of the *varkari* movement and locates Chokhamela's life and poetry within it. Part two attempts an exploration of the interface between the working castes and literature. Part three is a note on translating Chokhamela's poetry.

Chokhamela: His Life and Poetry

The bhakti movement, though largely associated with medieval India, began as a recognizable movement with the Alvar saints of south India somewhere in the seventh century CE and moved in a seemingly random and arbitrary fashion across the subcontinent, inspiring different regions and communities with an incandescent fire lit by previous movements, so that many aspects of the movement are alive even today. It was a wave of social, religious, and spiritual enquiry. This deeply spiritual and democratizing movement was characterized by the emergence of many religious communities and groups, revolutionary in spirit, in almost every region of the country. Perhaps this new spirit in some areas was a result of exposure to a more egalitarian religion–Islam–which had been introduced by the Muslim invaders. The bhakti movement was a questioning of the orthodox and repressive brahminical understanding of Hinduism, and as such made it possible for the lower castes and women to give a form to their religious aspirations, emphasizing devotion and love, not knowledge, as a means of salvation. In a newfound burst of confidence, it relocated the bhakti marg, the way of devotion, in the pursuit of salvation. In Maharashtra this democratizing devotional passion seems to have mainly precipitated the *varkari* community in the thirteenth century.

The *varkaris* are devotees of Vitthal, affectionately known as Vithoba, the deity at Pandharpur, a small town on the banks of the Chandrabhaga, a tributary of the river Bhima. Not much is known about the history of the temple, when it was built or who built it. But there is a poignant story about how Vithoba came to stay at Pandharpur, which attests to the mysterious nature of spiritual experience. Vithoba the god himself came to see Pundalik, a reformed rake from the neighbouring state of Karnataka, well known, after his conversion from a life of dissipation, for his extreme piety and goodness. Pundalik, who was devoted to his parents, was attending to their needs when Vitthal appeared. Throwing a brick for the god to stand on, for the Chandrabhaga was then in spate, Pundalik promised to return after finishing his work. He never managed to come back; and Vithoba is caught in stone, hands on hips, standing on a brick, endlessly waiting for his *bhakta*. The story, the image, the river, and the sands evoke a powerful emotional response, and year after year, thousands of *varkaris* make a pilgrimage on foot to have a darshan of the god. In fact, to be a *varkari* is to make this pilgrimage at regular intervals, not alone, but amongst a community of pilgrims belonging to various castes–high and low, and hailing from different parts of Maharashtra–all converging towards Pandharpur singing the *abhangas*, the hymns that the saint-poets of this tradition wrote or sang. *Varkari* literally means one who makes the to and fro journey at a specific time, the *vari*. For the fifty odd saint-poets belonging to this tradition, drawn from almost all castes of the region of those times, the *abhanga* is the most important medium of comprehending, reaching, and expressing the sense of divine mystery and joy; it is also the means of articulating pain and anger against injustice. It is a modification of the folk verse form–the *ovi*–which is traditionally the form of women's songs. Like most bhakti poetry, the *abhangas*, too are signed off by the poet composing them. *Abhangas* are sung by entire groups of people, even today, when on foot on the yearly pilgrimage to Pandharpur and at kirtans. A kirtan is a kind of prayer meeting where songs are invariably sung. The word kirtan itself means song in Carnatic music.

The fascination that Vithoba holds for these saint-poets is apparent, most clearly illustrated by the story of Pundalik. The story reverses the normative understanding of the divine; the divinity here waits endlessly for the *bhakta*, the devotee. It is this divine lack, in a sense, which empowers the *varkaris*' sense of overwhelming devotion. In a curious fashion, and unlike the luxuriant descriptions of godheads in Hinduism, Vitthal is identified not by myths and stories surrounding him, but by stories about the saint-poets. The mythology of Vitthal is in a sense the mythology of the saint-poets. He is given shape and form and substance by the devotion of the *varkaris*; by himself he is almost qualityless. The physical image of the god, too, is unlike most other images in Hindu iconography. He stands arms akimbo, without the terrifying arsenal carried by the many-armed Hindu deities. Though Vitthal is a *swarup* of Vishnu, not an avatar, he is identified sometimes with the child Krishna and is called, oddly enough for an image in black stone, Pandurang, which means the white one, and which is the name for Shiva. The main temple of Vitthal is surrounded by Shiva temples in the temple complex at Pandharpur; and the name Pandharpur, too, is etymologically derived from Pandurang. Obviously Vithoba is the later deity, replacing the earlier Shaivite godhead. But the perplexing confusion over the identity of Vitthal contributes to a feeling that it is, in the beautiful words of Prof. Fred Dallmayr, 'intriguingly placed at the crossroads between the manifest and the non-manifest, between revealment and concealment, familiarity and non-familiarity, or in Indian terminology between '*saguna*' and '*nirguna*' conceptions'.[1]

We now have to change tracks and look, not at metaphysical profundities, but at the saint-poets themselves, their lives, and how their hearts turned in devotion to Vithoba, at the Untouchable saint-poet Chokhamela in particular whose life captures the paradigmatic ambiguity of Hinduism: its liberating intellectual plurality and its equally restricting social construction. His is perhaps one of the first, if not the very first, marginalized voices in Indian history. There is very little in the way of recorded history of Chokhamela's life. The figure who emerges from the mists of the last seven centuries takes shape from legends and fleeting references to seemingly real-life situations in his own poetry and that of the other saint-poets of his times. Chokha was a Mahar, one of the lowest in the Hindu hierarchy of castes, and as such his duties, too, seem to have involved, like others in his situation, tasks menial in nature. Mahârs, as other Untouchables, are considered outcastes in the sense of being outside the four-fold varna system, although they are all members of various Untouchable castes. Their identity in society is shaped through a series of negations.

Perhaps it is important at this juncture to stress the difference between the lower castes, who form the fourth varna or category of four varnas (of which the upper three are the superior twice-born categories) in Hindu society, the Shudras, and those who form the unnamed fifth varna and are not reckoned as a respectable part of society. The Mahars were thought to be impure because traditionally some of their tasks, such as dragging out dead cows from the village, were unclean. They were Untouchable because their touch, or even proximity to them, was considered polluting. Generally, an Untouchable was not paid; he was expected to live off the leftovers given by the upper castes. He was denied education, knowledge of the scriptures, access to the facilities of the village such as the use of the well, and, crucially, he was forbidden entry into the temple. These denials, especially the last, are important preoccupations in Chokha's poetry.

Chokhamela, then, was an Untouchable saint of this tradition; that he wrote poetry at all is a matter of astonishment. Amongst his contemporaries are the important figures of Dnyaneshwar, the late thirteenth-century revolutionary Brahmin philosopher and saint-poet with whom the *varkari* tradition really begins, and Namdev, the lower-caste rebel saint and poet, a tailor by profession, under whose wide and generous understanding of spirituality blossomed many saint-poets largely drawn from the lower and marginalized ranks of society. Dnyaneshwar, the author of the celebrated *Dnyaneshwari*, an interpretation of the *Bhagvad Gita* in Marathi, was, in the words of James Edwards, 'an outcaste Brahmin'; his family suffered ostracism and he took samadhi when barely twenty-two years of age.[2] Namdev his close friend outlived him by about fifty years.

Presumably Chokha's spiritual leanings were given direction by Namdev: Chokha acknowledges him as his guru in many of his poems. He seems to have been instrumental in recognizing Chokha's devotion and getting him as far as the great doors of the temple at Pandharpur,

Plate 5.1: The samadhi of Chokhamela at the foot of the stairs of the Pandharpur temple to Vithoba. The painting above shows the legend of Ranya Mahar serving food to Eknath, Krishna and the *bhaktas* in Paithan. Photograph by Eleanor Zelliot.

Plate 5.2: Chokhamela's image at his samadhi at the foot of the stairs of the Pandharpur temple to Vithoba. The metal head is brought out and placed over a stone on holy days. Photograph by Eleanor Zelliot.

but either even Namdev lacked total conviction, or the Brahmin priests, who loom large in Chokha's poems, thrust him out, unable to countenance the 'Untouchable' Mahar polluting the divinity in the temple. Chokha's habitual place seems to have been at the foot of the outer doors of the temple, on the threshold. His poems quite simply and humbly refer to his standing there, quite without self-pity and certainly without rancour. This literal and symbolic stance of the saint-poet and the quietude in his voice are devastatingly moving. It may perhaps be noted that there exists a body of well-known stories, orally handed down for generations, narrating incidents from his life. It is quite probable that the poems have fed the stories and that these have acquired colour and depth over the years. However, there seems to be an individual voice and personality in the collection of his *abhangas*, numbering over three hundred, which is real and authentic. It is the quality of this voice and the stories around the person that have to serve in place of documented history. It is interesting to see how the poems merge into legend, so that in the popular imagination of the *varkaris* the two exist in a seamless continuum.

One may perhaps examine an instance of how myth and poem are woven into each other. A well-known story goes like this. One day Chokha had been standing at the door of the temple from morning till late in the evening, somewhat hopeless and unusually downcast. Towards nightfall, the priests locked up the doors and went away. As Chokha stood there, still and alone, Vithoba himself came out, exclaimed in distress on seeing Chokha waiting patiently, embraced him and led him by the hand to the innermost sanctum, where he lovingly held him to his breast. The night was spent in the union of the *bhakta* with the god, after which Vithoba playfully removed his *tulsi* garland (a garland made of basil seeds which the *varkaris* wear as a mark of their identity), and put it around Chokha's neck. When the day dawned, he led him out of the temple, still with the garland. Chokha, in a state of bliss after this vouchsafing of divine love, lay down on the sands of the river in a trance. At the temple the priests discovered that Vithoba's gold necklace had disappeared and, remembering that Chokha had been at the temple doors last, went into transports of rage over the fact that the temple and the deity had both been polluted and the necklace stolen. Search parties found Chokha still dazed and uncomprehending, but with a gold necklace around his neck. He was punished; he was tied to bullocks and was about to be dragged to death but for the animals who stood their ground, despite the whip lashing them. The story ends with Vithoba revealing himself to the entire company, holding the bullocks by the horns.

The poem, however, dramatizes Chokha's plea to Vithoba in the midst of his humiliation. The incensed priests lashing the whip, the bullocks, the crowd of people, all are frozen in the background. A curtain of silence is drawn on the flurry of activity. Instead, what is voiced are Chokha's anguished words to his god. The poem makes no mention of Vitthal's revelation or appearance in public; nevertheless, it makes an ambiguous reference to a secret shared between them.

They thrash me, Vithu,
now don't walk so slow.
The pandits whip,
    some crime,
    don't know what:
How did Vithoba's necklace come round your throat?
They curse and strike
and say I polluted you.
Do not send the cur at your door
    away,
    Giver of everything.
    You,
Chakrapani,
yours is the deed.
With folded hands,
    Chokha begs.
I revealed our secret,
don't turn away.

(*Abhanga* 82)

This poem is one of a few that dramatize situations. But the entire collection, of which some poems must be latter-day interpolations and additions mentioning as they do the names of saints who were not contemporaries of Chokhamela, communicates a range and depth of spiritual experience that is surely of immense value. The deprivations, material and religious, which constantly hemmed him in, and the humiliations that pushed him beyond the caste boundaries, evoke by turns a resigned wonder at unjust and hypocritical human constructions, a philosophic calm, despair, and sometimes anguish. Some poems reveal bliss, an ecstasy of affirmation. They work towards an awareness that it is not only divine love that empowers him, but also, perhaps more importantly, *his* devotion that empowers Vithoba. Some poems subtly play up the paradox that Vithoba, the holiest of the holy, touches, eats with, and embraces him, Chokha, the impure outcaste, a loving favour not extended to the touchable Brahmin priests. He is rarely angry, but sometimes he does strip away the facades of religious humbug to expose human cruelties. Chokhamela's poetry, in short, quietly reverses the normative understanding of divinity and social structure.

What about posterity? In the living tradition of the *varkari* community, Chokha's *abhangas* continue to be sung, not only by the 'lower' castes but also by communities of pilgrims. He remains in popular memory and currency. But he has never received as much prominence as, say, Namdev or Tukaram, other lower caste saint-poets. It is not difficult to see that his Mahar identity is the main reason for the half-neglect. Where secular politics is concerned, the scene changes significantly. In the twentieth century, especially during the Indian nationalist movement and after Independence, there has been a great mobilization of the former Untouchables under the leadership of Dr B.R. Ambedkar. Dr Ambedkar, who was from the Mahar community, was an outstanding leader of the independence movement. He was perhaps the most radical and committed leader of the marginalized. Today many former Untouchables call themselves Dalit, which literally means 'ground down' and can also be translated as 'oppressed', but implies no pollution.

A very significant outcome of the Dalit movement, primarily a struggle for social and political empowerment, was the mass conversion of thousands of Dalits, a majority of whom were Mahars, to Buddhism in the lifetime of Ambedkar. The Dalit movement is still a strong presence in contemporary Maharashtra, especially in the work of a group of revolutionary writers called the Dalit Panthers. This movement which could have given Chokhamela his rightful place has largely ignored him because Chokha's protest is contained in bhakti and because he accepts his karma, his birth as an Untouchable due to his previous deeds. If Chokhamela's Dalit identity lessens his importance as a *varkari* saint-poet, his association with Hinduism detracts from his Dalit identity.[3] It is clear that the peculiar dichotomy in which Chokha was caught within his lifetime–his outcaste identity, on the one hand, and his Vithoba bhakti, on the other–seems to spill over and continue down the centuries with paradoxical ramifications. This conjunction of bhakti and marginalization is embodied in the tone of his poems. Chokha questions pollution and untouchability. He is too intelligent not to perceive the self-interest of the powerful classes behind the façade of religion, but his heart full of love seems to melt anger into understanding. His joyous belief in God is weighed down by the sorrow of things, his anguish contained in quietude.

It is said that Chokha died along with other Mahar labourers when a part of the wall they were repairing in the town of Mangalvedhe collapsed on them. The legend goes that Chokha's friend Namdev went to find his remains and picked up those bones that murmured 'Vitthal, Vitthal'. The bones were buried at the bottom of the steps *outside* the great door of the main temple where Chokha was accustomed to stand all day long in worship. A shrine is built there today in Chokha's honour and there is still a great deal of obeisance to the samadhi from the crowds. In a way, Chokha continues to be at the threshold; from another perspective, the devotee has to visit Chokha's shrine before climbing up to Vithoba.

Literature, Religion, and the Working Castes

A distinguishing feature of the *varkari* movement is its grounding in the gamut of rural professions. This poem by Chokha illustrates my point:

> The saviour of his devotees,
> who never turns away,
> hurries to help them
> with their chores.
> He dusts and cleans,
> and fetches water,
> the upholder of dharma;
> saves from the searing
> flames of nirvana.
> He keeps the cows
> at the milkman's house
> and happily with others
> breaks the pot of curds.

He pulled a wall for
Dnyaneshwar; made Changdev
famous; weeded the beds
for Savata the gardener,
and fired pots for Gora.
He loves more than his own self
goldsmith, cobbler
and Namdev the tailor.
He grinds the grain
at Jani's home, sweeps the dirt
and brings the cow dung in.
Says Chokha, he is so tender:
his devotees know him
as a fond mother.

(*Abhanga* 284)

Dnyaneshwar the outcaste Brahmin, Changdev the yogi turned saint, Namdev the tailor, Gora the potter, Savata the gardener, Chokha the Mahar, Janabai the servant/nurse at Namdev's house, Joga the oilman, Narahari the goldsmith, Sena the barber, Kanhopatra the courtesan, and later, after a couple of centuries, there is Eknath the liberal Brahmin scholar-saint and then, the flower of the *varkari* movement, Tukaram, who was a peasant/grocer, a lower-caste Kunbi: these are the saint-poets.

At the other end, a reading of D.B. Mokashi's immensely valuable book, *Palkhi*, a first-hand account of travelling along with the *varkaris* to Pandharpur on their annual pilgrimage, shows the full scale and extent of the influence of this bhakti movement in contemporary Maharashtra, rural and semi-urban.[4] A brief sketch of the organization of the pilgrimage is in order here. Hundreds of travelling groups called *dindis* start from the many towns of Maharashtra along with the *palkhi* (the palanquin carrying silver representations of the saint-poet's foot prints); most of these towns are the birthplaces of the saints. For instance, the *palkhi* of Dnyaneshwar starts from Alandi, that of Tukaram from Dehu, that of Eknath from Paithan, and so on. The *dindis* walk according to a perfect time schedule of arrival, departure, and halts; they cater to the essential physical requirements of the devotees along the way on the payment of a fee. The *varkaris* sing *abhangas* as they walk. More *dindis* join along the way, different forms of musical-dramatic group performances such as the *bharud*, *goph*, *shej arati*, *lalit*, and *bhedik* are performed on certain occasions. There are kirtans and bhajans, again involving entire *dindis*. The villagers on the way take darshan as the *palkhis* pass. The most important of the two annual pilgrimages take place during Ashadh, a month of the Hindu calendar roughly corresponding to the month of August, the time of the year when heavy showers and strong winds play with the sunshine. Mokashi's book brings alive the days of travel and the rain-drenched, sun-soaked pilgrims walking towards the shrine in Pandharpur. This is the time when the *varkari* farmers have finished their sowing operations and are at leisure to travel, returning home well in time for the harvesting. The poorer *varkaris*—peasants, elders, housewives carrying babies on their hips, too poor to afford the modest fees of the *dindis*—walk alongside, eating whatever they are given in charity and sleeping in the open at night halts; *varkari* barbers who pay for the expenses of the travel by offering their services at the halts; *varkari* tea hawkers and bangle sellers who peddle their wares to pay for their way. It is literally religion and literature in the midst of work.

The *varkari* cult is clearly the most quietly influential mass movement of rural Maharashtra. It is based on autonomy and decentralization. The code enjoined upon a *varkari* is simple: clean clothes and a bath, a *tulsi* necklace, fasts on certain days, vegetarian food, doing good to others, and most importantly, the reiteration of the Name. Meditation or singing of the *abhangas* is enough to observe the code; there is no punitive measure for breaking it; only self-punishment is suggested.[5] No expensive and time-consuming pilgrimage to the distant shrines of Benares or Kedarnath is required, only the yearly yatra on foot to nearby Pandharpur. No priests mediate between the devotee and his bhakta; no rigorous individual rituals such as elaborate pujas are needed. It is a code most suited to poor, illiterate, labouring castes and peasants who can afford neither money nor leisure nor learning. By discarding the knowledge of the scriptures and mocking renunciation of the family or society, it emphasizes religion within the world, within relationships, and, most importantly, religion within labour. It is a movement of householder, artisan, peasant, and labouring saints and devotees; the story of Pundalik who asked Vithoba to wait because he was loath to leave his parents illustrates the point. All the names of the saint-poets mentioned at the beginning of this section sang from the hearth, so to speak; and being common men and women themselves they sang in the common man's language. Their words were picked up and retained orally through the centuries; there are illiterate farmers even today who can recite the whole of Tukaram and much of the other saint-poets besides. Like other bhakti literature, *varkari* poetry, too, is oral and it is in vernacular Marathi.

To come back to Chokha's poem quoted a little earlier, it throws up another significant aspect. Not only are the various saint-poets presented in their workaday worlds, but Vithoba, too, is shown lovingly participating in all their labours. Especially in poems relating to Janabai, the god combs her hair killing lice, feeds her mouthful by mouthful, grinds grain, and collects cowdung, for all the world as if he were a tender mother lessening the burden of work for his offspring. In the poem the original term is *lalla palloo*, which means a loving parent, someone who pets and spoils, and takes care. I have taken the liberty of translating this term as fond mother, taking my cue from countless *abhangas* where Vitthal is addressed as mother, *mauli*. If, to quote A.K. Ramanujan, in bhakti poetry men are like women before god,[6] in *varkari* poetry, not only is the poet a woman before god but also god himself is a loving, endlessly giving mother, who, like his mortal counterpart, has little control over the injustices and cruelties of the patriarchal family. Divinity becomes a powerless feminine principle, thus turning the traditional hierarchy topsy turvy.

Finally, we have to address the question of the gap between precept and practice. Though the *varkari* movement through its saint poetry movingly advocates egalitarianism and though all castes walk together to Pandharpur, yet different castes walk and, crucially, eat together amongst their own groups. As Irawati Karve notes, the *dindi* in which she was walking sang Chokha's *abhangas*, but observed all the purity rituals of the Brahmins, not eating together with the other lower-caste members of the *dindi*.[7]

While recognizing the need for equality, does the expression and articulation of inequity take the place of action amongst the *varkaris*? Is it the only possible revolt? Historically, one must remember that for Chokha there was no entering the temple in spite of his own and others saints' poems. But before dismissing the *varkaris*, it is important to note that this quieter movement was perhaps the only one possible within the economic and political history of the region; and that by being quiet it was more flexible and has lasted longer than more radical and short-lived manifestos. The range of its influence has been wider and deeper; the association between Tukaram and the great Maratha king Shivaji has been a strong and powerful legend. The Dalit movement, it must be remembered, originated and took root here. The contribution of *varkari* saint poetry to Marathi literature is acknowledged to be immense; more subtly, this oral literature has perhaps infused in the Marathi language a marked capacity for irony.

To conclude, a significant change in the arrangement of the *dindis* in the Pandharpur pilgrimage must be noted. The *palkhi* of the Chambhars in honour of the Hindu saint and the Chamar Rohidas (Ravidas), which used to be placed by itself in front of the horse representing Dnyaneshwar, now may walk *behind* the horse, still far from the Brahmin *palkhi* at the very end of the *dindi*, but no longer isolated. While this might not amount to a huge change, it is still a small gain.

A Note on the Translations

Abhangas are living sources of religion, literature, and music in contemporary Maharashtra. Their primary impulse is spiritual; they are literature only afterwards. They belong not to airy venues of literary meets but to communities of singing *varkaris* walking with their god. I have tried to remember this while translating Chokhamela's *abhangas*.

I have also tried to remember that Chokha's voice as it speaks from his poems is proof of his spiritual aspirations as well as his physical deprivations. In the act of translating, pure fidelity to the spirit of the text is bound to result in mushiness. The word is a more reliable guide and I have tried to work from the letter to the spirit. Even when the dropping of a word, or sometimes even a line, of the original seemed to fit in better with the sound and effect of the translation, I have preferred to remain true even to the point of sounding tedious in English. The syntax of medieval Marathi and especially Chokha's Mahar variant is naturally at odds with English. Without attempting to render the poems in the rhymed and metered verse of the originals, these translations are in modern English idiom, seeking to simulate only Chokha's tone of voice. Towards this end, I have permitted myself some liberties in punctuation and breaks in line.

Abhangas are oral literature and as such there exists no final and completely authoritative edition of Chokhamela's poetry. *Srisakalsantgatha* edited by K.A. Joshi (rept. 1967) contains the lives and poems of all the *varkari* saints and is more easily available. But the collection edited by S.B. Kadam in his *Shri Sant Chokhamela: Charitra ani Abhang* (rept. 1998) is a painstakingly sincere effort to collate all of Chokha's poems. The following translations are based on this edition; the numbering also follows the Kadam collection:

The Vedas and the shastras
polluted; the puranas inauspicious,
impure; the body, the soul
contaminated; the manifest
Being is the same.
Brahma polluted, Vishnu too;
Shankar is impure, inauspicious.
Birth impure, dying is impure.
Says Chokha,
pollution stretches
without beginning
and end.

(*Abhanga* 282)

Five elements compound the impure body;
all things mix,
thrive in the world.
Then who is pure and who impure?
The body is rooted in impurity.
From the beginning to the end,
endless impurities
heap themselves.
Who is it can be made pure?
Says Chokha,
I am struck with wonder.
Can there be any such
beyond pollution?

(*Abhanga* 279)

Something wonderful happened once:
God dropped in unannounced.
He walked in pell-mell, sat
down and said, get some

breakfast, won't you.
Jani said, O my lordly one,
won't you help yourself,
my friend?
God looked everywhere, raised
lids and clattered them on;
hurried away in the burning
sun, came back with a lidful
of gruel and drawing Jani
by her hand, fed her
mouthful by mouthful.
    Both fulfilled quite, belched satisfied.

        Chokha, standing on the threshold,
        hands outspread for the leftovers.[8]

(*Abhanga* 285)

Filled with joy is the whole self,
I saw he himself within me.
Seeing ceased,
looking was erased,
he filled my being
with wonder
Emptiness ahead and behind,
where locate?
The heart meets,
    in mine own self.
    Says Chokha,

I saw Pandhari[9]
    waiting
        on a brick
        by the Bhim

(*Abhanga* 80)

My father and begetter of the world,
how are you not moved?
why the weight of this world
on my shoulders?
why are you and I
severed like this?

Our joy and sorrow in this:
birth, age and death.
Why
do you look on
with such fond pride?
    Overcome, Chokha stands
    at the great door,
    hands folded for Vithoba.

(*Abhanga* 84)

Johar, mai-bap, johar.[10]
I am the Mahar of your Mahars.
I am come,
starved
for your leavings.
The servant of your servants
waits with hope.
I have brought, says Chokha,
my bowl
for your leavings.

(*Abhanga* 343)

You take care of yourself now; you
know, are informed of every
thing, what is or not.
A waste
to sing of your glory:
how long, after
all, can one praise.
What you couldn't
stick, I bore without murmur:
took in, ate,
digested and all for my good.
Says Chokha, if I
narrate these home truths,
how can they
lessen me in any way?[11]

(*Abhanga* 139)

Sitting by ourselves once,
deep in talk,
he held my chin and
soothed me. The world
and its worries,
he said, don't
take them to heart.
I'll give you
a key:
what must be, will be;
what will not, cannot.
All joy and sorrow you'll see
are based in karma.
Don't fret, Chokhya,
says God,
this is my promise:
you are the best of devotees.[12]

(*Abhanga* 164)

NOTES

* This study is reproduced with a few changes from the introduction to *On the Threshold: Songs of Chokhamela*, New Delhi: The Book Review Literary Trust, 2002, by the same author, with the permission of the publishers. Republished as a world edition with additional translations by Alta Mira Press, New York in cooperation with the International Sacred Literature Trust in April 2005.

1. Fred Dallmayr, 'Walking humbly with your God: Jnaneshwar and the Warkaris', *Journal of Contemporary Thought*, vol. 13, Summer 2001, pp. 33–53.
2. James F. Edwards, *Dhyaneshwar: The Out-Caste Brahmin*, Poona: Aryabhushan Press, 1941. Dnyaneshwar was outcasted because his father had returned from sannyas to take married life and had fathered him and his three siblings.
3. For a thorough analysis of the place of Chokhamela in the Dalit movement, see Eleanor Zelliot, *From Untouchable to Dalit: Essays on the Ambedkar Movement*, New Delhi: Manohar, 1992, 3rd edn., 2001, pp. 10–14.
4. D.B. Mokashi, *Palkhi: An Indian Pilgrimage*, trans. Philip. C. Engblom, Albany, New York: State University of New York Press, 1987.
5. For an excellent discussion of the *varkari* movement and literature from a socio-economic perspective, see Bhalchandra Nemade, 'The Revolt of the Underprivileged: Style in the Expression of the Warkari Movement in Maharashtra', in Jayant Lele, ed., *Tradition and Modernity in the Bhakti Movement*, Leiden: E.J. Brill, 1981.
6. A.K. Ramanujan, 'On Women Saints', in John S. Hawley and Donna M. Wulff, eds., *The Divine Consort: Radha and the Goddesses of India*, Berkeley, California: Berkeley Religious Studies, 1982, p. 316.

7. Irawati Karve, 'On the Road: A Maharashtrian Pilgrimage', *Journal of Asian Studies*, vol. 22, 1962, pp. 16–19. Reprinted in *The Experience of Hinduism: Essays on Religion in Maharashtra*, Albany: State University of New York Press, 1988.
8. This is a deeply interesting poem. It refers to Janabai, a contemporary lower-caste woman saint-poet, who considered Namdev her guru, and who was also a servant in his house. Jani's poems relate Vitthal's coming to help and comfort her—lending a hand with her tasks and combing her hair as a mother would. This poem shows us Chokha looking on the scene of Vitthal's loving care of Jani. It is significant that even here Chokha sees himself on the threshold. The poem is extremely sophisticated from a formal aspect.
9. The god of Pandharpur and hence Pandhari.
10. The term 'johar' was used by an outcaste to greet the uppercaste. It was, in effect, a way of making the outcaste reveal his identity himself. 'Mai-bap' can be translated as mother-father, though the original is retained in the translation. This is perhaps the most severe of Chokha's poems, and works by means of a controlled paring down to essentials.
11. This poem, as the one before, is significant in that it incorporates a critique of the social condition within the critique of the godhead. The laconic tone and the precision are devastating.
12. Chokhya is the affectionate diminutive of Chokhamela. If all *abhangas* end with the respective saint-poet's signature, so to speak, this one is signed off by Vitthal himself.

6

Banka Mahar and Karmamela

ROHINI MOKASHI-PUNEKAR

It is generally accepted that Banka and Soyrabai, Chokhamela's wife, were brother and sister. S.B. Kadam in *Sri Sant Chokhamela: Charitra v Abhang* (1998: 77) writes that to Krishna Mahar and his wife Bhima, both of Pandharpur, were born two children, Banka and Soyra. The name Banka is probably a diminutive of Venkatesh. It was Namdev, according to Kadam, who was instrumental in arranging the joint marriages of Soyra and Banka with the other pair of brother and sister: Chokhamela and Nirmala. This family, later with the addition of Karmamela, the son of Chokamela and Soyrabai, is an unusually well-knit family. It is closely bonded together, and not only by the ties of blood. Eleanor Zelliot's discussion of Soyra and Nirmala[1] analyses the nature of the loving friendship that characterizes the relationship between the pair of sisters-in-law twice over. If Nirmala is the symbol of love and devotion for Soyra, Chokhamela is the guru of her brother Banka.

Each family member is remembered by a fairly large number of *abhangas* ascribed to them; these poems shape a voice and take a particular stance that is useful, confronted as we are with the lack of any historic documentation. Banka Mahar has some thirty-nine *abhangas* to his name. He and Nirmala seem to have lived in Mehunpuri, about two hundred miles from Pandharpur, where they are still remembered.[2] Banka's poems follow, in a way, the stock themes of the *varkari* tradition: *stuti* or praise (of Vitthal), the woes of the world, caste and pollution, his own sins and weaknesses, and Vitthal's mercy and deliverance. Many of his poems refer to his beloved guru Chokhamela, and to his sister Soyra, and wife Nirmala; one poem sequence, of about eleven poems, describes the miraculous conception of Karmamela, contributing yet one more thread to the story of the birth of Karmamela. One interesting poem draws the lineage of the gurus, tracing the tradition behind his own guru Chokhamela. Gods are often given a feminine, and maternal, identity in the Marathi bhakti tradition, but 'mother guru' is somewhat unusual:

> Mother Dnyaneshwar is the king of wisdom.
> He engulfed Kechar in a flood of mercy.
> Kechar came to shelter at Dnyaneshwar's feet and
> graced Namdev.
> With his hand on Chokha's head, Namdev taught
> him these syllables: Vi th th la.
> Chokha is my guru mother, says Banka.
> I prostrate myself at his feet.[3]
>
> (*Abhanga* 39)

Kechar in this poem is Visoba Kechar, who did not, in the beginning, believe in Dnyaneshwar, but later became his disciple. He is also supposed to have accompanied Dnyaneshwar and Namdev on their pilgrimage to the north. Another *abhanga* describes Chokha with overflowing love:

> Chokha is pure; there is no dirt or flaw in him.
> He is an ocean of bliss, a store of bhakti.
> He is the mother of love; a haven of mercy:
> he draws my mind. Banka prostrates himself
> before him.
>
> (*Abhanga* 22)

The poem sequence (from poem 5 to 15) about the conception of Karmamela describes in graphic style the miraculous happenings at his sister's house. In Banka's tale, Soyrabai was anxious and sad because there was no child in the house. Vitthal, the king of Pandhari, heard her plea and came in the guise of a poor old Brahmin. Standing near the *tulsi* plant in her front yard, trembling with exhaustion and hunger, he begged for some food and water. Soyrabai was deeply troubled, caught between pity and fear. If she gave him food, people would beat her because she was an impure Mahar. How could she give food to a Brahmin? If he went away with nothing, her husband would be angry.

She told him her caste and her dilemma, but the god said, 'You can save my life by giving me some food. Don't think about what might happen.' She gave him some rice and curd that she had, probably some leavings that had been given to her, and he said, 'Ask me for whatever you want and I will give it to you.' Soyrabai asked for nothing but Vitthal gave her prasad and said, 'You will have a child.' When Chokha came home, she is of course told that she had behaved improperly. 'Who wanted what child?' says Chokha. But when the time of birth came near, Chokha went to his sister's house for help, a well-known story that is often narrated. However, instead of the birth story, Banka tells us that Hari came to Chokha's house, to the great joy of Soyra and Nirmala, who were both at home, and 'stayed happily in the house of Chokha'.

Banka's long narration is deft and realistic; Chokha does not come off very well here. He is a grouchy husband. But such a picture fits into the accepted pattern of *bhaktas* giving up everything for God, even, in the case of Gora the Potter, a son's life. A lovely poem by Banka is centred on Gora though he does not narrate the traditional tale of Gora trampling his son to death as he mixed the clay so engrossed was he meditating on the Name. Banka's *abhanga* tells of God helping Gora the Potter whose necessary beast of burden was a donkey. Vitthal's *vahan* (vehicle) becomes the donkey in this telling; Banka also manages a swift swipe at the scriptures:

> Look at this miracle:
> Hari has turned a potter in Gora's yard.
> His eagle that flies over the three worlds
> is now a donkey; and his glory is kept aside.
> Filling the gunny sacks with clay,
> he heaves them in, helped by Rukhmai.
> Banka wonders at the silence of the Vedas
> on Hari's love for his devotees.

(*Abhanga* 31)

In a manner typical of the *varkari* bhakti tradition, Banka shows how God grants physical and practical help to all his *bhaktas* who are, most of them, householder-saints.[4] But Banka, again in a way peculiar to the Marathi bhakti tradition, does not seem to recognize any conflict between the *nirgun* and *sagun* forms that is such a major source of controversy in other regions. Banka's opening lines from an *abhanga*, in a simple yet profound way, seem to indicate that both *sagun* or *nirgun* are a matter of perception, and more significantly, that God is merely fulfilling the wishes of the *bhaktas* in showing himself to them in whatever form *they* think appropriate:

Honouring his *bhaktas*,
keeping in mind their yearnings,
he fulfils their desires
appearing in *sagun*
or *nirgun* form.

(*Abhanga* 33)

Banka Mahar is characterized by loving devotion to Vitthal, and to the members of his family. There is more angst in the twenty-seven *abhangas* of Karmamela than in the poetry of any other member of this family. Karmamela's poems question and rebuke Vitthal; he is bitter and scornful in a few and only in some does he seem to have made some peace with his god, himself, and the world. His poems provide a perfect foil to the resigned sorrow and piety of his parents, and his uncle and aunt. One seems to expect that a hot-blooded young man would not accept so easily the humiliating slights and wrongs of the world, especially if the bhakti tradition to which his family belonged claimed something contrary. Kadam dramatizes glimpses into Chokhamela's life; one of these is a situation where Karmamela is angry and frustrated with his lot, but is soothed by his father's rather modern-sounding perspective on history and change in social norms (1998: 99–102). That, however, is a piece of fictionalized narrative; Karmamela's *abhangas* evoke an authentic voice that takes us straight into the middle of a confrontation, an on-going argument that Karmamela seems to have had with Vitthal:

How, Narayana, do you forget?
My father is your ward. You
bathed me as an infant. Why is
everything so hard now?
Take care, your reputation is at stake.
Your good name has to survive.

Says Chokha's Karmamela,
Please god, you must never forget me.[5]

(*Abhanga* 1)

And again:

You have made us low caste: Why
don't you understand the fact,
O god of gods? Our whole life:
spent in scrounging for leavings.
Have you no shame?
You ate rice and curd
In our house: do you dare to deny?
Says Chokha's Karmamela,
why have you given me this life?

(*Abhanga* 3)

The following *abhanga* works in an interesting way to depict a god almost powerless to change the world. The anger is put aside and, working half-ironically, Karmamela sketches a god who is as controlled by a preordained fate as he, a mortal, is. In a sense, this poem exonerates God of the evil and cruelty in the world; a decent god could not have created this awful world. God himself is helpless; he has no power over this third entity, fate. Hence, there is no point in blaming him for the injustice created by fate:

From now onwards, Hari,
don't reproach me. You look after
your interests and I'll manage
mine. What is the point
of blaming you for our destiny?
My heart is my witness.
I won't waste more words.
Says Karmamela, you should know,
Narayana,
both our hearts.

(*Abhanga* 15)

It is also clear that Karmamela equates his own heart with God; his heart is his witness, and God knows his heart. In different times perhaps

Karmamela would have been an agnostic; suffering the injustices of the world, all he can vouch for as divine is the purity of his own heart.

NOTES

1. See Eleanor Zelliot's 'Untouchable Women Saints' in this volume, where she examines the poetry of Soyrabai and Nirmala, wife and sister respectively of Chokhamela.
2. Ibid.
3. *Abhang* 39 (1: 1004) in *Srisakalsantgatha* in two volumes. Collected by Nanamaharaj Sakhare, edited by Kashinath Anant Joshi, Pune: Srisantwangmaya Prakashan Mandir, 1967. First published in 1923. The numbering in this paper follows that of the poems in these volumes. All translations are mine.
4. See Rohini Mokashi-Punekar's 'On the Threshold', in this volume for a full discussion on the *varkari* tradition emerging from a particular kind of economic background.
5. *Srisakalsantgatha*, 1967, 1: 1011.

7

The Story of Karmamela's Birth[1]

ELEANOR ZELLIOT

The Marathi saints are householders, and two especially, Namdev and Chokhamela, have important families in the bhakti tradition. Namdev's own *abhangas* occasionally concern his family of fourteen, and there are *abhangas* by his wife, mother, daughter, and Janabai, his serving maid who was considered part of the family. However, the family of Chokhamela, a man much beloved by Namdev, is much more involved in bhakti. In the same *Srisakalsantgatha*,[2] in which the *abhangas* of Namdev's family appear, are the songs of not only Chokhamela, but also of his wife, his son, his sister and her husband. It is a smaller family than Namdev's, but it is impressive in that every person in the family is represented by significant numbers of *abhangas*. Chokhamela's family was smaller, perhaps because, according to various *abhangas* and legends, Chokhamela was too busy in devotion to father sons, and a little miracle had to be performed in order for Karmamela to be conceived at all. But that story is told elsewhere. This story, pieced together from several sources, is the story of Karmamela's birth. It is extracted here from my article, 'Women in the Homes of the Saints', which appeared in *Home, Family and Kinship in Maharashtra.*[3]

In Chokhamela's family, Karmamela is the bitter Untouchable, not because of his father's inattention but because of the treatment he receives as an Untouchable. But that, too, is another story. The women, Soyrabai, Chokhamela's wife, and Nirmala, Chokhamela's sister, rarely sing about their social situation, although Soyrabai does refer to herself as a Mahari, using the name of their Untouchable caste, whereas the women of Namdev's family do not use their caste name, Shimpi or tailor. The songs of Soyrabai and Nirmala for the most part concern their devotion to God, their ways of dealing with the duties of household life, and their sense of mystical union with the *nirgun* divinity, the formless god. They also refer briefly to the birth of Soyrabai's son Karmamela, a story which is a wonderful example of how the women saints in a saint's family deal with *samsar*–and how God helps them.

The story of the birth of Karmamela, the son of Chokhamela and Soyrabai and a saint-poet in his own right, is one that has to be pieced together from several sources. References to the incident are found in Soyra's poetry but in a very abbreviated form. She simply sings:

> Karmamela was born, by the grace of the Dark Lord.
>
> The name of Vitthal is shouted. The husband of
> Rukmini comes running.
>
> Vitthal-Rukmini does the *barsa*[4] with joy,
> With all that is needed in their hands,
> says Chokha's Mahari. (15)

Soyrabai doesn't tell the whole story. Chokhamela's sister Nirmala adds some rather damaging evidence of Chokha's behaviour as a useless husband:

> Conscious of the threat of samsara,[5]
> Chokha went to Mehunpuri.[6]
>
> Seeing him, Nirmala was joyous,
> And ran to embrace his feet.
>
> She sat near him, asked him how he was,
> if his wife was well.
>
> Nirmala said, 'Tell me what to do now.' (12)
>
> Listening to her, Chokha said,
> 'She is nine months pregnant.
>
> There is no provision for this in the house,
> she told me.

To find out what to do in this great difficulty,
I have come quickly to your place.'

Nirmala said, 'What can I say to you?
You are at fault. (13)

Tell me, elder brother,
how could you act so thoughtlessly?

How could you come running here without asking her?
My sister-in-law will cry wildly.'

Chokha said, 'Vithu will take care of everything.
I have put my burden on him.'

Nirmala said, 'It is not fair to give Vithoba
such trouble.' (14)

But he stayed there happily for one month,
his mind entangled in Pandurang.

Night and day, his only passion was the Name of Vitthal.
There was no thought of samsara in his mind.

After dinner, he sat alone.
Nirmala said to him

'Many days have passed. I remember the king of
Pandhari and I feel sad.

Nothing tastes sweet to me. When will I place my head
on His feet?'
Nirmala said, 'O King of Gods, meet me soon.' (15)

Chokha said to Nirmala, 'Sing the Name day and night.
That makes samsara happy, truly, both here and in the
other world.

This is the great way: peace, pardon, and mercy will
dwell in you.'

Nirmala heard this joyously and embraced his feet. (16)

Meanwhile, back at their home, which was probably in Pandharpur, Soyrabai was having a baby. We have to turn to the *abhangas* of Namdev to find out the end of the story. Namdev's 'biography' of Chokhamela, his beloved fellow *bhakta*, includes a very lengthy *abhanga* about Chokhamela's birth, life, and death. *Abhanga* 2353 is about the birth of Chokha's son Karmamela, and here is the story, in Namdev's narrative version:

> Chokha's wife was pregnant.
> She completed nine months.
>
> She asked her husband
> for the necessities for the birth.
>
> He heard her request and thought:
> who will take care of this bloody mess?
>
> Without telling her, he went to his sister's place,
> thinking joyfully about God.
>
> Afternoon came, and he didn't come to eat.
> His wife inquired everywhere.
>
> She searched and searched; it became evening.
> She said to herself, Where has my husband gone?
>
> Then she thought: I have asked one who is non-attached.
> Why didn't I realize that?
>
> O Pandurang, please bring him back.
> I won't tell him about household affairs.
>
> She became very weary. The time of birth came.
> Mother Vithu[7] came running to her.
>
> Vithoba became Chokha's sister and called,
> 'O sister-in-law, open the door.'
>
> The two saw each other joyously,
> and Chokha's wife started weeping.

'Oh, it's so good that God has sent you.
My husband has gone somewhere.'. . .

'So, sister-in-law, everything we need is here.
Don't worry about anything at all.' . . .

Soyrabai gave birth, and it was a son.
Pandurang was very happy.

Soyra gave sugar to everyone in the caste,
saying, 'My Chokha has a son.'

Nirmala bathed her, applying fragrant powder;
the ache was gone from her whole body. . . .

Chokha stayed for a month in his sister's place,
and then he said to himself:

'I was afraid of household duties and so I left them and
came here, but I have lost the feet of God.'

His mind was overwhelmed with emotion.
Tears of love came to his eyes . . .

'I take your leave, sister. Bless me.'
She sent him back with her own hands.

[Vitthal as Nirmala said:]
'Now, sister-in-law, let me go back to my own village.
My husband will scold me.'

Hearing this, Chokha's wife said,
'Don't leave me now, sister.

Let my husband come and he will send you back.
How can I repay your kindness?' . . .

[Nirmala said:] 'My brother is a devotee of Pandurang;
his mind is always on God.

Honour him, my sister. Accept what he says;
in that lies your well-being . . .

Take care of my Karmamela;
your Chokhamela will come home.'

'Wait, sister, I'm sewing you a blouse'.
Pandurang said, 'No need for it.'

The Lord said goodbye to all and left;
Chokhamela came home.

When he entered, his wife touched his feet
and put the baby in his arms.

'Your sister just now went,
Did you meet her on the way?
I feel bad that you missed her.'. . .

'O wife, Pandurang himself came here.
It is your great fortune that you met him.' . . .

God does not let his devotees fall into trouble;
he runs to their help when they need him.

It seems to me that the main lesson this tale is meant to convey is that God will take care of you. But it also contains some very human touches, even humour–the husband leaving to avoid a 'bloody mess', a sister shocked at the brother's behaviour, a saint whose non-attachment makes him ignore his householder duties, a god who comes in the form of a loving relative, a wife who forgives her husband, whatever he does. The other interesting thing to me about this family is the pure love and admiration Soyrabai shows to Chokhamela's sister, just as Nirmala adores and honours Chokhamela. Neither mentions Nirmala's husband Banka, who very likely was Soyrabai's brother. Soyrabai finds in Nirmala the perfection of bhakti. It is very appropriate that the God of Pandharpur comes to Soyrabai in the form of her sister-in-law Nirmala for the birthing of Karmamela. And here the use of 'Mother' for God, which is a common way of referring to Vitthal, and often to the saints themselves, is doubly appropriate.

NOTES

1. For another version of this tale and other stories, see 'Women in the Homes of the Saints' in *Home, Family and Kinship in Maharashtra*, edited by Irina Glushkova and Rajendra Vora, New Delhi: Oxford University Press, 1999, pp. 89–100.
2. *Srisakalsantgatha*, collected by Srinanamaharaj Sakhare and edited by Kashinath Anant Joshi, vol. I, Pune: Srisantwangmaya Prakashan Mandir, 1967 (1923). The poetry was translated by Vijaya Deo, Sucheta Paranjpye, and Eleanor Zelliot with the advice of the late S.G. Tulpule.
3. *Home, Family and Kinship in Maharashtra*, 1999, pp. 89–100.
4. *Barsa:* the naming ceremony.
5. Samsara is used throughout Maharashtrian bhakti poetry as shorthand for the cares of the material world, which for women is the married life.
6. Mehunpuri near Buldana was the village home of Nirmala and her husband Banka, also a saint-poet. Together with Dr Prabhakar Mande, driver Gaikwad, and research assistant S.Y. Waghmare, I found the village and learned that the names of Nirmala and Banka are not only remembered, but also that the saints are spoken of as if they took samadhi in the Nirmala river only yesterday instead of in the fourteenth century.
7. Vithoba and many of the saints are often addressed as 'mother'.

8
Soyrabai and Nirmala

ELEANOR ZELLIOT

The *varkari* movement is characterized by an openness to all castes and many women. It was also, almost inclusively, a householder phenomenon. Both points are illustrated by the stories and songs of Soyrabai and Nirmala, two women from the Untouchable caste of Mahars, the wife and sister of Chokhamela.

Nirmala and Soyrabai lived in the late thirteenth-early fouteenth-century, Nirmala in Mehunpuri near Aurangabad and Soyrabai probably in Pandharpur, the centre of the bhakti tradition in Maharashtra. Whoever preserved their songs is unknown, and there are no early manuscripts, but their *abhangas* (the flexible metre used in Marathi for devotional songs) ring true in terms of the tradition of that period and what we know of the place of women and the role of caste in medieval Maharashtra. Their voices seem to be true women's voices in the Marathi style. For instance, there is no great personal passionate love for Krishna as in the case of Mirabai and Antal; there is no scathing (and amusing) denunciation of husbands as in the poetry of Mahadeviyakka, the three best-known women poets from other language areas.[1] The typology developed by A.K. Ramanujan for women saints—early dedication to God, denial of marriage, defying societal norms, initiation, marrying the Lord—does not apply to either Soyrabai or Nirmala as it does not to Muktabai or Janabai, other women poets of the period, nor do they qualify as being 'superior to their husbands', which Ramanujan notes is the pattern of saints' wives. Like many other of the women *bhaktas* of the Marathi tradition, Soyrabai and Nirmala write of family, of their devotion to the god

Vithoba, of the joyous pilgrimage to Pandharpur, of the various ways of maintaining the household and still finding true freedom.

Although sixty-two *abhangas* of Soyrabai and twenty-four of Nirmala appear in the collected works of all the saints,[2] they have received very little popular or scholarly attention. Only two of Soyrabai's *abhangas* have found their way into the popular Maharashtrian tradition. Vinayak Lakshman Bhave, in the first edition of his *Maharashtra Saraswat* (introduction to Maharashtra), used the third and fourth lines of Soyrabai's first *abhanga* in the *Srisakalsantgatha* as an invocation:

> I'll place a leaf before you and I will serve you family food.
> O God, it's not fit for you, but imagine it sweet and accept it.

The lines well illustrate Soyrabai's humility (as well as the Brahmin Bhave's), but the whole *abhanga* indicates another quality: Soyrabai's knowledge of the Mahabharata legends:

> Come, come, you who bear the flag of Garuda,
> I will worship you along with the brick.
> O Gopala, I will present you with incense, lights and garlands.
> I will place a leaf before you and I will serve you family food.
> O God, it's not fit for you, but imagine it sweet and accept it.
> Vidur served watered broken rice, O my mother and father, O Lord.
> O Narayana, Draupadi's one leaf smeared with leftover food satisfied you.
> It's just like that here, says the Mahari of Chokha.[3]

Another of Soyrabai's *abhangas* has been widely sung and recorded by Bhimsen Joshi, Maharashtra's beloved classical and *bhavgit* (devotional song) singer:

> Sing this joyous Name lovingly, chant a prayer to Vithoba.
> This worldly life will be happy if you chant the Name again and again.
> Lust and anger become helpless. Look! Desires and longings flee.
> Say Hari Hari lovingly, says Chokha's Mahari.[4]

These well-known songs illustrate some of the messages of Soyrabai:

her sense of her own poverty although she will give God all she has, the common *varkari* understanding of God as father *and* mother (*mai-bap*, written as one word), chanting the Name of God as the cure for the emotions and woes of *samsara*, the worldly or married life. There are other themes in Soyrabai's songs. Among the *abhangas* that deal with the 'dark night of the soul', a sense of the inaccessibility of the divine common to all saints, is one which interests me especially because one of my interpreters, Jayant Karve, said while we translated: 'She's speaking to God as if he were a Brahmin, not really sounding angry, just reproachful':

> Why have you saddened me so?
> Who would call you the Just?
> We sit at your doorstep,
> asking for alms, saying 'Give, give'.
> And you have taken from so many.
> How can you feel good about it?
> This is not decent conduct
> says the Mahari of Chokha.[5]

There seems to be nothing specific of caste in the song above, unless sitting at God's doorstep refers to the fact that the Mahar could not enter the temple of Vithoba and asking for alms indicates a low status. In fact, caste does not enter into the majority of her songs. However, in some *abhangas* Soyrabai is very conscious of her low status and her untouchability. In one *abhanga* she clearly protests the very basis of untouchability, pollution, in explicit and moving terms:

> A body is unclean, they say, only the soul is untainted.
> But the impurity of the body is born with the body.
> By which rule has a body become pure?
> Not a creature in the world has been born
> except in a gory womb.
> This is the glory of God: defilement exists within.
> The body is polluted from within.
> Be sure of it, says the Mahari of Chokha.[6]

There is no stronger statement of the *bhaktas* against the very idea of hereditary pollution except for the anguished cry of Soyrabai's husband in one of his *abhangas*, 'O Lord, who is born pure?' However, the Marathi for 'Untouchable' or 'untouchability' is not used. Soyrabai refers to herself as *hin*, i.e. low or base. But she does refer in an indirect way to the restrictions to which the Mahars were subjected. Both Nirmala and Soyrabai speak joyfully of coming to the great door of the temple at Pandharpur, implying but not saying directly that they could not go inside to see the image itself. Indeed, the samadhi of Chokhamela is at the very foot of the steps leading to the great door and until Independence, no Untouchable could go farther than that memorial stone. In many *abhangas*, Soyrabai refers to 'leftover food', food ritually and perhaps actually unclean, which was one of the Mahar's perquisites after higher caste feasts and rituals. The word is used in a religious context in addressing God, 'I will accept your leftovers' (*abhanga* 32) and 'I can only wish for your discarded food' (*abhanga* 55).

Perhaps one should not wonder that there is so little reference to untouchability. The songs of the saints must have been kept orally for generations, sung by pilgrims going to Pandharpur, so those specifically about untouchability might have been considered inappropriate for the joyous pilgrimage. There is, however, a curious partial story in *abhanga* 19 that begins with trouble in Pandharpur from the temple priests but then ends very happily:

> The Brahmins of Pandhari harassed Chokha;
> God was surprised at this.
> Everyone gathered at Chokha's house;
> Wealth and Power stood at the door.
> Rangoli at the entrance, flags on the gate,
> Joyous kirtan of the Vaishnavas.
> The celebration was like Divali and Dussehra
> Soyra waves the lights of *arati* before Chokha.[7]

One of the most unusual characteristics of Soyrabai's poetry is that she often refers to her sister-in-law, Nirmala, Chokhamela's sister. Although she calls herself Chokha's Mahari, she does not really refer to her husband in any meaningful way. For instance, Soyra tells us that she and Chokhameia and their son Karmamela went to see Nirmala in her far-away village of Mehunpuri, but then her attention turns solely to Nirmala. Soyra embraces her feet saying, 'Great is the woman of

Mehunpuri' (*abhanga* 12). As Soyra and Nirmala sit together, 'By the grace of the Father, Vitthal and Nirmala became one' (*abhanga* 13). She sees God in her husband's sister. And she sings in *abhanga* 15 'Taking a bath at Nirmala's place is like visiting Prayag crores of times.' The affection between the two women and the clear religious guidance of Nirmala brings a sense of realism to the lives of these women and gives an idea of the importance of extended family relationships.

Nirmala herself is also an accomplished poet and *bhakta*. She speaks of her brother, Chokhamela, as her guide, although she does not hesitate to chide him when he leaves Soyrabai as she is about to give birth to their son. She never mentions her husband Banka, even though he is thought to have been Soyrabai's brother, and does not use his name in her signature line, although she does occasionally end with, 'the sister of Chokha says'. Banka himself was also a poet and a *bhakta*, and when Prabhakar Mande, a folklorist, my research assistant Sudhir Waghmare, and I went to Mehunpuri, we found that both Banka and Nirmala were remembered as if they had died yesterday. The spot in the river where they took samadhi was obliterated in a flood, but a hut where a contemporary guru came to set himself up as a modern Chokhamela is still preserved. The villagers also think that Chokhamela lived there, although it is two hundred miles from Pandharpur as the crow flies. At one time a *palkhi* (palanquin bearing the footprints of the saint) left Mehunpuri for Pandharpur, but since the great conversion of the Mahars (and some others) to Buddhism in 1956, such devotion to Pandharpur has ceased.

Nirmala seems to have a more personal relationship with the God Vithoba than Soyrabai. In one *abhanga* she sings:

> I am certain of you; I surrender to your feet.
> Now, do what you think is right; I have put down my burden.
> I have put my head in your lap, knowing what the future holds.
> Nirmala says, Save me or kill me; now the burden is yours.[8]

She often compares the closeness of her brother Chokhamela to God with her sense of less worth but just as much need:

> You have protected Chokha then and now, bearing all his faults.
> O merciful one, tell me, after that, why are you weary of me?

I am low-born and poor, a heap of sins, but with heart and soul
I fall at your feet.
Nirmala says, You are merciful, so take care of me.[9]

I read Nirmala's poetry with the late S.G. Tulpule, whose work on classical Marathi literature is indispensable.[10] He had not read the *abhangas* of the Untouchable saints before, although he is very familiar with other bhakti literature. I was touched and amused when he looked, up at me after we had worked on the following *abhanga* and said, 'This is a very intelligent woman!'

People say you should gain the ultimate goal, but they don't
have the skill at all.
Pure bhakti feeling, meditation on the Name--this is the
source of spirituality.
Censure, fault finding, praise, honour, dishonour–treat all these
as vomit!
In spirituality, others' food, others' money, others' women
should be considered polluting.
Nirmala says, This is the way to the ultimate goal: the companionship of the saints night and day.[11]

There is nothing in this *abhanga* that could not be sung by any high-caste saint, except perhaps the rather vulgar word vomit. Like Soyrabai, Nirmala rarely refers to her Untouchable status except in a roundabout way, here perhaps with the word 'polluting' for the sin of covetousness, a use very different from the idea that a human could be polluting by birth.

An *abhanga* that illustrates why the Mahar Untouchable saints have been rejected in the modern movement of Untouchables led by B.R. Ambedkar is the following one, which indicates Soyrabai's belief in rebirth. The Ambedkar movement, which culminated in a mass Buddhist conversion,[12] totally rejected the concept that Untouchable status was the result of karma, birth according to past deeds. It is not clear whether Soyrabai traces her status to 'sin' or whether she is simply using the traditional idea of many births before moksha (salvation or freedom) can be attained.

The name of Hari is on the lips only of the one who has merit
tied in his garments throughout innumerable births.

The name of Hari is on the lips only of the one who carries
in his purse the good deeds of innumerable births.
The chanting of Narayan's name is only for the one who has
practised discipline throughout innumerable births.
The sweetness of *Harinama* is only for the one who has left
worldly attachments throughout innumerable births.
Nirmala says, the sin of innumerable births disappears
as you chant the Name.[13]

Here Nirmala speaks of 'innumerable' births rather than the traditional number of eighty-four hundred thousand births before one reaches moksha, the ultimate union with *brahman*, the universal substance.

In contrast to most of the Marathi *bhaktas*, Nirmala does not use the stuff of her daily life in her poetry. Gora the potter refers to pots, Janabai the maidservant to her daily work, but Nirmala's *abhangas* (and Soyrabai's for the most part) contain no household images. What both women do, and this may be in part the reason for the neglect of their work, is to sing of their daily life, their *samsara*, as a great burden. Nirmala indicates that she has some understanding of meditation in this *abhanga*, but that her daily existence prevents her from reaching the presence of God:

Ocean of mercy, listen to my prayer.
Let me lay my head at your feet.
There are many ways, but I do not know them.
I can only embrace your feet with all my strength.
My body, my mind, my thoughts are restless.
What can I do? I have no strength to quiet my mind.
I cannot free myself from *samsara*.
it embraces me, it takes you far from me.
Nirmala says, what shall I do? You have left me far behind.[14]

Nirmala is even more tormented by *samsara* in this *abhanga*, in which not even Chokhamela is called upon to relieve her weariness:

O God, the forest fire blazes all around;
why don't you have pity on me?
I am caught in the midst of *samsara*;
help me now, O mother and father.

O God, I am weary to death of this *samsara.*
  O Keshava, come now!
Who is my family other than you?
  O God, you are my support.
Nirmala says, embracing your feet,
  don't send me away, you who are mother and father.[15]

Soyrabai has an even more negative *abhanga*, but one which offers also a sense of her imagination and of the possibility that the power of the mind can overcome meaninglessness:

House and home are meaningless; samsara is meaningless,
  the corporeal body is meaningless.
Your name is meaningful, all else is meaningless;
  if people don't drown, it is only because of the Name.
All things are meaningless.
  Ideas are meaningless.
  Great wisdom is meaningless. Who cares?
The science of words is meaningless.
  Words themselves are meaningless.
  Knowledge is meaningless.
  Why speak of these things?
If your mind is not steady, that's also meaningless,
  and then how will you come to Hari?
Till then, there's no meaning in speaking speech
  says Chokha's Mahari.[16]

The antidote to all this misery is the chanting of the name of God. But there are also other kinds of relief that these women sing of. One is the great pilgrimage to Pandharpur, that joyous occasion which has in the twentieth century became the central event in the religious life for many people in Maharashtra, and the culmination of that pilgrimage in the celebrations near the temple or at the river that flows by the city. Soyrabai begins *abhanga* 18 with 'There's a celebration of joy in the month of Ashad in Pandhari, kirtan and shouting on the river's sands' and ends the song with 'Soyra prostrates herself with devotion'. Another *abhanga* sparkles with joy as she describes the dancing and singing of the *bhaktas*:

They shout, they dance, they sway in joy.
They bubble up the name of Vitthal with love.
Even Brahma and all those Gods don't know such happiness;
this Pundalik has them in ecstasy.
They dislike Vaikunta, dislike jewels, dislike household comforts.
Sri Hari dances in the kirtan, says Chokha's Mahari.[17]

While reading the entire body of Soyrabai's poems, one also occasionally has a feeling that she is a true mystic, finding at times the words to describe the indescribable, words that recall the poetry of mystics in many cultures. A fourteenth-century Untouchable woman seems to have risen above the problems of *samsara* and the humiliation of low birth to sing of immersion in the divine:

All colours have merged into one. The Lord of Colour himself
is immersed in that colour.
When I saw the Lord of Pandhari, the I–you feeling also
disappeared.
Distinctions have no work here. Anger and lust have run away.
You who have a body are not embodied. Look! You are
always in samadhi.
I who look and the looking itself are one, says Chokha's Mahari.[18]

NOTES

1. Mirabai sang in Rajasthani Hindi, Antal in Tamil, Mahadeviyakka in Kannada. For a compilation of many women saint-poets, see the tenth anniversary triple issue of *Manushi*, nos. 50, 51, 52, January–June 1989, on the theme of Women Bhakta Poets. The Maharashtrian women sants included are Muktabai, Janabai, and Bahinabai.
2. *Srisakalsantgatha* in two volumes. Collected by Nanamaharaj Sakhare, edited by Kashinath Anant Joshi, Pune: Srisantwangmaya Prakashan Mandir, 1967. First published in 1923.
3. *Yei yei garudadhvaja vite sahit karin puja*. The flag of Garuda is a symbol of Vishnu and Narayana is another of his names. Vithoba is almost always referred to in Vaishnava terms. The brick is a symbol of Vithoba, who stood on a brick thrown him by the devotee Pundalik to keep his feet from the mud while Pundalik finished paying loving attention to his parents. It symbolizes Vithoba's patient love for his devotees. The poems of Soyrabai were translated primarily with the help of Vijaya Deo.

4. *Sukhace he nam avadine gave/vace alvave vithobasi. Abhanga* 43 in *Srisakalsantgatha.* Giving a human quality to the deadly sins of lust and anger and the desires and longings which hinder devotion is typical of Soyrabai. She sometimes signs her work in her own name, more often as her husband's wife.
5. *Ka ba udas maj kele/kon mhane tumhhi bhale. Abhanga* 28 in *Srisakalsantgatha.*
6. *Dehasi vital mhanti sakal/atma to nirmal shuddhbuddh. Abhanga* 6 in *Srisakalsantgatha.*
7. *Pandharice brahmane cokhapasi chalile/tayalagi kele naval deve. Abhanga* 19 in *Srisakalsantgatha.* Temple priests in Pandharpur are not often *bhaktas* in the Maharashtrian tradition and they do not join in the pilgrimage. The other references in this song are to kirtan, the song-and-sermon sessions common to bhakti groups; to the Hindu holidays of Diwali and Dussehra; to *arati,* the ceremony of waving a tray of lights in circles before the face of someone being honoured; and to the chalk drawings made for special occasions called *rangoli.*
8. *Tumca bharanvasa dharoni manasi/dradh payasi sharan ale. Abhanga* 23 in *Srisakalsantgatha.*
9. *Ajivari tumhi tayasi palile/apradh sahile cokhiyace. Abhanga* 21 in *Srisakalsantgatha.*
10. *Classical Marathi Literature from the Beginning to A.D. 1818* (A History of Indian Literature, vol. IX, fasc. 4), Wiesbaden: Otto Harrassowitz, 1979. The late Dr Tulpule refers only briefly to Chokhamela and quotes one *abhanga,* but his work sets the bhakti literature in its historical context. S.G. Tulpule is also the author of *Mysticism in Medieval India,* Wiesbaden: Otto Harrassowitz, 1984.
11. *Parmarth sadhava bolti ya gosti/pari na ye hatwati kahi tyaci. Abhanga* 10 in *Srisakalsantgatha. Parmarth* has here been translated both 'ultimate goal' and, in accordance with Tulpule's suggestion, 'spirituality'.
12. See my *From Untouchable to Dalit: Essays on the Ambedkar Movement,* New Delhi: Manohar, 2001 (1992) for the history of the long path to conversion.
13. *Ananda janmace sukrt pandari/toci uccari harinam. Abhanga* 9 in *Srisakalsantgatha.* The early Mahar movement rejoiced in the presence of a Mahar saint, Chokhamela, as an important part of the Pandharpur pantheon of religious figures. Chokhamela, however, explained in one *abhanga* that his Untouchable status was due to a previous sin, and this has meant that he no longer serves as a religious icon or source of pride. Ravidas, the Untouchable saint of north India, does fill the role of one who allows a claim of religious worth for the Maharashtrian Chamarkars (Chambhars).
14. *Krpecya sagara parisa vinvani/mastak charni aso majha. Abhanga* 5 in *Srisakalsantgatha.*
15. *Cahukade deva datla vanva/ka na ye kanva tujlagi. Abhanga* 1 in *Srisakalsantgatha.*
16. *Vauge ghardar vauga sansar/vauge sarir nasivant. Abhanga* 10 in *Srisakalsantgatha.*
17. *Garjati nacti anande dolti/saprem phundati viththal name. Abhanga* 17 in *Srisakalsantgatha.* The three classic sources of information on the Pandharpur pilgrimage are G.A. Deleury, *The Cult of Vithoba,* Poona: Deccan College Postgraduate Research Centre, 1960; Irawati Karve, 'On the Road', *Journal of Asian Studies,* vol. 22, 1962, pp. 13–29, reprinted in *The Experience of Hinduism: Essays on Religion in Maharashtra,* edited by Eleanor Zelliot and Maxine Berntsen,

Albany: State University of New York Press, 1988; D.B. Mokashi, *Palkhi: A Pilgrimage to Pandharpur*, translated by Philip C. Engblom, Albany: State University of New York Press, 1987. Reprinted in India by Orient Longman, 1990.

18. *Avagha rang ek jhala/rangi rangala shrirang. Abhanga* 5 in *Srisakalsantgatha*. Samadhi here means a state of immersion in the divine that transcends consciousness.

9
The Search for Chokhamela

ELEANOR ZELLIOT

Several years ago, V.L. Manjul and I began a search for the way in which over four hundred poems of an illiterate Untouchable and his entire family had been preserved and carried through six centuries. There was no old collection such as that existing for Ravidas in the Sikh Granth or the sixteentnth-century Rajasthan *vani* of five important *bhaktas*. But in contrast to the Untouchable saints from south India, there was a great body of songs of all sorts, critical as well as devotional, in Maharashtra. There was a legend that the son of an orthodox Kannada Brahmin, one Anant Bhat, had served as Chokhamela's scribe, but there is nothing to show how the writing had been preserved.

In the end, we found only a few poems jotted down in the notebooks of some Brahmin *kirtankars* of fairly recent times. Not even a page from the manuscripts that had been used by the authors of the *Srisakalsantgatha* a hundred years ago, or by S.B. Kadam in the 1960s as he assembled his remarkable collection of Chokhamela's songs, could be found. And since the Mahars, Chokhamela's caste, had by and large converted to Buddhism fifty years ago, there were few Mahar *kirtankars* whom we could interview about their tradition. And the one who knew the most *abhangas* had memorized them from a written source.

Our search was futile in terms of manuscripts and so I am still curious about that fundamental question; but the outcome in the end was very rewarding because we found a great deal of current material about Chokhamela. There is a revival of interest in this saint that has resulted in Ph.D. theses, popular pamphlets, and semi-scholarly studies in considerable quantity. This revival is not a symbol of caste pride, as it was in the 1920s when Kisan Fago Bansode (1879–1946) and others found Chokhamela to be a heroic symbol for the progress of the Mahars. Bansode, a very important leader in the Nagpur area until he opposed the conversion announcement of Dr B.R. Ambedkar in 1935, named one of his newspapers *Chokhamela*, tried to collect the *abhangas* of Chokhamela in Pandharpur, and urged protest in a poem that asked:

> Why do you endure curses?
> Chokha went into the temple resolutely.
> You are the descendants of Chokha.
> Why do you fear to enter the temple?
> Brace yourself like a wrestler.
> Come, together let us conquer pollution.

Those of Chokhamela's caste now have by and large rejected him, and for two reasons: the Buddhist conversion initiated by Dr B.R. Ambedkar in 1956 has meant a rejection of most things Hindu on the part of many. Second, Chokhamela himself, in one *abhanga*, said that he was Untouchable because in a previous life he had insulted Krishna, and this karmic reasoning is totally unacceptable to Untouchables now. The devout Chokhamela who could not enter the temple can be admired as a historic phenomenon but not worshipped or held up as a hero to be emulated.

In the end, we collected a publishable selection of tributes to Chokhamela and his family.[1] It was certainly not meant to win Ambedkar's followers back to bhakti Hinduism, the most tolerant and accepting facet of that religion, although this may have been the motive of some authors we included. Our only purpose was to honour this astonishing family of saint-poets as creative members of the human race. Chokhamela, his wife Soyrabai, their son Karmamela, Chokhamela's sister Nirmala, and her husband Banka, are figures of great historic importance. Ambedkar himself honoured Chokhamela as he dedicated his book entitled *The Untouchables* to Chokhamela, Nandanar, and Ravidas, even though the book's purpose was to show that Untouchables had been Buddhists, forced into degradation when a brahminical revival in the fourth century CE had marginalized that religion.[2]

The songs of Chokhamela and his family tell us what was known of the philosophic knowledge of the time among the lowest of the low, and what stories were important. Their songs reveal great unhappiness with the treatment given them and state in the strongest terms their disbelief in the dichotomy of purity and pollution. The fact that all five members of the family are represented by a considerable quantity of poetry, a fact not apparent in any other *bhakta*'s body of work, gives us great insight into the lives of a family of devotees.

Several of the essays in our Marathi volume were taken from the first independent edition of Chokhamela's poems, that of S.B. Kadam, a civil servant, someone who was not a Mahar but who sacrificed a great deal to collect and publish his work. When Bhalchandra Nemade, one of Maharashtra's most prominent writers and also not a Mahar or Buddhist, went to the Kadam home to talk about bringing out a second edition, he found Kadam's widow in such a precarious condition and with such little space that she had been unable to keep any of his material. But in spite of poverty, Kadam had been able to collect songs sung by all of Chokhamela's family members; poems from the work of other saint-poets on Chokhamela; a statement from one of the temple priests, Bhagwan Panharinath Badve, and one from a hereditary Mahar pujari of the Chokhamela samadhi, Bhaskar Soma Sarvagoda; essays by two Brahmin scholars, B.P. Bahirat of Pandharpur and R.G. Karandikar of Mangalvedhe; and a foreword by the most important Brahmin reviver of the Dnyaneshwar *palkhi*, Sonapant Dandekar. Kadam's devotion in assembling this tribute to Chokhamela was almost matched by that of Balchandra Nemade, who reprinted Kadam's collected work and added his own introduction.

The *dindi* (group of pilgrims travelling together) to Pandharpur of Chokhamela has been diminished to a few old folk and the once crowded dharmashala in Pandharpur is empty except for three or four *varkaris*. The Chokhamela temple in Dehu was at one time a place of worship, but only Mahars came. Now it is empty and has become a *hatbhatti*, a place selling illicit liquor, but as Sadanand More writes ironically, all castes now come to the temple which they once used to shun.

For the Untouchable Chamars (Chamarkars) of Maharashtra, Rohidas, known as Ravidas in his own Hindi-speaking territory, is ever more important; his *dindi* in the procession that moves from Alandi to Pandharpur every year is impressive and growing, and the Chamar dharmashala in Pandharpur contains the samadhi of a Chamar woman saint, Shantabai, and a tribute to Rohidas, and also offers educational classes for the young as well as a place for pilgrims to stay. The only demand of the Chamars for equality seems to have been a plea for a place behind the horse of Dnyaneshwar along with all the other *dindis* in the great *palkhi* that leaves from Alandi for Pandharpur rather than as isolated pilgrims in front of the horse. They won a legal case for this limited privilege. The Mahars chose another way, losing the colour and beauty and spirituality of Chokhamela's world but gaining the self-respect, humanism, and freedom from religious restrictions so important to them through a Buddhist conversion.

The story of Chokhamela is preserved in legend. He was born miraculously, it is said, as his Mahar parents were on their way to the town with a basket of mangoes for the *patil*, the headman, a duty traditionally given to Mahars. An old Brahmin begged a mango, bit it, and gave it back to Chokhamela's mother. When she pulled it out from her sari to show the *patil* that it had been spoiled and that was why the count of mangoes was less by one, the mango had turned into a beautiful baby, Chokhamela. Chokhamela's home is given variously as Mehunpuri (near Buldana), Mangalvedhe (near Pandharpur), and Pandharpur itself. His sister and her husband are clearly identified with Mehunpuri, and Ambedkar himself thought Chokhamela came from that area.

Unlike the legends surrounding Ravidas that make him out as a Brahmin come down in Untouchable form to teach, Chokhamela is always seen as an Untouchable Mahar. Chokhamela's death came about because he was doing his Mahar duties, mending the wall at Mangalvedhe. The wall collapsed, burying Chokhamela. Namdev found the bones, which whispered 'Vitthal, Vitthal' and buried them below the steps to the great door, the spot at which Chokhamela had to stand because he could not enter the temple. No Mahar could go beyond the samadhi built at that spot until a Gandhian, Sane Guruji, on the birth of India's independence, fasted in front of the great door until the Untouchables were permitted to enter the temple. V.L. Manjul's story of certain Brahmins who removed the spirit of the God at this juncture has been translated into English for this volume.

There is not much to add that is not in Rohini Mokashi-Punekar's Introduction to Chokhamela, but there were and still are some physical signs of Chokhamela's presence in Pandharpur. Until recently, a *dip mal*, a pillar of lights, which was identified as Chokhamela's, stood across the river Chandrabhaga from the Vithoba temple, marking the spot to which Chokhamela had been banished. There is a photograph of a broken column in Kadam's book.[3] A non-Maharashtrian individual who bought the land on which the column stood destroyed it and all that is left is a legend. The samadhi itself, on the other hand, has been greatly improved, with inscriptions of donations added within the last few years. The *dip mal* is no more, but Chokhamela's samadhi at the foot of the great door has been both preserved and enhanced, and hundreds pay their respects as they enter the temple.

A partial review of some of the new books in Marathi on the saint indicates the current interest in Chokhamela. Anantrao Patil, then a newspaper editor, went to see all the places that appear in the Chokhamela story, in Pandharpur, Mangalvedhe, and Dehu. He was disappointed by the neglect of Chokhamela, and decided to write something that would allow others to know something of Chokhamela, to decide whether they were going to accept 'fellow feeling' with Chokhamela, or see him as opposed to Hinduism. The cover of his little book features the most realistic image of Chokhamela of any of the tributes we have seen, a rough image, barely clothed, with the traditional Mahar blanket over one shoulder.

Another new and popular study is that of Nirmal Kumar Phadkule, who has written his book after contemplating Chokhamela 'sitting in darkness but singing songs of light'. Much to our surprise, we found a third recent popular study, that of Shantaram Govardhan Bute, who has not only commented on a number of *abhangas* and given the modern reader a glossary of medieval terms, but also illustrated his book with photographs from Mehunpuri, Mangalvedhe, and Pandharpur.

Three Ph.D. theses have been published, raising the study of Chokhamela to a very scholarly level. We have not seen V.R. Gharge's thesis, submitted to Kolhapur University, but the works of Sarita Haridas Jambhule and the late Padmavati Shrotiye, done at the Universities of Nagpur and Pune respectively, are very impressive. Both place the poetry and the story of Chokhamela in the context of the times, the *varkari sampradaya*, and the influences on the saint. Both studies have been published and are valuable additions for those who read Marathi to gain knowledge of Chokhamela and his world.

These six new works indicate a new level of interest in Chokhamela. All six are from outside the Ambedkar movement. From inside is the work of the late Shankarrao Kharat, one of the earliest of the Dalit Sahitya writers and a long-time associate of Dr Ambedkar. Kharat found Chokhamela different from all other saint-poets in his belief in social equality. The Pandharpur tradition itself has been a humanizing, not a revolutionary tradition. It is difficult to see Chokhamela as a revolutionary figure; it is easy to see him and his family as proof of two things: first, creativity dwells at all levels; second, the idea of pollution is rejected in no uncertain terms by even the most devout of Untouchables. B.C. Shinde, a Buddhist dramatist, has also written a small book in Marathi on his impresssions of Chokhamela.

The search for Chokhamela turned up no manuscripts, but revealed a tradition that is living and changing. Chokhamela and his family have been marginalized figures in the bhakti movement. But our search indicates that after almost seven centuries, he still commands interest, affection, wonderment. He and his family still have the power to speak to us of pain and piety, of devotion and degradation, of the ever-lasting hope that *manuski*, Dr Ambedkar's favourite word, will triumph. *Manuski* means human-ness, humaneness, the honouring of all humans.

NOTES

1. See *Sant Chokhamela Vividh Darshan* (in Marathi), Pune: Sugawa Prakashan, 2002.
2. B.R. Ambedkar, *The Untouchables*, New Delhi: Amrit Book Company, 1948.
3. S.B. Kadam, *Srisant Chokamela Maharaj yance caritra va abhang gatha*, Mumbai: Mrs Mandakini S. Kadam, *c.* 1969.

10

Representations of Chokhamela in Marathi Film and Drama

ANIL SAPKAL

Translated from the Marathi by Dinesh Kulkarni,
abridged by Eleanor Zelliot*

Chokhamela's position in the galaxy of bhakti saints has remained a constant source of inspiration and interest to modern creative thinkers. The image of Chokhoba has emerged from numerous anecdotes, the poetry of and about Chokhoba, and through the praises bestowed upon him by his contemporaries. Here we review the image of Chokhoba as it is projected in popular media. This article deals with the musical play *Sangit Uhshap* (Antidote to the Curse), the drama *Yugayatra* (Epic March of an Era), and the films *Chokhamela* or *Hi Wat Pandharichi*, and *Johar May-bap*. We can only mention that there was also a *tamasha* (folk drama) called *Vaga-natya* (the fourth act of a performance) on Chokhamela for which there is no surviving script.

Sangit Uhshap by Veer Savarkar was written with a view to theatrical presentation, and its opening show was performed on 9 April 1927. It was written when Savarkar was pursuing social reform after 1920, when he was sentenced to detention at Ratnagiri by the British for his revolutionary activities. The play was not performed according to the script; a tragic ending was changed to a happy ending at the suggestion of the Censor Board, a change Savarkar accepted.

Savarkar seems to have utilized the image and character of Chokhamela to project his own ideas and theories about social and political reform. Anti-Islamic sentiments go hand in hand with the message of eradication of untouchability as the central themes of this play. It seems to have been written with the clear aim of invoking a feeling of affection and loyalty towards Hinduism among the Untouchables and at the same time inciting them towards hatred and anger against Christianity and Islam and provoking them to take revenge on the followers of these religions. The play represents Savarkar's political doctrine. He draws an affectionate picture of Mahar children in the play, telling of the experiences they must have as Mahars but also invoking a sense of pride in being a Mahar because it means being a Hindu. Introducing the theme of forced Muslim and Christian conversions, the playwright tries to impress upon the audience the idea that it is more glorious to live and die a Hindu than convert to Christianity or Islam.

The greatness of Hinduism is expressed through the character of Chokhoba, who hails Hinduism as the truly superior religion and the one that provides true salvation to the downtrodden. In the play, Chokhamela explains to his fellow Untouchables the importance of virtues such as cleanliness, devotion, and the willingness to serve God. He expects his fellow Untouchables to be clean and also to be the cleaners of society, this being their destined sacred duty. He also praises Brahminism and the Brahmin caste. For example, he tells his rebellious son Karmamela:

> Now, dear son, don't make such unbecoming poisonous remarks against the Brahmin caste. A Brahmin is the third eye of knowledge of Lord Mahadev of our great Hindu Dharma. It is only because of the Brahmins that the divine knowledge of *Brahmadnyana* has been kept alive to this day. (Act I, Entry 3)

In truth, Chokhoba's poems refer to the exploitation of the masses in general and the Untouchables in particular by the Brahmins and the hereditary priests, the Badves. In an *abhanga,* Chokhamela wrote: 'Come fast, run, dear Vithu, do not come slowly. The priests are almost killing me over such a petty offence.' Savarkar does not refer to this.

Savarkar constructs his play as high drama and the climax is reached when Chokhoba is expected to meet Lord Vitthal in his divine image. Chokhoba frees himself from the burden of karma by shifting it from his weak shoulders to place it at the feet of Lord Vitthal, as he submits himself entirely to the God in complete devotion (Act III, Entry 8).

Savarkar includes incidents of his own devising in the play. He attacks the hypocrisy and false pride of Hindus, baring the ugly face of casteism, but also viciously attacks the practice of conversions of Hindus by Muslims. Even though it is completely out of both place and time for the historical period of Chokhamela in Maharashtra, Savarkar denounces Christianity and makes use of the Mahar characters to implant the thought of vibrant Hinduism. In the play, the Mahar girl Kamalini scorns her Mahar lover Shankar because he renounces Hinduism in favour of conversion. She claims to be a follower of Chokhamela and for her, her Hindu dharma is of the utmost importance; she is willing to lay down her life for her beliefs.

Chokhamela is shown being harassed by some communal, opportunistic, and selfish characters created by Savarkar from among the affluent upper castes, the Brahmins, Kshatriyas, and Vaishyas. These vile characters drag Chokhoba before the Muslim king, complaining that Chokhoba is corrupting the Hindu dharma by trying to enter the temple. The king encourages Chokhoba to convert to Islam. But in the play Savarkar's Chokhamela confirms his loyalty to Hinduism and says: 'Yes, I am a Hindu. I am a lowly cushion for the feet of Hindu society to step upon. I am a Mahar, a sweeper who cleans the traditional circular path around Lord Vitthal's shrine.' Chokhoba prefers Hinduism with its practice of casteism and untouchability to Islam or Christianity. He says in a statement that evidently reflects Savarkar's understanding of Islam and Christianity:

> Compared to Islam and Christianity, the concept of our Naramabhat [an important priest] is much more caring and compassionate. According to Naramabhat's logic, it is sufficient for only humans to practise the concept of untouchability. But in your alien religions the concept of untouchability is followed by God himself. He won't even touch an Untouchable after death, and won't bless his soul. The upper caste people won't touch our bodies as low and impure, but your Muslim or Christian ideology will tell you to avoid the touch of the soul of an Untouchable.

Instead of social justice, the play shows Chokhoba receiving divine justice at the hands of Lord Krishna himself. Through the character of Chokhamela, his devotion, sentiments, poetry, and saintliness, Savarkar spreads his idea of Hindu dharma and its greatness.

* * * * *

M.B. Chitnis's play *Yugayatra* (1956) is regarded as a milestone in the gradual cultural progress of the Ambedkar movement. Chitnis was an upper-caste lieutenant of Dr Ambedkar, important in Ambedkar's educational institutions. In drawing a graph of social exploitation, his play gives voice to the struggles of the exploited and the oppressed.

The character of a heavenly narrator explains the social situation with the help of incidents from the life of Chokhoba. The character of Chokhamela is portrayed as a toiling bonded labourer working for the local village headman. He is not able to enter the shrine of Vithoba of Pandharpur, which is evidently quite close to his village. Chokhoba is shown standing outside the great door of the temple, trying to send a message to his beloved god with Janabai, who can go into the temple even though she is a low-caste servant. She is not an Untouchable. Chokhoba's message is: 'Convey my last *johar* (the Mahar greeting) to God. Tell him that this devoted servant remained loyal to him till the end.'

In the play, the character of Chokhoba accepts the theory of karma without any protest. He says, 'Who has escaped the destined duty? Hasn't our beloved Dnyaneshwar himself said that the omnipresent God is pleased when we worship him by religiously following our destined caste-found duties? And God also helps us in carrying out these duties.'

Chokhoba is shown as the casteless one in the sense that he is the representative of the countless oppressed masses; he is separated from the label of any particular caste. In the play, he emerges as the one with yearning devotion, the one who really craves to see his beloved Vithoba. His character is absorbed in his duties and his assigned work. But he is aware of casteism. He exclaims, 'Defilement! Defilement! From birth to death we are shooed away for the defilement that might be caused by our touch.' He says that the life of Untouchables has become defilement embodied throughout, devoid of even a flicker of refinement or a humane touch.

The play dramatizes Chokhoba's exploitation at the hands of the deshpande and the patil (upper-caste village officials). It also shows the last moments of his life: crushed under the village wall that he is repairing. Chitnis has sketched Chokhoba's image as a devotee engrossed in the chanting of verses in praise of Vithoba along with the traditional paraphernalia of cymbals, saffron flag, and all, waiting endlessly outside the great door of Vithoba's temple. Chokhamela's experience of life reflects his helplessness. The hypocrisy of the upper castes in their behaviour towards Chokhamela is also one of the themes of the play.

* * * * *

The early era of Marathi films witnessed the attempt to create a realistic picture of the life and times of various saints and their beloved deity, Lord Vitthal. The films available today are *Sant Eknath*, called *Dharmahatma* before the censors demanded that the title be changed since it was reminiscent of Gandhi's title of Mahatma (1935); *Sant Tukaram* (1936); *Sant Namdeo* (1937); *Sant Kanhopatra* (1937); *Sant Janabai* (1938); *Sant Dnyaneshwar* (1941); *Sant Chokhamela* (1941); *Sant Savata Mali* (1944); *Johar May-bap* (1950), renamed *Hi Wat Pandharichi* (The Way to Pandharpur) in 1981 for better audience acceptance; and *Sant Gora Kumbhar* (1967). *Sant Eknath* was the first important film that addressed the social issue of the uplift of the Untouchables. The films on the great saints proved a boon to the music-oriented film industry. But the prospect of making a film on Chokhamela's life was quite a challenge from the point of view of the economics of filmmaking, i.e. ensuring viable returns. To explain Chokhoba's views on the caste system and to express them effectively on the screen was really the acid test for the effectiveness of this medium. It must be said that the subject of Chokhoba's life remained rather less explored than the films related to women's issues, such as *Sant Sakhu*, *Sant Janabai* and *Sant Kanhopatra*.

Sant Chokhamela was the first film based on the life of Chokhamela. It was directed by the well-known D.K. Kale, its dialogue was written by Shivaram Vashikar, and the lyrics were penned by S.A. Shukla. The film is based on the standard version of Chokhamela's life and shows him working dutifully as a Mahar, but engrossed in devotion to Lord Vitthal. In one scene, Chokhoba's shadow inadvertently falls on Bindumadhav of the Brahmin caste. The enraged Bindumadhav treats this as an act of defilement, a grave offence by Chokhoba, and denies him entry onto the street leading to the Pandharpur temple. Chokhoba is denied even a view of the great door of the temple.

But Chokhoba carries on his devotion to Vithoba through *nama-smaran*, the continual recital of the name of God. Anant Bhat, the son of the orthodox Brahmin Bindumadhav, becomes a follower of Chokhoba and a fellow devotee of the *varkari sampradaya*. This is the result of Chokhoba's unflagging devotion to Vithoba. He is filled with compassion towards all living beings and stops the Mahar tradition of sacrificing a male buffalo before the deity Mariai. His fellow Mahars are alarmed at this development and regard it as a blow to their pride. They, as well as the upper castes, oppose Chokhoba. But Lord Vitthal craves Chokhoba's true devotion and helps him. He appears as a Mahar before Chokhoba to share his meal. And the Brahmin Anant Bhat coming forward to help Chokhoba is a revolution indeed. While underlining the caste conflict, the film gives central stage to the story of Anant Bhat's life.

In the end, the bones of Chokhoba repeat the name of Vithoba after he is crushed under the wall. Namdev, who finds the bones, says: 'The bones of Chokhoba that chant the name of Vitthal are proclaiming today the fact that Chokha, the greatest saint, has become God incarnate.'

A tape of the film was not available to this writer, but the published screen play helped in understanding the nature of the film. Chokhoba emerges as a sensible, and conscientious man, a man of discretion. He is a humane character in search of humanity: 'What kind of a Brahmin is he if he has no mercy, no compassion.' But Chokhoba feels the pain of his birth into the Mahar caste. At one point in the film he says, 'No time to sing praises to Lord Vitthal in the morning, not able to seek the blessing of a Brahmin in the morning–what kind of a wretched life is mine.' Chokhoba is shown obediently carrying out the duties assigned to him by the caste system. He accepts the theory of karma. He says, 'It is our credo, our duty to serve. The son serves his parents, the breadwinner serves his family, and the lowest of society serves the Brahmin. One community serves the other. I serve you, you serve me–this is the basis of the credo of service.'

* * * * *

A Marathi film based on the devotion of Chokhamela that is available today is Mangal Pictures' *Johar May-bap* or *Sant Chokha Mela* (1950), directed by Ram Gabale. The same film was released again in 1981 under the title *Hi Wat Pandharichi* (The Road to Pandharpur) in order to attract a larger audience. A number of very famous persons from Maharashtra were involved in the making of the film. The writer P.L. Deshpande played the part of Chokhamela and Sulochana enacted the part of his wife, Soyrabai. The story of the film was by the writer Venkatesh Madgulkar, and the screenplay, dialogue, and verses were by another well-known writer, G.D. Madgulkar.

In the film, the story of the life of Chokhamela and his family are played out against the backdrop of the town of Mangalvedhe. The warmth and affection in Chokhoba's relationship with his wife, his sister Nirmala, his brother-in-law Banka, and his son Karmamela are expressed beautifully in the film, as is the dire poverty of the family. Vithoba's earthly appearance before Chokhoba is shown as a sign of approval of the measure of his devotion. The film shows Banka as the one who introduces Chokhoba to the practice of *bhagavat dharma*, whereas in fact Banka himself tells us in his poems that he regards Chokhoba as his guru. The film shows Chokhoba as a bonded labourer of the local village head working on a yearly basis, doing hard labour and odd jobs such as looking after cattle, cutting wood, and working as a farmhand. The warm and harmonious relationship between Chokhoba and Soyrabai is depicted against the backdrop of his hard labour.

After learning the essence of *bhagavat dharma* from Banka, Chokhoba begins to sing *abhangas*. His progress into total absorption through the devotion of *namasankirtan* (the continual remembrance of the god by name) provides Chokhoba with a rare sense of the elevated status of the soul. The transformation of Chokhoba into Saint Chokhamela is shown through the parable of Valya Koli, the legend of a highwayman, although this is not a very fitting comparison. Lord Vitthal is shown helping Chokhoba in his hard labour.

The film shows Chokhoba's awareness of the evils and travails of the caste system, but more frequent references are to poverty as the cause of all troubles. There is no depiction of the pain suffered as a result of the humiliation caused by charges of defilement merely because one is born into a low caste. On the contrary, the life of Chokhoba is seen against an idealistic and liberal background, which avoids showing the harsh reality of the contemporary inhuman caste system. In the scene that shows the meeting of Chokhoba and Namdev on the bank of the Chandrabhaga, Namdev says: 'All of you are Vitthal,' indicating Chokhoba's high status as an integral, accepted, and revered member of the fraternity of contemporary saints.

In the film, Chokhoba emerges as a virtuous and moral person. He is opposed by the village head but, on the other hand, Anant Bhat, who belongs to the priestly caste, is shown as being close to Chokhoba, regarding him with an almost devotional affection. The character of Bindumadhav, father of Anant Bhat and an orthodox Brahmin, is absent. On the contrary, Chokhoba is shown accompanying Anant Bhat's mother to Pandharpur.

The depiction of Chokhoba's poetry as a true reflection of his life and experiences and the uniqueness of the character of Anant Bhat are important features of the film. The sheer down-to-earth sense of life in Chokhoba's poetry, the reflection of his daily chores and experiences, is conveyed very effectively in the film.

The film shows Chokhoba deeply engrossed in devotion when he is dragged away by the village head and ordered to construct a boundary wall around Mangelvedhe. The wall collapses and Chokhoba dies under it. To be precise, Chokhoba is shown performing samadhi, the state of leaving one's earthly body for heaven, at one's own will, in a yogic posture. Lord Vitthal appears in person before Namdev and sends him to fetch the bones of Chokhoba to place in the samadhi of Chokhamela, which was to be constructed in front of the great door at Pandharpur. Here there is an effective use of music in the film. An atmosphere of intense devotion is created by brilliant and moving performances, but missing from the film is a sense that Chokhoba faces the humiliation of being regarded as polluting.

* * * * *

The playwrights, writers and directors who created the character of Chokhoba in the plays and on film seem to have painted a Chokhoba based on their own ideologies. Therefore, a kaleidoscopic image of Chokhoba emerges as all these works represent the authors' understanding of Chokhoba's life. Only a part of what Chokhoba preached and practised is projected in each particular work and Chokhoba is made into a complementary figure in order to propagate that particular theory or aspect. Therefore, despite the existence of four sources, a true representation of the life of Chokhoba has not yet been produced. But these works do have one thing in common: Chokhoba's complete devotion to Vithoba. The uplift of the Untouchables and devotion to Lord Vitthal were what Chokhoba preached and practised, and these aspects of his life are projected in both drama and film. They are, however, influenced by movements seeking the uplift of the Untouchables led by Gandhi, Dr Ambedkar, and Savarkar. These works can be seen as attempts to depict Chokhoba's life from the perspectives of specific ideologies or movements.

NOTE

* Published in Eleanor Zelliot and V.L. Manjul, ed., *Sant Chokhamela Vividh Darshan*, Pune: Sugawa Prakashan, 2002.

REFERENCES

Drama

'Sangit Uhshap' (Antidote to the Curse), by Veer Savarkar, manuscript form, performed 9 April 1927.

'Yugayatra', by M.B. Chitnis (The Epic March of an Era), manuscript form, performed 1956.

Films

Chokhamela. Script by Shivram Vashikar. Lyrics by S.A. Shukla. Directed by D.K. Kale. Mohan Pictures, Bombay, 1941. The script has been published by S.S. Vashikar, Mohan Pictures, Andheri, Bombay.

Johar May-bap. Story by Vyankatesh Madgulkar. Screenplay, dialogue, and lyrics by G.D. Madgulkar. Directed by Ram Gabade. Starring P.L. Deshpande and Sulochana. Mangal Pictures, Poona, 1950. Also released in 1981 under the title *Hi Wat Pandharichi* (The Way to Pandharpur). Available from the Film Archives, Pune.

11
God in a Copper Pot

V.L. MANJUL
(Translated by Sudhakar Kulkarni)

This paper is an eyewitness account of one of the most significant social and religious events in the history of modern India. Its value, it is hoped, lies in the power of its immediacy and its closeness to the event described through the eyes of a twelve-year old. The second part of the essay looks at the persistence of social structures through the years. The two defining ends of time–the first, the year 1947; the second fifty years later, 1997–are significant as markers of independence and what independence has been able to achieve or not achieve over half a century. The event is the fast unto death undertaken by Sane Guruji[1] (one of the foremost and most well-loved social reformists of India, from Maharashtra) in 1947 on a mission to open the doors of the Vithoba temple at Pandharpur to the Untouchables, and the celebration of the golden jubilee of this movement in 1997.

* * * * *

When Sane Guruji launched his fast, the orthodox priests put up a very strong fight. They used Ram Rajya Parishad, a political party, to campaign against the entry of the Untouchables. Local orthodox leaders such as Pandit Bhagwanshastri Dharurkar, Pandit Gopalshastri Gore, and Dhundamaharaj actively opposed Sane Guruji's demand. They organized public meetings and seminars against him. These leaders obtained the support of other important priests such as the Shankaracharya from other parts of India. They also countered Sane Guruji's fast by observing fasts themselves, as well as getting themselves arrested. However, their efforts proved futile and a law was finally enacted that allowed the Untouchables entry into the temple. This law, however, triggered off a very peculiar act. The fast took place in May 1947; on 10 November 1947, these orthodox people performed a *maha* puja, including in it a ritual that claimed to remove the divinity of Lord Vitthal's idol, which they then stored in a copper vessel. This was done to impress upon the devotees that the God whom they were worshipping had lost his original divinity and what they were really doing was worshipping a stone statue. The stubborn orthodox people of Pandharpur even observed a day of mourning fifty years later, in 1997, to counter the golden jubilee function. Led by Agnihotri Bhimacharya Varkhedkar, they repeated the ritual of storing Vitthal in a pot.

The period between 1 May and 10 May 1947 was, however, memorable for the Pandharpur residents. The Rashtra Seva Dal, a social organization, conducted *prabhat pherey*, morning marches, entire groups singing bhajans, to impress upon the people the importance of Sane Guruji's demand. Slogans calling out to the priests to open up the doors resounded amongst the people. Political leaders visited Sane Guruji, expressing their support to his cause as well as to enquire about his health.

Pandharpur in the 1940s was a stronghold of Hindu orthodoxy. The Ram Rajya Parishad and the Hindu Mahasabha were the two political parties that had large followings. Both these parties held very strong views on preserving traditional Hindu values. The Hindu Mahasabha, however, was against untouchability. The managing committee of the Pandharpur temple had Hindu Mahasabha activists as members. These members favoured allowing the 'depressed castes' into the temple. But the orthodox Hindus resisted with daily public meetings, raising slogans against Sane Guruji. I was then a schoolboy of twelve, and this tussle made a strong impression on my mind; passing to and fro near the steps of the temple known as Namdeo Payari, the steps of Namdev, I even tried penning a poem on this event. My family has had the right to recite religious scriptures in the temple since many generations; they were in a sense counted amongst the temple priests. Thus, when the Untouchables were allowed into the temple, my grandfather, Tryambakrao Manjul, and father, Baburao Manjul, participated in the boycott of the temple. They, along with other orthodox priests, decided, in an astonishing ritual, to remove the divinity of Lord Vitthal from the idol, put it in a copper vessel, and take the pot to a Brahmin's home.

The assumption they made was that the temple would be purified subsequently and the same divinity could be re-installed in the idol. But the ritual purification of the temple was impossible after the passing of the act, and hence the divinity of Lord Vitthal remained in the copper pot for fifty years. Over the years though some of the orthodox devotees began revisiting the temple, by and large the majority still believes that the temple has been polluted by the act of lifting the restrictions on the former Untouchables.

According to the Hindu calendar, the divinity was removed on Ashwin Vadya Tritiya, Shak 1869 (or 1947). Mantras were recited by Gopalshastri Gore; the mantras for the removal were recited by his master, another Gopalshastri, one of the seven 'authorized' priests of the temple. Balacharya Varkhedkar was another religious authority in Pandharpur. He claimed to have found religious sanction for this process of divinity removal. There is no doubt that this act was not only absurd but was also against the basic spirit of religious teaching. Once the act was performed, the copper pot containing Vithoba's divinity was taken by one of the temple priests to his own house, since which time his house has become the alternative orthodox Vithoba temple. It remains a mystery how orthodoxy could tolerate this profanity of two Vitthals worshipped in Pandharpur. Who is the real lord of the devotees? How do the peaceful *varkaris* accept this impossible situation? Orthodox Hindus maintain that the copper pot contains the real God; they offer puja, prasad, and prayers to the pot. How do the *varkaris* continue to respect them?

Be that as it may, the whole episode is nothing but pure madness. It so happened that once a cat pounced on this vessel and its contents flowed out. The cat jumped on the food offered to the 'divinity' of Lord Vitthal at Pandit Dharurkar's residence. The 'divinity' was washed away, but the family poured fresh water into the vessel.

It is, however, important to note that despite the so-called divinity removal, there is no change in the devotion of Lord Vitthal's followers. Millions of *varkaris* throng the temple every year. Initially, the different heads of even the *varkaris* kept away, but slowly they, too, began to visit the temple. One pandit entered the temple as late as February 2002. Even today, some orthodox people do not go to the temple. But, paradoxically, these very people worship Vitthal's temples at Dehu and Alandi. These temples have been open to everyone, including the former Untouchables, since ages but that does not deter them. How can one explain this paradox?

Sane Guruji's fast unto death and the enactment of the new law are historic events.

The devotees continue to pour into the temple every year. But Vithoba still remains 'arrested' in the copper vessel.

NOTE

1. Sane Guruji (Pandurang Sadashiv Sane) was born in 1899, and died in 1950. He wrote extensively, often for children. His most famous novel is *Shyamchi Ai* (The Mother of Shyam), published in 1935 and very influential in shaping attitudes towards Untouchables. He was a political worker and spent several terms in jail for undertaking non-violent direct action, but his written work is not political.

12

Chokhamela and His Revilers

MAHIPATI

Mahipati (1715–90) was 'the most prominent and the most profuse among the Marathi hagiographers' (Tulpule, 1979: 430). In his Bhaktavijaya *(Victory to the Bhaktas),* Bhaktalilamrita *(The Nectar of the Divine Play of the Bhaktas),* Santalilamrita *(Nectar of the Divine Play of the Saints), and* Santavijaya *(Victory to the Saints), he told the lives and legends of dozens of saints from the Marathi, Hindi, and even Gujarati traditions. Born near Ahmadnagar, he devoted his whole life to performing kirtans and to do this he composed story-sermons on the lives of the saints. Much of his work was translated by a Christian missionary, Justin Abbott, often with the help of a Brahmin pandit, N.R. Godbole, and it is from these translations that the stories of Chokhamela and Rohidas (Marathi for Ravidas or Raidas) are taken. The selections have been slightly abridged and edited, and the numbers for each sentence omitted. The oral story-telling quality of Mahipati's work and the way in which the kirtan could capture the attention of an audience should still be clear, even in translation. The economic reasons the Brahmin gives for not allowing Untouchables into the temple and the lengthy, rather radical, answer Chokha gives the Brahmins are very unusual elements of this story. It should also be said that Chokha's own abhangas do not refer to any entry into the temple, nor were Untouchables allowed in until Sane Guruji's fasting before the temple at the time of Independence in 1947. There was, however, until recently a pillar for lights on the side of the Chandrabhaga river opposite the temple that was said to be Chokhamela's pillar.*

Chokhamela and His Revilers

It now happened that all the saints on the Ekadashi (the eleventh day of the fortnight) proceeded to Pandharpur. Chokhamela was a Vaishnava *bhakta* and chief among the outcastes. The Dark-Complexioned One showed His favour to him, seeing the loving emotion of his heart. Pandhari (Pandharpur) was his birthplace and there he lived with his family. He had continually the Husband of Rukmini in his heart and was constantly repeating His name. He was accustomed to bathe by the bank of the Bhima and to circumambulate the whole of the city of Pandhari. Then he would go to the main door of the temple and prostrate himself there. He had no authority to go within the temple and meet the god; so, bringing the Life of the World into his thoughts, he worshipped Him from afar.

On one occasion he was seated at the great door of the temple and some evil-minded people saw him there. Listen to what they said to him:

If Vithoba had any love for you, he would have taken you into the temple. If you do not actually see the Husband of Rukmini, why do you worship Him in vain? When the dainty food has been cooked in the house of a Brahmin, dogs are not allowed to sit by the ceremonially clean plates. So outcastes have no authority to worship Pandurang. How can beggars enter into the pleasure-house of kings? Therefore, Chokhamela should not go into the temple. Just as an unfortunate man wanders about in the jungle, but does not see there a wish-tree, so Krishna is not seen by the eyes of Chokhamela. Just as any man whose life is coming to an end in vain licks his chops with the desire of seeing a well of nectar, so although the Lord of the World is in His temple, He will never meet with you.

Hearing them say this, Chokhamela prostrated himself before them and said,

My mother and father, why should I want in vain so great an honour? Although the sun is one hundred thousand towns [or miles] high, yet from that distance it cares for the lotus. So Krishna being in His temple, He cares for me from there. The moon is two hundred thousand towns [miles] away, yet its intense love is upon the *chakor* bird; so He who is the Helper of the helpless, and the Personification of compassion, He remembers me. Just as the mother tortoise cares for her little ones from afar, so Krishna looks upon His servants with a look of compassion. Though seeing one who is continually near Him, yet if that one does not love Him, nothing whatever is accomplished by a still closer contact.

Saying this, he hastened back to his home, but he was remembering the Husband of Rukmini in his heart, and he continued worshipping Him with love.

KRISHNA TAKES CHOKHA INTO THE INNER SHRINE

Now when it was night, the Lord of Pandhari said to Chokhamela, 'I intend tonight to take you into My temple.' The Husband of Rukmini having said this, He took him by the hand and lovingly led him into the innermost shrine. The Eagle-Bannered One then spoke to Chokhamela of His heart's secrets. He said to him, 'I cannot endure a single moment without you. I might be eating with Nama, or drinking nectar with delight, but even at such times the memory of you is in my heart.' Krishna having said this, Chokhamela fell at His feet and said, 'You call yourself the Helper of the helpless and fulfil the desires of your servants.'

The priest who was sleeping near the door heard this conversation and, full of amazement, he arose. He called the others to come and bear witness to this and told them all that had happened.

Someone very much like Chokha is speaking to Krishna. The Dweller in Vaikunth (Heaven) is evidently the supreme Brahm, and yet an outcaste has touched Him. The locks on the doors are just the same. I cannot understand how he could have entered. If a man of low caste can touch the God on whom are garments and ornaments, then our duties as Brahmins will cease. What shall we do? Just as at the full moon its brilliance is at its highest, then it is that the monster Rahu comes and in love embraces it; or as when the sun in the dark half of the month rolls around in the heavens, the monster Ketu suddenly appears and dims its light; so is the Husband of Rukmini glorious in His six qualities. That He Who is described in the Vedas and Shastras should in love have been embraced by an outcaste going into the shrine at night, how can this be remedied? How can this hindrance be put away?

One remarked, 'Let us call him and ask him.' Then removing the lock of the door they questioned Chokha in reference to the whole affair. They said, 'How did you come into the temple? Tell us exactly how it happened.' Hearing them say this, Chokhamela replied, 'I am your child. The Dark-Complexioned One took me by the hand and forcibly brought me into the temple. Forgive me of wrongdoing and let your eye of favour rest upon me.' Saying this, he at once started to depart.

PRIESTS ORDER CHOKHA OUT OF PANDHARI

The priests said to him,

You should remain no longer in Pandhari. For if you are here, the Lord of Pandhari brings you into the temple. So you must dwell on the other side of the Chandrabhaga river a short distance away. If you do not do so, we shall certainly punish you. You have done a very great wrong. You have defiled the supreme God and because of all this sin you will have to experience hell.

To these words of the Brahmins, Chokha replied,

That I have defiled the Husband of Rukmini is a false charge. If an outcaste and a Brahmin both bathe in the Ganga, one should not blame the Ganga. The earth is regarded as pure and on it all castes walk. How is it defiled? And in what Shastra is it written that it can be defiled? If the wind strikes an evil man, his evil qualities will not attach themselves to the wind. It is a wrong thought to blame the wind. If space fills the washerman's vessel and an earthen jar, still it is quite detached from the two. It is not entangled in them. So to God supreme, the Lord of Rukmini, all castes are alike. How can you think that He is defiled? The Lord of Vaikunth fills all the universe but is unattached to it. You therefore have wrong thoughts in your mind and have become worthy of blame.

INSULTED BRAHMINS EXCOMMUNICATE CHOKHAMELA

While he was thus speaking and giving illustrations, the Brahmins became full of rage and said,

He is from a low and dirty caste and yet he teaches us knowledge. A locust proud of itself tries to teach an eagle how to fly. A shepherd comes and gives knowledge to Brihaspati (the guru of the gods). Or it is like a thin coating of tin showing its bright qualities to the gold. It is like common serpents showing their jewels before the great serpent Shesha; or as when other elephants show off their gait before the elephant Airavat (Indra's elephant); or as if before Shiva His servants should perform the *tandav* (dance) to show Him how it should be done; or seeing the sun, the firefly shows off its brightness; or as if the ocean, on seeing the muni Agasti, should begin to roar. We are Brahmins of high caste. We are expert in every Shastra, but you are of low caste, and though an outcaste you are attempting to give us knowledge. So now go to the other side of the Bhim river and live there. If on the morrow you are seen here, we shall give you a good punishment.

Hearing these words of the Brahmins, Chokhamela replied. He said, 'Mother, father, I am your servant and truly call myself your sweeper.

You have taken care of me for many days but now you drive me off.' Having said this, his eyes became full of tears. He then exclaimed, 'O merciful Mother Vitthal, from today I am separated from Thy feet. My fate is very powerful. What am I to do?' Saying this, he hastened as fast as he could to his home, at the same time remembering the form of Hari in his heart and in love repeating His name. He told his wife all that had happened and said, 'The Lord of Pandhari has neglected us. Let us now go to the other side of the river and there we shall live.'

Chokha in Exile

Then looking for a spot straight in front of the temple, on the other side of the river, he built there a pillar for lights. There it was that Chokhamela lived, contemplating the cloud-complexioned Krishna in his heart. Even today, when anyone goes on a pilgrimage to Pandharpur he sees there the pillar for lights. At that place, then, the chief of *bhaktas* lived, indifferent to all earthly things. Bringing the Husband of Rukmini to mind, he continued to worship Him with love, saying 'God has abandoned me and cast off His love; so it seems.'

On a certain day, this God-loving *bhakta* Chokhamela was eating his meal when suddenly the Cloud-Dark One appeared and sat down beside him. Underneath the *nimb* tree there was a dense shade. Sitting in this shade, Krishna ate along with Chokha. Just then a priest suddenly came on some business or the other, and for a moment stood looking at the astonishing sight. At that moment his wife was serving curds to the God and the food rose up and fell down. Chokha said to his wife, 'A great fault has been committed by you. The Husband of Rukmini is dining with us and you have soiled His yellow robe.'

Hearing this conversation, the Brahmin was full of amazement. Chokha turned to a crow in the tree eating the fruit of the *nimb* tree and throwing it down and he said, 'Krishna is sitting here and it is falling on His body. Go at once from here and sit on another branch.' While the *bhakta* of Vishnu was saying these things, the priest became very angry. Said he, 'Seeing me here, he is talking at random. For how can the Lord of the World have dined with one who is an outcaste.'

Chokha Restored to the Temple

The Brahmin hastened to come near Chokha and slapping him over the mouth he immediately went away. Then after bathing by the bank of the Bhima, the Brahmin went into the temple of the God and there saw a most wonderful sight, which astonished him. There was Krishna standing on the brick but His yellow robe was all soiled with curds. Seeing this, the Brahmin looked straight at the God's face. He saw that the cheek of the God was swollen. His eyes were closed by the swelling. The Brahmin was full of astonishment as he came to understand the meaning of it. Said he,

I have persecuted Chokha and God has made me realize this. Just as when an evil man troubles an infant and this troubles the mother, so when anyone persecutes a *bhakta* the Life of the World becomes sorrowful. Then punishing the ones who are not *bhaktas*, He increases the glory of His servants.

Thinking thus in his mind, the priest went back to the bank of the Bhim and there said to Chokha,

Come with me into the temple. I did not know the glory of bhakti. I have persecuted you needlessly, just as if one should hammer a diamond on an anvil and only weary himself. I punished you but the Lord of Pandhari felt the force of it in His temple. When I saw that His cheek was swollen, I became full of fear. Therefore, O dear *bhakta* of His, come at once with me. Perform some means or other and reconcile the Lord of Pandhari to me.

Then taking Chokha by the hand, the priest came into the temple and there, seeing the Lord of Pandhari, Chokha's mind became filled with peace. When he embraced the God, his heart felt great comfort. The face of Hari that was swollen now lost its swelling. The Lord of Vaikunth had become weary through the strain of separation from His *bhakta*, but just as soon as He met him again, His joy was unlimited. From that time Chokhamela began to go into the temple always, just as when the Ganga accepts a streamlet, it becomes holy. All the saints, sadhus, and Vaishnavas became full of joy and said, 'The Life of the World takes pride in His saints.'

[From *Stories of Indian Saints: An English Translation of Mahipati's Marathi Bhaktavijaya* by Dr Justin E. Abbot and Pandit Narhar R. Godbole, Poona: The Poet-Saints of Maharashtra Series, no. 9, 1933, pp. 377–84.]

III

RAIDAS, RAVIDAS, ROHIDAS

13

The Poems of Ravidas

TRANSLATED BY ANNE MURPHY

I

In whatever family a good Vaishnav is found,
whether they be high caste or outcaste, lord or pauper,
the world will know the one by his flawless fragrance.
Whether one's heart is Brahmin or Vaisya,
Shudra or Kshatriya,
Dom, Chandal, or Malech,
through the worship of the Lord, one becomes pure, and
liberates the self and both family lines.
Auspicious is that village, auspicious is that place,
auspicious is that entire holy family,
of the one who has drunk of the nectar's essence,
who has abandoned other pleasures,
and–immersed in this essence–abandons all other poisons.
Scholars, heroes, kings great and small,
none are equal to the one truly devoted.
Just as the water plant's leaf remains near the water
[but untouched by it],
in this way, says Ravidas,
is the life [of the blessed] in this world.[1]

II

The baby calf makes the cow's udder unclean,
the bee spoils the flower and the fish, the sea.

Oh mother! What can I bring to offer in worship to Govind?
There is no perfect flower to be found! (refrain)

The snake has spoiled the sandalwood tree;
the poison and the nectar are as one.
Incense, lamps, offerings of food, fragrances:
how can I, your servant, offer these?
I would offer my body, my mind;
through the grace of the Guru I will find the one without stain.
I cannot worship you and offer rituals.
So, Ravidas says: what is to be my end?[2]

III

Oh people of the city! My notorious caste is Chamar!
In my heart is the essence of all good qualities, Ram-Govind. (refrain)
If the water of the Ganga were made into wine,
the good people would not drink it.
Low, unclean wine is water, just the same;
if it mixes with the sacred river,
does the river's water lose its honour?
Consider the palm tree, which we see as impure.
If thought of as paper
on which a devotee writes the Bhagavata,
we worship it and show our respect.
My caste is *kutabadhala*. I carry cattlehides
all around Benaras, always.
Now the Brahmins and leaders bow down before me.
Ravidas, your servant, has taken the refuge of your name.[3]

IV

Those who recite the name of Hari:
there is none who can compare with them,
not even the lords of Kailash and Lakshmi.
He is only One, although divided into many parts.
Come, come–he that fills everything. (refrain)
He who wrote of the Lord, and saw nothing else,

he was one of the Untouchable caste of calico-printers.
As was written in Vyas and seen in Sanak,
his name is known in the seven lands.
He whose family sacrificed cows at Id and Bakr Id,
and accepted Sheikhs, Shahids, and Pirs;
he whose father is like that, is a son like this
whom people now call the accomplished one, Kabir.
He whose family of *dhedhs* bears cattle hides,
then and now, all around Benares.
The Brahmins and the Teachers bow down low before [him]–
that one, the servant of servants, Ravidas.[4]

V

Who could be so beloved without you?
You are the protector of the poor, my Gosai.
Over my head you hold the royal umbrella. (refrain)
Those whose bad influence comes to the world,
you shield them in you.
You make the low high, my Govind
They are afraid of none.
Namdev, Kabir, Trilochan, Sadhana, and Sain:
all were saved by you.
Ravidas says: Oh pious ones,
All comes to fruition in Hari.[5]

NOTES

* References are given for textual sources of two types: the standard version of the *Adi Granth*–volumes generally follow a fixed page numbering pattern–which is referred to below as *AG*, and Callewaert and Friedlander (referred to as CF). Other translations available are also referenced for comparative purposes: Callewaert and Friedlander, Hawley and Jurgensmeyer (referred to as HJ), and Jassi and Suman, the most recent, from the Ravidas centre located outside Jalandhar in Bala (referred to as JS).

1. #106 in CF.
   AG, p. 858, Rag Bilavalu, Bani Ravidas Bhagat Ki.
   See JS, pp. 246 ff; CF, pp. 164–5, 231; HJ, p. 25.
2. #39 in CF.
   AG, p. 525, Rag Gujari, Sri Ravidas Ji Ke Pade Gharu, p. 3.
   See JS, pp. 152 ff; CF, pp. 127–8, 199–200; HJ, p. 26.

Many different names are used by Ravidas for the Lord. In these examples, we see Govind, Bhagvant, Ram, and others. See CF, pp. 82 ff. In keeping with contemporary colloquial pronunciation, I give these names without their final short 'a'.

3. #47 in CF.
   AG, p. 1293, Rag Malhar, Bani Bhagat Ravidas Ji Ki.
   See JS, pp. 311 ff; CF, pp. 132–3, 203; HJ, p. 25.
4. #111 in CF.
   AG, p. 1295, Rag Malhar, Bani Bhagat Ravidas Ji Ki.
   See JS, pp. 318 ff; CF, pp. 167–8, 234.
5. #109 in CF.
   AG, Rag Maru, Bani Bhagat Ravidas Ji Ki.
   See JS, pp. 276 ff; CF, pp. 166–7, 233; HJ, p. 24.

REFERENCES

Winand M. Callewaert and Peter G. Friedlander, *The Life and Works of Ravidas*, New Delhi: Manohar, 1992.

J.S. Hawley and Mark Juergensmeyer, *Songs of the Saints of India*, New York/Oxford: Oxford University Press, 1988.

Sat Pal Jassi and Chain Ram Suman, *Holy Hymns and Miracles of Guru Ravidass Ji*, Jalandhar: Shri Guru Ravidass Janam Asthan Public Charitable Trust, 2001.

14

The Saintly Chamar: Perspectives on the Life of Ravidas

JAMES G. LOCHTEFELD

The specific subject of this essay is the Hindu poet-saint Ravidas, but the more general theme has to do with religious biography, and the ways that a single person can assume distinct personae in the hands of different biographers. The different ways in which people portray a saint can reveal volumes about their own concerns and the issues troubling their societies. This is particularly true in India, where the genre of biography has been employed less to inform than to teach and prescribe; it is not only the biography of a person, but also biography with a purpose.

* * * * *

Ravidas must have been profoundly troubling to the orthodox Hindus of his time, for he came from one of the lowest Untouchable groups, the Chamars or tanners. Chamars were considered physically impure because of their occupational contact with dead animals, but it is also important to recognize the moral taint associated with untouchability. Given the prevailing belief in karma, according to which people got what they deserved, birth as a Chamar bore witness to grave sins in one's past. This sinful past also influenced one's present moral tendencies, while one's 'sinful' company (fellow Chamars) made it unlikely that one could ever reform. The notion of a saintly Chamar must have been hard for his contemporaries to accept, as it was for at least one of his biographers.

Although in the past Ravidas's low status may have presented a problem, his present-day admirers strive to affirm it, not deny it. Ravidas has become an important symbol for certain low-caste groups, particularly Chamars, in their struggle for social and religious equality. Hawley's reports on the activities of B.R. Ghera and the Chamars of Shri Govardhanpur are only two examples of this trend.[1] As a Chamar saint, Ravidas is their model in the effort to define a new religious identity, as well as a useful figure for those who wish to bypass the hierarchical assumptions of traditional Hinduism.

This essay will look at six 'portraits' of Ravidas. Three of these come from older sources–the accounts by Nabhadas and Priyadas in the *Bhaktamal* and by Anantadas in the *Raidas Parchai.*

Two of these portrayals are much more recently drawn; the first comes from *Sant Pravar Raidas Saheb*, written in 1956 by Chandrikaprasad Jijnasu; the second comes from 1986 and is a comic book in the *Amar Chitra Katha* series. The final source can be found in the poems ascribed to Ravidas in the *Adi Granth* and the Fatehpur manuscript. All except the last are distinctly coloured by the writers' religious, social, and economic concerns.[2] It is more difficult to draw concrete conclusions from the poems, since their intent is devotional rather than biographical. For this reason I will consider them last of all.

NABHADAS

The first portrayal of Ravidas comes from Nabhadas's *Bhaktamal* (Garland of Devotees), which was written at about the turn of the seventeenth century. His two hundred-odd portraits include saints of all the different sects, and in a few verses he deftly outlines each individual's character. Modern editions of the *Bhaktamal* usually include the *Bhaktirasabodhini*, a commentary written by Priyadas about a century later, in 1712. Priyadas gives a much longer story about each devotee, but his accounts share little with those of Nabhadas. Even a cursory comparison reveals that Priyadas's actual source–at least for Ravidas–was the *Raidas Parchai* of Anantadas, who was roughly contemporary with Nabhadas. Anantadas wrote *parchais* (introductions) for many bhakti saints, but because his work has never been published–unlike that of Priyadas–he remains virtually unknown.[3]

The descriptions of Ravidas in the *Bhaktamal* clearly show that these are two distinct narratives that should be evaluated separately. Nabhadas's description is brief and circumspect, but his very brevity makes the account more credible.

The pure verses (*bani*) of Raidas [were] skilled in breaking the bonds (*granthi*) of doubt, but [were] not opposed to the Vedas, the *shastras* and the practice of good [people]. The best *hamsa* bird, separating water and milk, takes [these verses] to heart. Through God's grace he attained the ultimate goal in this body. Seated on a king's throne, he showed pride in [his own] lineage (*jnati*). [People] worshipped the dust of his feet, giving up pride in caste (*varna*) and station (*ashrama*). The pure verses (*bani*) of Raidas [were] skilled in breaking the knots (*granthi*) of doubt.[4]

The description here is quite spare. The word *granthi* (bonds, knots) may refer to shoemaking, but aside from this there is no explicit reference to Ravidas's caste. Presumably it was not high, since Nabhadas speaks of others having to abandon their pride, but he also insists that Ravidas was not ashamed of his birth. The statements about being seated on a king's throne, and attaining the highest goal in this body, point to a person of rare spiritual accomplishment. This is sustained by the statement that higher-caste people would bow at his feet, since only a very charismatic person could invert the social hierarchy so dramatically.

Nabhadas mentions that Ravidas's verses did not conflict with the accepted Hindu standards (the Vedas, the shastras, and the conduct of virtuous people), which at least does not exclude him from the Hindu fold. One of the lines implies devotion and surrender to God, since he attained the highest state through God's grace. Finally, there is the call to the discerning listener, the *hamsa* bird, to take these pure verses to heart. Besides the obvious exhortation to heed the words of such a man, it also points to a body of verses. This admittedly sketchy portrayal does not betray an obvious agenda, and although Nabhadas identified himself as a Ramanandi, his accounts are generally considered objective and non-sectarian.[5] Yet beyond the general qualities he mentions—many of which could belong to almost any saint—this account contains virtually no concrete detail.

Anantadas and Priyadas

Both Anantadas and Priyadas recount the life of Ravidas in far greater detail. Their accounts are so laden with miracles that one cannot regard them as literal biography, but beneath the veneer of magic and miracle there are important messages. The most obvious message is that Ravidas was a great saint—a judgement buttressed by the miracles—but they are also clearly responding to the problem of Ravidaṣ's caste. As mentioned earlier, tanners were among the lowest of low-caste people; not only did their work involve habitual contact with polluting substances–dead animals and their skins–but birth as a Chamar was also seen as evidence of prior depravity. Given these assumptions, the notion of a saint coming from such a debased caste doubtless seemed contrary to the karmic process, and the anomaly of a Chamar saint–and his relations with established religious authorities–are central themes in both narratives, although the writers treat them differently.

Anantadas responds matter-of-factly to the problem of a Chamar saint, declaring that his birth was the result of his former actions. He reports that Ravidas had been a Brahmin in his previous birth, but he had eaten meat and had kept an Untouchable co-wife. The bad karma arising from these actions led to his birth as a Chamar, but he also carried other signs (*chinha*) from his former life, as his first actions clearly show. Distressed because his parents are not religiously inclined, and convinced that death is preferable to a life lived among irreligious people, the infant Ravidas refuses to suckle for four days. The impasse is finally resolved by the dramatic appearance of Ramanand, a well-known saint, who had been directed there by a heavenly voice. Ramanand initiates the entire family, and Ravidas begins to eat. As Ravidas grows older, his devotion develops and deepens, becoming more established with each year. Unfortunately, his family does not share this devotion, or even appreciate it. Very early in the narrative Ravidas has been sent out of the family home, denied his share of the family property, and completely ignored by his family, who are never mentioned again.

This is an unflattering picture of his family, who seem to have taken initiation merely to save his life, but their failing stems from their lack of devotion, rather than their status as Chamars. The important standard for Anantadas is consistently individual: that individuals reap the consequences of their good and evil actions, and that nobility or depravity comes not from birth, but from the depth of one's devotion. The infant was distressed not because he was born a Chamar, but because his family was irreligious. Ravidas's devotion makes him a saint despite his social standing, while his parents, despite their initiation, remain enmeshed in the affairs of the world.

The notion of a Chamar saint seems far more troubling to Priyadas, who explains it not as the fruition of past karma, but by invoking the mechanism of a curse. Priyadas relates that in his previous birth Ravidas had been a Brahmin disciple of Ramanand, and that one of the ways Ravidas served his teacher was by begging food from certain specific households. One day a storm deterred him from his usual rounds, and he foolishly accepted food from a merchant who did business with Chamars. Ramanand immediately sensed that something was wrong with the food, and when he discovered the source he cursed his disciple to be born a Chamar.

This device resolves the cognitive dissonance of a Chamar saint. Despite his birth as a Chamar, Ravidas is 'really' the Brahmin disciple of a powerful saint, and this accounts for his spiritual attainments. Priyadas's account also reinforces conventional opinions of Chamars as being extremely polluting. Ramanand curses his disciple not for taking food directly from Chamars, but from a person who merely does business with them. Yet even such indirect contact is enough to render the food impure.

Negative attitudes towards Chamars persist throughout the entire account. According to Priyadas, the infant Ravidas is so horrified at being born a Chamar that he refuses to suckle, and is repulsed by his mother's mere touch. Ravidas is again saved by Ramanand, who in this version initiates Ravidas alone. Since initiation is considered a second birth, and one's guru a parent, this makes Ramanand Ravidas's 'real' father. Priyadas's message is clear–Ravidas was born into a low family, but does not belong to them.

Priyadas also reports that Ravidas's father was displeased by his son's devotional bent; here, too, the father disinherits Ravidas, kicks him out of the house, and is never mentioned again. Yet in the context that Priyadas has already established, this episode reinforces the lack of any real connection between Ravidas and his biological parents. In the end, he is never really their son; they are merely the instruments for fulfilling Ramanand's curse.

Beginning with the tale of Ramanand's curse, Priyadas shows far greater ambivalence about Ravidas's birth than Anantadas. Whereas for the latter Ramanand's appearance is merely dramatic, Priyadas portrays it as the continuation of an established guru–disciple bond, confirming that Ravidas is not really a Chamar. Whereas Anantadas reports that Ramanand initiated the entire family, showing the availability of devotion to all, Priyadas uses this second birth as a way to remove the stigma of being a Chamar. Finally, although both writers relate that his family treated him shabbily, for Anantadas this reflects their individual shortcomings, whereas for Priyadas it is one more sign that Ravidas never really belonged to 'those' people.

Despite their differences on the issue of whether Ravidas was really a Chamar, both of them consider him a saint, as the wonders they recount clearly show. In both accounts Ravidas is born with full consciousness–Priyadas adds that he felt sharp regret for his error–and refuses to suckle until he has received initiation. This is no ordinary child! Further testimony to his saintliness comes from stories in which Hari himself tests Ravidas's devotion. In one he comes disguised as a devotee, and shows Ravidas a *paras*, the philosopher's stone that changes iron into gold. Ravidas scorns the stone–Anantadas has him deliver a long speech on the danger that gold (representing wealth) presents to a sadhu–but agrees to hold it for safe keeping until the 'devotee' returns. When the 'devotee' comes back thirteen months later, he finds that the stone has never been touched in his absence.

To reward Ravidas, Anantadas reports that Hari left five gold coins, telling Ravidas (in a dream) to use the money for worship, which he does without hesitation. Priyadas reworks the coin motif into other incidents as further evidence of Ravidas's probity. In his version, Ravidas finds five golden coins every day. He is troubled by this unexplained wealth and refuses to keep it, until finally Hari appears in a dream, and tells him to use the money. In all these cases Ravidas refuses to be seduced by wealth, showing his freedom from greed and worldly entanglements.

Further testimony to Ravidas's holiness comes from the tales of his disputes with the Brahmins of Benaras. On one occasion they denounce Ravidas to the king, who puts them all to the test before an image of Hari. When the Brahmins chant Sanskrit mantras, the image remains unmoved, but when Ravidas speaks a single verse, it leaps into his arms as a sign of divine favour.[6] Later in his narrative Anantadas uses this motif a second time, but also has the image speak to the crowd, blessing Ravidas as his devotee, and cursing the lying (*jhuthe*) Brahmins.

Both writers conclude with a tale in which Ravidas himself displays superhuman powers. Ravidas goes to visit Jhali, the queen of Chittor, who has taken him as her guru. This provokes the ire of the local Brahmins, who want to assert their spiritual superiority. Yet as the Brahmins sit down in rows for a banquet at the queen's palace, they are horrified to see the figure of Ravidas appear between each one of them, defiling their ritually pure meal. After this display of power, Ravidas peels back his flesh to reveal a golden sacred thread under his skin.

Priyadas tells this story as evidence of spiritual one-upmanship; Ravidas is present at the banquet, although he is banished to a corner of the hall; his multiple forms and subcutaneous sacred thread demonstrate his superiority, and also his brahminhood. Anantadas uses the story to convey Ravidas's personal qualities, and to stress yet again the primacy of devotion. Even though the Brahmins have abused and insulted him, Ravidas asks the queen to sponsor a banquet for them, showing generosity in exchange for spite. He does not attend the banquet, but remains in the garden where he has been staying. After seeing his multiple forms the Brahmins rush to the garden, only to discover that Ravidas has never left his seat, and it is only then that he produces the sacred thread.

Whereas Priyadas concludes his account with the retrieval of the sacred thread, Anantadas describes how the Brahmins humble themselves before Ravidas, and beg to become his disciples. At first Ravidas feigns reluctance, reminding them of their higher status, but concludes by speaking of the power of devotion, which overturns all human boundaries.[7] Anantadas takes a much more radical position than Priyadas. Rather than simply transforming Ravidas into a Brahmin, thereby elevating his status to that of his tormentors, his stress on the primacy of devotion completely overturns the social hierarchy.

By reporting Ravidas as Ramanand's disciple, both Anantadas and Priyadas set him squarely in the Hindu tradition. But though they spend a lot of time relating wonders and miracles–and Anantadas continually stresses devotion–both accounts tell us surprisingly little about the particulars of Ravidas's spiritual life. The things mentioned seem like ordinary devotional fare: giving gifts (shoes) to ascetics and devotees, sharing food, congregational singing (kirtan), loving and serving God. Both writers mention Ravidas using an image in worship, and Anantadas explicitly describes him as a *sagun* devotee.[8] Since Ravidas is normally described as worshipping a *nirgun* God, that is, a God without attributes, this last claim is surprising.[9]

It is interesting that the villains in both accounts are none other than the local Brahmins, who are especially enraged when Ravidas worships images. They continually oppose and harass Ravidas, but they are always defeated in the end. As conventional religious authorities, Brahmins are stock villains in many tales of the saints, and harass the devotees even when the devotees are Brahmins![10] Yet the way that both men portray this conflict highlights their larger concerns. Priyadas castigates the Brahmins for their inability to see the obvious, namely, that Ravidas is a saint. Yet in their inability to accept that a Chamar could be spiritual adept, the Brahmins are the mirror image of Priyadas, who denies that Ravidas was not 'really' a Chamar. Both Priyadas and the Brahmins, resolve this anomaly by affirming only one aspect: the Brahmins, his caste status; and Priyadas, his sainthood. In condemning the Brahmins, Priyadas seems curiously blind to his own assumptions.

Anantadas has no such problem with the notion of a Chamar saint, and his account points to something much more fundamental–the tension between dharma and bhakti, between a hierarchical social structure and an essentially egalitarian religious practice. The real conflict is not rooted in caste, but in differing standards of religious and spiritual worth. Anantadas continually affirms the importance of devotion, and highlights this on the two occasions when the Brahmins abuse Ravidas for transgressing caste boundaries–once for worshipping a *saligram*, and later for having the audacity to initiate disciples. In each case Ravidas responds with genuine anger–once warning the Brahmins that their false devotion will send them to hell–and undercuts the assumptions behind their perceived superiority, particularly those of relative purity and impurity. Whereas Priyadas tries to rehabilitate Ravidas as an individual, leaving the social system intact, Anantadas tries to subvert it completely.

Both of these accounts are clearly hagiographic; the miracles alone render them suspect as biography. Both stories convey important themes–Priyadas's ambivalence about Ravidas being both a saint and a Chamar, and Anantadas's emphasis on devotion. The events they relate can also provide a point of comparison with later accounts.

Sant Pravar Raidas Saheb

The first modern portrait is painted by Chandrikaprasad Jijnasu, author of *Sant Pravar Raidas Saheb*.[11] Jijnasu openly admits that he has an agenda, for the book is subtitled 'A Discriminating Biography: Written from a Buddhist Point of View'. Jijnasu aims to portray Ravidas not as a Hindu, but as a Buddhist who has been drawn into the Hindu tradition.

Jijnasu's book clearly shows the influence of Dr B.R. Ambedkar. Ambedkar was the architect of the Indian Constitution, and a highly educated man, but he was also an Untouchable Mahar. He knew the indignities of untouchability from personal experience, and devoted his life to destroying this ignoble practice. At the end of his life Ambedkar finally rejected Hinduism, urging his followers to convert to Buddhism to escape the degrading aspects of the caste system.

Jijnasu's book was not only published the same year that Ambedkar converted to Hinduism, but Jijnasu also mentions Ambedkar (1956: 9) as an example of the fact that great spiritual leaders can come from any community. What better saint to further support his point than Ravidas, who was born a tanner? Jijnasu is speaking to the lower-caste people of 1956, trying to give them some basis for self-respect. He urges them to embrace Buddhism, which he claims is identical to sant religion, and to abandon Hinduism as one abandons 'urine and faeces' (10). Throughout the book he seizes every opportunity to demonstrate that Ravidas was not a Hindu, but a Buddhist; he magnifies every possible difference in an effort to distance Ravidas from the Hindu tradition.

Given these aims, it is not surprising that he rejects Priyadas's account of Ravidas's birth as 'unnatural and fabricated' (7). He ridicules the claim that Ravidas was a Brahmin, that a person could be born through a curse alone, or that an infant would refuse the breast until given initiation. Jijnasu stresses that Ravidas was actually a Chamar, and that he never claimed to be anything else. The real motive behind Priyadas's story, he contends, is Brahmin arrogance. He claims that Brahmins cannot accept the thought that 'low-caste' people can know God by themselves, and he rightly notes that similar tales of Brahmin descent were also spread about Kabir (2–3).

Jijnasu's account of Ravidas's birth shows an intimate connection with Buddhism. According to his story, one day Ravidas's father was passing through the deer park at Sarnath, the place where the Buddha preached his first sermon. There was an ascetic staying there who was very fond of rice pudding (khir). Ravidas's parents happily supplied this, and in return for their devotion the ascetic promised them a son. Besides the location, which carries strong Buddhist overtones, the ascetic is said to be a *dhyanayogi*, that is, a person realized through meditation, like the Buddha. Such a person would be free from any Brahmin influence, and thus an ideal figure to associate with the birth of Ravidas. Jijnasu claims that an old sadhu in Benares told him this story (5–9), and that he includes it because it seems so believable. This may well be true, but it is also true that sadhus often tell stories that one finds nowhere else, such as this one.

Jijnasu differs from with Priyadas on other fundamental points. The first concerns Ravidas's guru. He notes that Ravidas never mentions Ramanand in his poetry, and that Ravidas's name does not appear in the traditional lists of Ramanand's disciples (11–12). Jijnasu therefore denies that Ravidas was Ramanand's disciple, asserting instead that he was realized solely by his own study and reflection, like the Buddha and Dr Ambedkar (14).

Another bone of contention is the claim that Ravidas worshipped images. Jijnasu denies this (101–6), citing as proof verses from Ravidas's own poetry. Because of this, he rejects the story about Ravidas finding five gold coins every day. According to the story, Ravidas found the coins in one of the articles used for worship (puja), but since Ravidas did not do puja, according to Jijnasu, this story is clearly fabricated.

Jijnasu's final argument is with Nabhadas. Although he agrees that Ravidas's poetry was not opposed to the conduct of the virtuous (*sadachara*), he takes issue with the statement that it was not opposed to the Vedas and the shastras. Jijnasu devotes a section (93–100) to disproving this latter assertion, again citing verses from Ravidas's own poetry. Jijnasu strongly emphasizes the differences between the picture of Ravidas in his poetry and the picture given in the *Bhaktamal*, trying to distance Ravidas as far as possible from the Hindu tradition.

It is interesting to note, however, that Jijnasu uses stories from the *Bhaktamal* when they can be made to serve his purpose. He cites Ravidas's refusal to use the philosopher's stone (*paras*) as evidence that Ravidas rejected parasitism and believed in honest labour. Jijnasu associates this work ethic with 'Right Livelihood', one of the steps on the Buddha's Eightfold Path (23). He also recounts that Ravidas's parents disowned their son, but uses it to illustrate the point that intelligent and hard-working people are soon rewarded. Although his parents didn't give him a thing, after a short while Ravidas had a successful business with a dozen employees! Jijnasu tells the story of the Brahmins complaining to the king of Benares, and Ravidas's audience with the king. Finally, he tells the tale of Queen Jhali's inviting Ravidas to the banquet, though he refrains from mentioning the golden sacred thread (30–6). For Jijnasu, the important thing about both these episodes was not the miracles associated with them, but the way in which they contrast Ravidas's humble saintliness with Brahmin pride and arrogance.

Jijnasu gives a full account of Ravidas's miracles and marvels; his third chapter is devoted entirely to miracle stories (41–54). But the introduction to the chapter is titled 'Buddhists are not convinced by miracles'. He notes that the Buddha forbade his disciples from performing miracles to convince people, and that all great beings shun such vulgar displays of power. According to Jijnasu, Ravidas's greatness stems not from his miracles, but from his moral qualities such as compassion, virtue, and purity, qualities that anyone can hope to emulate. He further claims that Ravidas never performed miracles for their own sake, but that these were always harsh tests of his devotion (41–2). This shows a curious tension. On the one hand, Jijnasu shows the rationality and rejection of the miraculous characterizing both early Buddhism and twentieth-century scientific thought. But on the other hand, he also gives a full account of these miracles, as if these could provide further proof of Ravidas's sanctity. It seems as if Jijnasu wants to simultaneously deny and affirm these miracles. Part of this tension may stem from the presence of an audience who may have been impressed by such stories.

Jijnasu's claim that Ravidas was a Buddhist is based on his analysis of India's religions (dharmas) into six groups. Three are indigenous (the sants, Buddhists, and Jains), while the other three are not (Muslims, Christians, and what he calls *vaidik-arya dharma*) (53). This differentiation between sant dharma and *vaidik-arya dharma* not only removes the sants from the Hindu fold, but also allows him to claim that there is no such thing as 'Hindu' religion (58, note). According to Jijnasu, sant dharma is the original religion of India; it was the religion of the Indus valley civilization, and the ultimate source of the other indigenous traditions (59). Finally, he traces the ultimate roots of the medieval sants to the Buddhist tradition, since the sants were influenced by Gorakhnath and the Naths, who were themselves influenced by the Buddhist Siddhas.

This analysis is unconvincing. A major flaw lies in polarizing the Hindu tradition into sant dharma and *vaidik-arya dharma*. At one time *vaidik-arya dharma* was certainly a discrete tradition, but non-Vedic elements have been working their way into the tradition since well before the beginning of the Common Era. This is why present-day Indologists distinguish between different stages of the tradition: an earlier period (Vedism or Brahmanism) and a later period (Hinduism). Another problem is his assertion that Jainism and Buddhism sprang from the religion of the Indus valley civilization, for which there is absolutely no evidence. Nor does he explain, why sant dharma, if it was the original religion of India, lay dormant for such a long time, and why it reappeared only through Buddhism. Finally, although Siddha influence on the Nath yogis is generally acknowledged, the Naths have generally considered themselves Hindus, not Buddhists. In the end, Jijnasu is not a dispassionate researcher, but a man trying to support a conclusion he has already reached, in the service of an ideal in which he fervently believes.

Amar Chitra Katha

The most recent description of Ravidas, published in 1988, comes from the comic book series, *Amar Chitra Katha.* Given the medium, it is unreasonable to expect a sophisticated portrayal. However, this account does betray certain concerns reflecting the social currents in present-day India.

Although untouchability is officially illegal in the Republic of India, it is no secret that discrimination based on caste status persists to this day. The main emphasis in this account is squarely on social issues, such as occupational status, purity, and impurity. The first part of the story sets the stage, showing the social discrimination suffered by Ravidas and the other Chamars. The primary evil is not poverty, for Ravidas and his family, through their honest labour, are able to make a living. The thing that really bothers them is the low status associated with their occupation: tanning and working leather.[12]

In two places, the comic book explicitly condemns judging people as pure or impure based on their occupation, implicitly condemning caste discrimination. The first is when Ravidas's teacher, Sandan Swami, tells him that the distinctions between pure and impure occupations are solely the product of ignorant men. Men have classified themselves by the work of their own hands, forgetting the hand that made them, that is, God's. Such distinctions are purely adventitious; they do not reflect any deeper reality about the humans performing such work.[13]

Later in the book, Ravidas himself tells his followers to detach their sense of self-worth from their occupation: 'Do not be ashamed of yourself. Do not be afraid of your caste. Do your work with dignity and bow before no-one but God' (Pai, 25).

Social and caste concerns are also reflected in the comic book's story about the origin of Ravidas's followers, the Ravidasis. According to the story, the sect is formed when a young man complains to Ravidas that ordinary people cannot escape from the burden of caste that society has laid upon them. He asks Ravidas to give him a new identity, and Ravidas makes him his disciple. In good comic-book fashion, the young man is immediately transformed, and stands up with pride to his former oppressors (Pai, 26–7).[14]

These oppressors could be seen as a cross-section of Indian society; one has the shaven head and topknot of a Hindu, another wears the skullcap and beard associated with Muslims, while the third is a non-descript Indian male. When the young man shows his new-found dignity and confidence, their expressions are dejected. The message is clear–there is a new social order in India, one in which all people have human dignity.

Despite rejecting caste distinctions, the comic book sets Ravidas's life in a distinctly Hindu context. The opening page shows his parents bathing in the Ganga, and mentions that they came every morning for a 'holy dip' (Pai, 1). His parents beseech Surya, the sun god, to fulfil their only wish, the desire for a son. An ascetic named Sandan Swami assures them their wish is granted, and in due time the child is born. This same swami gives Ravidas his first instruction about God, and later becomes his guru (Pai, 9–10).

However, any religious beliefs portrayed in the book must also be compatible with the comic book's message of social equality. Sandan Swami's teaching (and later, Ravidas's) is heavily influenced by *advaita vedanta* (non-dual monism), according to which all distinctions are ultimately false. The swami tells Ravidas that because God and the human being are one and the same, Ravidas should see himself as he really is (that is, God), and not according to the label applied by society (Chamar). In the next episodes, Ravidas breaks down his mental constructions; he first stops thinking of himself as a Chamar, then destroys the distinction between 'self' and 'other'. This latter point is shown by his charity, especially to the poor (Pai, 11–13). The book's cover shows Ravidas meditating in the lotus position (*padmasana*), lost in yogic contemplation of the Absolute. Finally, after Ravidas realizes God, he never shows the slightest uncertainty, hesitation, or self-doubt. This unshakeable confidence accords with Shankara's conception of the liberated state as permanent and irrevocable.[15]

Based on this perspective, the comic book criticizes other types of Hindu practice. Image worship and sectarianism are criticized as ideas limiting God based on human conceptions. Though Ravidas does not deny that God is represented in an image, he sees God everywhere else as well. Seeing God only in an image, he says, puts the image between oneself and God. It is the same with the different names for God. To name is to limit and particularize, but God transcends human conceptual capacities. For this reason, Ravidas says, he refers to him solely as 'Name' (Pai, 24–5).

The ultimate identity of God and devotee are re-emphasized at the end of the story, when the famous Krishna devotee Mirabai visits Ravidas. Mira constantly carries an image of Lord Krishna, and says that she cannot bear to be separated from him (that is, Krishna) for even a moment. In response, Ravidas says that since she is already one with God, how could there be any separation? After some days in Ravidas's presence, Mira finally sets the image down, presumably having been liberated from slavery to a statue (Pai, 30–1).

Given the communal and sectarian problems in present-day India, it is not surprising to find the message that God transcends particular names and forms, but there are also other reasons for this stand. The issues of ritual purity and impurity are less likely to be emphasized in a practice that does not have sacred images, whereas these issues will probably be important if images are used. The lack of emphasis on images is thus consonant with the comic book's social concerns.

The comic book also criticizes the mechanical performing of ritual action (*karmakanda*). There is an episode late in the story where a Brahmin goes to the Ganga to make a ritual offering. In the process he spurns a poor beggar, one of the only dark-skinned people in the comic book. Though the beggar falls into the river and calls for help, the Brahmin ignores him, concentrating solely on his ritual. Ravidas helps pull the man from the water, then tells his disciples:

Unless you know the Supreme Essence, what use is shaving the head . . . dancing, singing and praying . . . Of what use is the lamp ceremony and fire worship to him whose hair contains crores of suns . . . if we do not also love our fellow-men? He would certainly prefer our kindness to our rituals. (Pai, 29)

The emphasis is clearly on one's inner attitude rather than mere external action, with the conviction that genuine devotion to God is intimately connected with concern and care for one's fellow human beings.

Like Anantadas, Priyadas, and Jijnasu, the comic book tells of conflict between Ravidas and his parents, but treats this story differently from the other sources. The problem comes from Ravidas's compassion for the poor, for whom he steals shoes and money from his parents. On one occasion when his father asks whether it was proper to give away their earnings, Ravidas replies: 'Her need was greater than ours' (Pai, 14). After a while, his despairing father sets him up in a separate household.

Thus far the story accords with tradition, but while the other sources portray Ravidas's father as a greedy and selfish man, he is given far nobler motives here. He is worried about Ravidas, and thinks that the burden of running a household will turn him into a responsible adult. In the end, he is only doing what he thinks is best for his son (Pai, 14). Unlike any of the other sources, Ravidas and his parents are eventually reconciled. His father not only apologizes, which Ravidas dismisses as unnecessary, but also becomes Ravidas's disciple. Thus, the stain on the name of Ravidas's parents is neatly erased, and the ultimate integrity of the Indian family is preserved.

The comic book gives an idealized account of Ravidas's life, strongly emphasizing twentieth-century ideals such as equality, compassion, and brotherhood. The only thing marring this picture comes in the exact centre of the magazine, where there is a full page advertisement for shoe polish! (Pai, 23–4) This may reflect the belief that leather workers would flock to buy a magazine portraying Ravidas, but at the very least it shows incredible insensitivity. The sad reality is that despite the comic book's cheery message of equality, one should have no illusions that caste, colour, and occupation are meaningless in present-day India. This may be true someday, but it will probably take a long time.

Poems of Ravidas

The final picture of Ravidas comes from his earliest known poems: thirty-nine poems attributed to him in the *Adi Granth* (*AG*), and eight in the Fatehpur manuscript. The Fatehpur manuscript was compiled in 1582 and the *Adi Granth* in 1604, which makes these poems at least contemporary with the Nabhadas and the Anantadas, the earliest biographical accounts. Since these poems are the benchmark against which other poems are judged for authenticity, they define (in a sense) the 'real' Ravidas.

Though it seems contrary to look at the earliest material last, there is good reason for this. On the whole, the poems address purely religious concerns, mentioning little or nothing about Ravidas's personal life—they are poems by him, rather than about him. For this reason, any picture drawn from them would be sketchy and highly speculative. It, therefore, seems better to use what can be drawn from these poems to criticize the other three portraits of Ravidas.

One thing that seems sure is that he was actually a Chamar. He mentions this many times (*AG* 3, 4, 5, 9, 20, 38, 39),[16] and seems quite open about it. Since most of his poetry stresses devotional (bhakti) themes, this may account for the reason he shows neither shame in his own caste, nor deference to another's. Since all human beings are equally insignificant compared to God, the most significant quality is not one's birth, but the depth of one's devotion.

A few of the verses substantiate the image of absolute identity with God portrayed by the comic book: 'What is the difference between you and me, me and you? [We are] like the gold and the bracelet, water and waves' (*AG* 1). Sometimes the identification is less direct, phrased in terms of things invariably associated with one another: 'If you are the mountain, I am the peacock; if you are the moon, I am the *chakora* bird' (18). There are also times when he shows great certainty that he has attained the highest state: 'Yama's rod will not strike me, I've abandoned all entanglements' (4, also 20).

Most of the poems, however, strike notes more consonant with the general themes in bhakti poetry. The dominant theme is a deep sense of unworthiness and distance from God: 'I am bound by the snare of delusion, you are bound by bonds of love; I can make no effort to free myself, if I am freed it is by devotion to you.'[17] Some other prominent themes are: praise of the saints, praise of God's Name, warnings not to fritter away the blessing of a human birth, and praise of devotion (bhakti) as the best means to realization. In the end, the dominant picture is of a humble man with little faith in his own capacities. His only hope lies in surrender to God, and the confidence that God will not abandon him: 'Tanner Ravidas says: My birth is low, my people are low, my caste is also low—Raja Ramachandra, I've come to you for refuge!' (19). The emphasis in these poems is very different from the picture in the other sources. The later stories begin with the assumption that Ravidas is a saint, and according to popular conceptions, saints are never afflicted by self-doubt.

Only one poem seems to have an overt social or political message. In it Ravidas tells about a place he calls 'The Sorrowless City' (*begampur*), in which there is no unhappiness or anxiety, no jealousy, taxes, or trade. There is 'no second or third' (i.e. no social hierarchy), all are equal. People live richly and comfortably, stroll wherever they please, and no one keeps them from the Beloved's house (*AG* 3). This is a utopian vision, although one can certainly imagine Ravidas comparing this ideal to the society he saw around him, and finding the latter wanting.

On the whole, however, Ravidas seems less interested in changing society than in transcending it altogether. In one poem he compares himself to a fish that never forgets its home; even after its body has been cut up for cooking, every piece still longs for the water.[18] In another poem he compares himself to a widow separated from her Beloved (146). These images convey a sense of alienation and displacement, a feeling that Ravidas did not consider this world his true home.

Ravidas's poems do not mentions his guru's name, though he does refer to the necessity of a guru: the guru is the philosopher's stone, transforming the disciple (*AG* 6); through the guru's grace one attains God (13) and does not go to hell (11); through the true guru (*sadguru*) one can know the saints (8); and, finally, he exhorts people to follow the guru's path (7). It is not clear whether these statements about a guru refer to his own experience, or are more general pronouncements about the need for a spiritual guide. But even if they refer to himself, one need not assume that Ravidas had a human preceptor. The word guru, especially *sădguru*, is often simply another way to refer to the Divine. From the limited evidence in the poems, there is no sure answer.

Ravidas's position is much clearer with regard to ritual action (*karmakanda*). Given his emphasis on devotion, he feels that ritual action without inner feeling is empty:

One cleans the outside [of one's] body with water, but inside [the heart] there are various faults. How can one become pure, this is [like] the elephant's bath (an expression for a useless activity, since the elephant throws dirt on itself immediately after a bath). (*AG* 6)

In another poem, he bluntly states that a man of good family performing ritual action without devotion is no better than an Untouchable. Although he would probably not denounce action performed with devotion, he clearly thinks that the latter is the more important.

Ravidas is more ambivalent about Hindu sacred texts, namely, the Vedas and the Puranas. Given his feelings about ritual action, it is not surprising that he denounces the sections in these texts that prescribe ritual action. Nor does he feel that they can even hope to convey the majesty of the Divine: 'O Lord, the Vedas call you the Inner Knower, [but] they do not know your glory.'[19] But he also speaks favourably of them when they are conducive to devotion: relating the weaknesses of the gods themselves (*AG* 24) or telling the stories of paradigmatic devotees. In the end, he does not reject them wholeheartedly (as Jijnasu claimed), but neither is he unopposed to them (as Nabhadas asserted). The final scale against which texts are measured is whether or not they lead one to true devotion.

Conclusion

Which of these pictures gives us the 'real' Ravidas? Of all the different perspectives available to us, his poems seem the most reliable, but they are also the sketchiest. And although the poems are the earliest sources for the life of Ravidas, they, too, have been selected and filtered. Ravidas himself was almost certainly illiterate, so the poems would have been transmitted orally until they were finally written down. Nor can we overlook the possibility that these collections may have been selectively compiled from a larger body of work that is now lost. But there is an important difference between the tone in these poems and the other accounts of his life. The other sources begin by assuming that Ravidas is a saint, which automatically makes him important. They then use his life story to advance their own concerns—whether highlighting the value of devotion, glorifying a devotee, creating a new religious identity, or exhorting one towards greater social justice—and their respective concerns affect the way that they interpret his life. The poems attributed to Ravidas himself carry no obvious agenda, but convey instead a living human being, full of doubt, despair, and sometimes joy. This human voice carries a ring of authenticity. Here there is no saint, no realized being, but only a man struggling to find his place in the world, and his relationship to the divine.

NOTES

1. Hawley, John Stratton and Mark Juergensmeyer, *Songs of the Saints of India*, New York: Oxford University Press, 1988, pp. 9–10, 19–23.
2. Not surprisingly, this pattern appears in the accounts of other bhakti saints, as D.N. Lorenzen, *Kabir Legends and Anantadas's Kabir Parchai*, Albany: State University of New York Press, 1991, notes in the case of Kabir.
3. For my remarks on Anantadas I am deeply indebted to Dr Winand Callewaert, who was kind enough to send me the text from four different manuscripts of the *Raidas Parchai*, and without whose help this analysis would have been impossible. In accordance with his wishes, I shall not quote the manuscript, except to clarify occasional words and phrases.
4. Nabhadas, *Sribhaktamal*, Lucknow: Tejkumar Press, 1964, p. 230.
5. C. Vaudeville, *Kabir*, vol. 1, London: Oxford University Press, 1974, p. 30.
6. Anantadas, Chap. 3; Nabhadas, 1964, pp. 477–8, v. 325. Anantadas specifies that the image Ravidas worshipped was a *saligram*, an aniconic form of Vishnu. Priyadas remains silent on the specific nature of the image.
7. Anantadas, Chaps. 11–12. The final discourse plays on the similarity between the words *sidha* (respectable) and sudra; Ravidas notes that the power of devotion has turned him from the latter to the former.
8. Anantadas, Chap. 5; Nabhadas, 1964, p. 476, v. 324. Anantadas says that Ravidas did puja before a *saligram*, which is aniconic, but still an image. The claim that Ravidas was a *sagun* devotee may simply reflect Anantadas's concern to promote devotion of every kind. In the *Raidas Parchai*, Anantadas contrasts Ravidas with Kabir, the quintessential *nirgun* devotee, but concludes by proclaiming that both forms of devotion are equally valid, although they appeal to people with differing inclinations.
9. Even if one discounts the claims that Ravidas worshipped images, in his poetry he often uses Vaishnava names for God, showing tendencies that seem to be *sagun*. Ravidas seems to show both *nirgun* and *sagun* tendencies, and the real problem may lie in the rigidity of the categories themselves.
10. Tulsidas and Eknath, though Brahmins themselves, were both greatly troubled by Brahmins. Priyadas (1964, p. 476, v. 325) gives the standard explanation that Hari himself inspires this opposition to magnify the fame of his devotees.
11. Chandrikaprasad Jijnasu, *Sant Pravar Raidas Saheb*, Lucknow: Bahujan Kalyan Prakashan, 1956.
12. Anant Pai, ed., 'Guru Ravidas', Amar Chitra Katha Series, no. 350, Bombay: IBH Publishers Pvt. Ltd., 1988, pp. 2–8.
13. Ibid., p. 10.
14. This is the only account that mentions the Ravidasis, recognizing it as a present-day religious movement.
15. The moment when Ravidas realized God is clearly shown to the readers by the halo surrounding his head from that point on, a portrayal probably influenced by

Christian iconography. It is also striking how much the picture of the realized Ravidas (light skin, long brown hair, and beard) corresponds to the picture-postcard images of Jesus. This may indicate something about the target readership for this series (the educated and economically better-off) as well as the continuing stigma associated with dark skin.

16. The numbers given to the poems come from the numbering scheme in P.G. Singh, *Sant Ravidas, Vicharak aur Kavi*, Jullundar: Nav Chintan Prakashan, 1977, pp. 191–204.
17. G.N. Bahura and K. Bryant, *Pada Suradasa Ji ki*, Jaipur: Maharaja Sawai Man Singh II Museum, 1982, p. 157.
18. Ibid.
19. Ibid., p. 146.

15

The Legends of Raidas in Word and Song: Satire and the Rhetoric of Reform

JOSEPH SCHALLER

The theme of 'satire and the rhetoric of reform' has been the focus of my present work on the legends of Sant Raidas or Ravidas (*c.* 1450–1520 CE). I have selected two different texts for discussion, each containing variant versions of the same episode. The first of these texts is the *Raidas-paracai*, a hagiographic text containing one of the standard accounts of Raidas's life. The date of the manuscript is 1843 VS, or 1786 CE.[1]

Anantdas is the author of the *Raidas-paracai* manuscript. Known to us primarily as the biographer of sants such as Raidas, Kabir, and others, he was historically associated with the Raivasa monastery of the Ramanandi sect, located near the town of Sikar in Rajasthan. Sikar was traditionally an important centre for the followers of Dadu (fifteenth century), as well as a centre for the adherents of the Niranjani *panth.*[2]

The second text is a devotional song (bhajan) authored by a Ravidas devotee named Arjun Lal (Aka Aughar Nath). It was recorded during a long, late-night bhajan singing session in mid-September 1990 in Jamuri village, which lies about 15 miles south-east of Varanasi off the Chunar–Allahabad road. Arjun Lal is a resident of the village and a farmer by profession; he also happens to be a mean hand at fixing bicycles, a talent he displayed the following morning! With great humility, he described himself simply as 'a very devout devotee of Raidas'.[3]

The description of the Raidas legends as hagiographic highlights one of the main issues in this essay. The term hagiography implies that the historicity of the legends contained in the aforementioned texts is not a primary concern. Most readers know that the tales of the lives of Indian saints are replete with elements that would hardly, if ever, pass the accepted norms of historiography. Critical issues aside, the use of the term hagiography itself remains problematic due to its linguistic and religious roots. I will revisit the question of problematic terminology in the conclusion of this essay. For now, suffice it to say that my reading of these texts seeks to decipher their respective author's concerns in the religious and social arenas, rather than attempting to verify their historical accuracy. As suggested in a relatively recent journal volume dedicated to Vaishnava hagiography, the primary goal of such readings is to gain insight into a tradition based upon a genuine attempt to understand the life of its 'spiritual exemplar(s)' in context.[4] Critical detachment aside, any such reading misses its mark if it fails to consider the emotional resonance of hagiographic tales for the tradition's followers.[5]

Both authors, that is, Anantdas and Arjun Lal, express their concerns predominantly in a satirical mode. The use of satire in this vein receives extensive commentary in the classical work of Indian dramaturgy, Bharata's *Natyashastra*. In Siegel's analysis of this work, satire as farce (*prahasana*) falls into two categories: pure and mixed. In pure farce, comic situations are created by having the characters dispute one another, characters such as Brahmins, priests, and religious devotees. Employed in this mode, satire reveals the 'ludicrousness of the venerated' by exposing the vulgar reality behind the religious ideal.[6] Both texts employ this pure form of farcical satire.

Another key issue in this essay concerns the multiple recensions that have been transmitted of Raidas's life. In this regard, I was struck by the much more strident satirical tone of the bhajan in comparison with the *Raidas-paracai* manuscript. This pointed use of satire invites an alternative reading to elicit the texts' socio-political critique masquerading under the guise of religious discourse. The essay's final section will suggest some fruitful avenues for this alternative reading, drawing upon the work of James Scott.

The Story of Queen Jhali and the Feast at Chittorgarh

This episode involves a queen named Jhali from Chittorgarh in Rajasthan.[7] Earlier in the story, the queen had already travelled to

Varanasi and accepted Raidas as her guru against the vehement opposition of her court Brahmins. Their opposition was based upon Raidas's Chamar caste status that rendered him unfit to grant initiation to the queen. Her acceptance in this case would cause them to suffer a great loss of face in the Byzantine intrigue of court politics.[8] Later, after returning to Chittor, the queen invites Raidas there. He accepts her invitation and, arriving near Chittorgarh, sets up his camp some way outside the city. In order to honour him, she plans a great feast.

CHAPTER (*VISHRAM*) 12

1. The queen enthusiastically decided to hold a feast. All the Brahmins met and hatched a plot to spoil her plans.
2. [They thought:] 'Having summoned this Shudra, she is showering him with hospitality but has abandoned us.'
3. All the Brahmins went to the court and there angrily threatened the queen.
   She responded, 'Why are you all so distraught, You act like your fields had been stolen.'
4. They replied, 'You have ruined everything, by arranging for a feast in the capital.'
6. 'Everywhere Brahmins wield authority, You made this base Chamar your guru.'
   The queen responded, 'Listen my friends. In my mind this was good.'
7. 'One who does evil deeds is a Shudra; one who performs good deeds is great . . . .'
8. 'Desire, greed, anger are faults. These are Chamars in the body.'
   'Great is the one who is victorious over these. Was Valmiki a Brahmin'?
9. 'Caste and kinship carry no weight. The beloved of Ram is he who worships him.'
   '. . . Rise up, you Brahmins, and get out of my sight'!
10. The Brahmins were dismayed. Angrily they demanded of the queen,
    'First give us food. Afterwards it will be as you wish.'
11. She replied, 'Why should I feed you when it is the guru who comes first?'
    Thus, a great quarrel ensued. Raidas then dispatched a disciple to the Queen.

12. His message was, 'For me there is neither victory nor defeat. Preserve the rights and privileges of the Brahmins.'
    Taking his words as a command, the queen consented . . .
13. She had the Brahmins summoned. They all rose up and ran towards the city.
    In order to take food they ran; seven hundred of them could be counted.
14. They thought to themselves: 'No one will be allowed to precede us . . . .'
15. Then, heedless of time, the Brahmins bathed in preparation for their meal, while the devotees of Hari sat singing songs of praise to him.
    When the food was ready, the Brahmins loosened their garments and prepared to eat.
16. All of them were pleased, unaware of their unfolding fate . . .

The foregoing passage exploits one of the oldest motifs in all of Indian literature: brahminic insatiability or, in brief, gluttony! The use of this motif is found as early as the Brahmana and Upanishad texts of the Vedic corpus, and becomes a joke in trade of later Sanskrit drama.[9]

As the Brahmins begin eating, two different miracles occur. First, a bodily image of Raidas appears between each and every one of them. A messenger is dispatched to Raidas's camp, only to find him there deep in meditation at that very moment. The Brahmins, deeply ashamed, fear some form of divine retribution for having so dishonoured him. Thus, they collectively decide upon the remedy of going to his camp, prostrating themselves fully the entire way. Once there they touch his feet, beg his forgiveness, and seek his counsel on how to attain spiritual liberation. Then, surrounded by a huge crowd that has gathered, the second and greater miracle occurs.

CHAPTER (*VISHRAM*) 13

5. Raidas spoke, telling the story of his previous birth.
6. 'I was a Brahmin but did not know god (i.e. Hari). Thus, I took birth as a Shudra.'
   [Ripping open his chest] he revealed his sacred thread of gold within; all present grew faint at the sight.
7. Raidas continue, 'Practising *bhakti* I was saved. Without god's love the world is base'.

'Caste and kinship confer no authority. Only he who practises devotion crosses over'.

9. Thus did Raidas speak, and his words took root in everyone's heart.
   The Brahmins spoke, 'You are our guru. Touching your feet we shall attain liberation.'
10. 'Please place your hand upon our heads' O Master. You know all. We are your followers.'
    Then Raidas, placing his hands upon their heads, accepted them as his disciples.

Let us now compare the *Raidas-paracai* version with the same episode as sung in Arjun Lal's bhajan. As almost all the bhajans I recorded tend to repeat the same lines for greater rhetorical effect, I have taken the liberty of eliminating the repetitions in this instance.

THE BHAJAN OF ARJUN LAL

O friends, Guru Ravidas tore open his chest in the king's court. He displayed in his chest the sacred thread representing the four ages. All the ritual priests (*pandas*) present there bowed their heads in shame.

On account of their defeat, the king announced the Brahmins' punishment: 'Bring a palanquin from the royal palace and seat the Supreme Guru on it. Parade him through the entire city.'

Look! Having lifted up the palanquin, the *pandas* have become Kahars! They traversed every corner of the city of Kashi.

Arranging themselves like a marriage party, the obese palanquin-carriers advanced slowly.
They shouted: 'Great is Guru Ravidas.'

Hearing this, the men and women of Kashi came running.
They celebrated the victory of Guru Ravidasji.

Having traversed the whole city the *pandas* returned to their homes, their shallowness fully revealed.

Today those *pandas* bowed their heads at the Guru's feet.

O compassionate one, please bestow your kindness on us everyday. Aughar says, 'Please give me the gift (lit. bag) of wisdom.'

A common theme emerges from these texts. This theme is how satire serves as an outlet for repressed feelings of hostility on the part of Raidas's low-caste followers towards the oppressive caste order. A prime example is when the king compels the *pandas* to do the traditional work of the Kahars and parade Ravidas around the city of Varanasi. In the bhajan, this line is sung repeatedly with great verve and delight. As Siegel comments, satire constitutes a form of verbal aggression that substitutes for the physical violence that ethical or legal codes prohibit; the verbal aggression is transformed into satire by aesthetic dictates and concerns. In this context, the appeal of satire is the release of tension it grants, a tension generated by the ceaseless 'repression of aggressive feelings' towards dominant figures in the society who are normally the ones compelling others to behave in a particular manner.[10]

From the satirical perspective, the greatest sin one can be guilty of is pretense.[11] Throughout the texts, the Brahmins are repeatedly guilty of the sin of pretense, but never more so than in the climactic episode where Raidas's sacred thread is revealed. The right to wear the sacred thread is, of course, one of the most tangible physical symbols signifying the Brahmin's privileged position at the apex of the social hierarchy. Raidas's possession of the same within simultaneously accuses the Brahmins of wearing it with false consciousness, and asserts his equality with them.

The final issue I want to touch upon is this assertion of the socio-religious equality of bhakti practitioners. As manifested in the climactic episode of Raidas's revealing his inner sacred thread, this egalitarianism features prominently throughout all the different genres of texts that I am researching. In both of the two short excerpts from the *Raidas-paracai* quoted above, this egalitarian claim is explicitly advanced. Queen Jhali makes the first such claim while arguing for the appropriateness of having accepted Raidas as her guru (*Raidas-paracai*: 12.9). The second example immediately follows the climactic episode in which Raidas stakes his claim to true brahminhood. He reiterates the argument that caste and kinship considerations are irrelevant; the practice of devotion is the key to crossing over the proverbial ocean of samsara. While such egalitarian claims are certainly not novel in the context of bhakti religiosity, I want to offer the following reading of their function with respect to the above two texts.

According to this reading, the egalitarian religious vision that both texts offer is simultaneously a critique of the socio-political order in which they are embedded. As Scott notes, in large-scale systems of domination such as caste, critiques of domination articulated by subordinates, or in our case subaltern Dalits, develop outside the spheres controlled directly by the dominant. The reason for this, of course, is that subordinates 'dare not contest the terms of their subordination openly' for fear of reprisal, the forms of which are all too painfully familiar.[12] In regard to my own texts, the late-night bhajan singing session constituted one such sphere where the overwhelmingly low-caste and Dalit participants felt free to voice their dissent. Such a reading helps to explain the far more strident satirical tone of the bhajan.

CONCLUSION

In a recent work on hagiography in the Indian tradition, Snell suggests a dualistic typology reflecting the two main approaches towards such religious literature: reverential and referential. In this context, reverential refers to 'traditional *pandita* scholarship' that depicts the life stories of its subjects as taking place in a non-temporal, ahistorical realm. Naturally, the reverential approach fails to satisfy the demands of critical scholarship designated by the term referential. He goes on to suggest that the rather unwieldy term 'poet-saints', often applied to figures such as Raidas, be abandoned in favour of the more simple and generic devotee (*bhakta*).[13] I question the proposed typology for two reasons. First, it does little to truly clarify hagiographic literature as a genre, whether renamed 'sacred biography' or something else. Second, the Hindu tradition itself provides perfectly workable distinctions for its sacred literature. As for the term *bhakta*, it strikes me as not adequately capturing the reverential attitude of actual devotees towards exemplary figures such as Raidas. In spite of questioning the proposed typology I now offer some final referential comments regarding this particular episode in Raidas's hagiography.

The *Raidas-paracai* of Anantdas exhibits many features characteristic of the genre of Indian hagiographic literature. A major purpose of the genre is to assert the superiority of one sect, tradition, or lineage over another. In the description of the *Raidas-paracai* manuscript, I noted that its author, Anantdas, was associated with a monastery belonging to a Ramanandi order. The story of Ramanand giving initiation to Raidas is recounted in virtually all of the traditional hagiographies of Raidas's life. Thus, Raidas is placed firmly in the sectarian Ramanandi orbit, which also puts him squarely into the Vaishnava *sagun* theological fold by extension. Yet, based upon an extensive review of the available sources, this purported *guru-shishya* relationship is highly tenuous, at best.[14]

The theological implications of Anantdas's claim also demand close scrutiny. Conventional wisdom in our field firmly places Raidas among the sant poet-saints. The sants, by definition, are those who conceive of and worship God in the *nirgun* mode. Yet, identifying Raidas as Ramanand's disciple clearly places him in the Vaishnava theological fold. This forces Anantdas to have Kabir come to the rescue in the *Paracai* to convince Raidas and his fellow *bhakta*, Sain, of the ultimate truth of the *nirgun* perspective. Such theological debates form an entire sub-class of part hagiographic, part didactic religious and philosophical literature known as *ghosti*. With respect to the analysis, this episode involving Anantdas reflects two related features employed by hagiographic literature in achieving its aims. The first of these is establishing a secure connection with pre-existing tradition that grants legitimacy to the position being advanced. In turn, this air of legitimacy reinforces the particular truth claims of the sectarian viewpoint in question.[15] My study of Raidas's hagiography is forcing me to re-formulate the main question I posed years ago at the outset of this project. Rather than asking what can this body of literature tell us about the authenticity of the core elements of his life story, now the question we should ask is, how does this literature in all its variety position Raidas in the universe of bhakti saints to which he belongs?

NOTES

1. I originally translated the text with Professor Sukhdev Singh of the Hindi Department at Benaras Hindu University, and later refined the translation with Professor Avadesh Mishra, one of my Hindi gurus from the AIIS Language programme.
2. B.P. Sinha, *Ram Bhakti me Rasik Sampraday*, Balrampur: Awadh Sahitya Mandir, 1957, pp. 334-52.
3. Arjun Lal, interview by author, tape recording, Jamuri village, Uttar Pradesh, 30 August 1990. Interestingly, Arjun had another village resident, Mochu Lal Yadav, sing this particular bhajan. Arjun Lal was unquestionably its author, however, as evidenced by the two notebooks he keeps close by him that contain the lyrics to the bhajans he sings.
4. Steven Rosen, 'Introduction', *Journal of Vaishnava Studies*, vol. 1, no. 2, 1993, p. iii.
5. Cf. here Kakar's comments on Satsangis in the Radhasoami movement for whom histories of the movement that do not evince a divine teleology, and biographies of

the movement's gurus that are not hagiographic, are 'essentially false'. Sudhir Kakar, *Shamans, Mystics and Doctors*, Chicago: University of Chicago Press, 1982, p. 125.

6. Lee Siegel, *Laughing Matters: Comic Tradition in India*, Chicago: University of Chicago Press, 1987, p. 58, citing Bharata, *Natyashastra* (18.103–4), edited with the commentary of Abhinavagupta by M. Ramakrishna Kavietal, 4 vols., Gaekwad Oriental Series, nos. 36, 68, 124, 145.
7. Winand M. Callewaert and Peter G. Friedlander, eds., *The Life and Works of Raidas*, New Delhi: Manohar, 1992, provides a summary of Raidas's hagiographic biography in English from the original Hindi sources. Callewaert and Friedlander, however, were primarily concerned in this work with producing a critical edition of Raidas's poetry, the Raidas-vani, and thus related Raidas's life story from the Paracai in very brief, summary fashion only.
8. Callewaert and Friedlander point out that as granting initiation is not a common hagiographic motif, this particular episode is likely rooted in fact, ibid., p. 34.
9. Siegel, *Laughing Matters*, p. 199, citing *Aitarey Brahmana* (7.29) and *Chandogya Upanishad* (1.13.4–5).
10. Ibid., p. 65.
11. Ibid., p. 61.
12. James C. Scott, *Domination and the Arts of Resistance: Hidden Transcripts*, New Haven CT: Yale University Press, 1990, p. xi.
13. Winand M. Callewaert and Rupert Snell, eds., *According to Tradition: Hagiographical Writing in India*, Wiesbaden: Harrassowitz Verlag, 1994, pp. 1–2.
14. Nabhadas, *Bhaktamal*, 3rd edn., with a commentary by Priyadas, Lucknow: Tej Kumar Press, 1951; P. Chaturvedi, *Uttari Bharat ki Sant Parampara*, Allahabad: Leader Press, 1951; Richard Burghart, 'The Founding of the Ramanandi Sect', *Ethnohistory*, vol. 25, 1978, pp. 121–39; Peter van der Veer, *Gods on Earth*, New Delhi: Oxford University Press, 1989; Charlotte Vaudeville, *Kabir*, vol. 1, Oxford: Clarendon Press, 1974; W.H. McLeod, *Guru Nanak and the Sikh Religion*, Oxford: Clarendon Press, 1968; David Lorenzen, *Kabir Legends and Anantdas's Kabir Paracai*, Albany: State University of New York Press, 1991.
15. Callewaert and Snell, *According to Tradition*, pp. 5–6.

16

Stories of Ravidas (Raidas)

ANANTADAS

One of the many sources on the life of Raidas is the Raidas Parcai *composed around 1588* CE.[1] *Anantadas's work exists only in manuscript form but its contents are widely used, as in the articles by Schaller and Lochtefeld in this volume. Like Mahipati, he was clearly within the tradition. Callewaert and Friedlander (1992:15) call him a sant who traced his guru tradition back to Ramanand, a bhakta from south India, who also figures in the legends about Kabir and Ravidas. They also note that both names, Raidas and Ravidas, are used in the all important Rajasthani sources on the sant, but that Ravidas is used most in the Punjab.*

The selections below are from The Hagiographies of Anantadas: The Bhakti Poets of North India *by Winand Callewaert in collaboration with Swapna Sharma, Richmond: Curzon, 2000, pp. 307-35. Some parts of the* Parcai *have been summarized, and only the parts significant to the theme of the present volume have been reproduced; likewise only a few of the notes, those necessary for the understanding of the text, appear here. Note the difference between this story of Raidas and Queen Jhali and that used in the Schaller article. Note also the rather radical stress to which Lochtefeld calls attention expressed in the humbling of the Brahmins.*

For his edition of the Raidas Parcai, *Callewaert has collated four manuscripts numbered 25 to 29. He has used as standard the version of Ms. 27, and gives indented only the important variants found in the other versions.*

ONE

RAIDAS

1. In Benaras, the best of cities
   no evil ever visits men.
   No one who dies ever goes to hell:
   Shankar himself comes with the Name of Ram.
2. Where Shruti and Smriti have authority
   there Raidas was reborn,
   in the home of a low-caste Shakta-
   his father and mother were both Chamars.
3. In his previous birth he was a Brahmin;
   he listened all the time to religious recitation, but did not give up meat.
   For this sin he was born into a low-caste family,
   but he remembered his previous birth.
4. He did not drink milk but only cried,
   causing anxiety in his family.
   'In great pain our son has been born.
   Has in pain the unique child of a great house been born here?'
5. The women did not sing auspicious songs, and
   in their anxiety they did not play any instruments.
   They summoned many a sorcerer and healer
   to work magic and minister potions.
6. 'Whoever saves this dying child, (they said),
   will be hailed as Dhanvantari.[2]
   We will do whatever he says
   and heap things in front of him.'
7. Four days passed,
   while the mother despaired
   and the father grieved with the rest of the family.
   Only Raidas found pleasure in dying.
8. Dying is better than living,
   for life without Hari is tasteless.
   The man who lives but has forgotten Hari
   is like one who drinks poison and is punished by the god of death.
9. Whether poor or wealthy,
   powerless or powerful,
   a fool or a wise man,

a king or a beggar, nobody can cross the ocean of being
without the grace of Hari.

10. As Raidas lay thinking of death,
Hari, the compassionate one, had mercy on his follower.

Raidas and Ramananda

In the night a heavenly voice was heard,
which in his heart Ramananda understood:

11. 'The son born in a Chamar's house
is my devotee born again,' and
Hari related the whole story
of what had happened in the past.
12. 'With great compassion, give him initiation.
You must by all means save this dying child.'
Then Ramananda decided
to enlighten the whole family:
13. 'If you become devotees, brothers,
Hari will revive your child.'
The Chamar touched Ramananda's feet, and said:
'Do what you like, O Goswami.'
14. Without further ado, Ramananda
put his hand on the Chamar's forehead.
He gave them understanding and had the child shaven,
removing and rubbing away his past.
15. And everyone's hearts were gladdened when
Raidas started to suckle at his mother's breast.
People congratulated them, while drums were beaten
and in every home the sacred pitchers were decorated.
16. In telling the birth story of Raidas
even the Lord finds pleasure.
The bonds of karma are severed:
so sings the devotee, Ananta.

[*Soon, however, the family starts to get weary of Raidas's devotion and he is relegated to the back of the house, where he toils away at his cobbler's trade, enduring many privations. Finally, Hari himself comes one day in the guise of a devotee and tempts him with a* paras *stone to allay his poverty. Raidas refuses, of course, and seeing him obdurate to all argument,*

Hari keeps the paras *stone tied up in a piece of cloth under the thatch of the hut, suspecting Raidas will use it later. Thirteen months after Hari returns to find the* paras *still tied up, and knowing Raidas will not accept it, appears in a dream, offering him five gold coins every day to help organize festivals and bhajans, which Raidas gladly accepts much to the ire of the Brahmins.*]

FOUR

RAIDAS AND THE BRAHMINS

12. 'From where is this low-caste man getting the money?
This stupid villager does not even know how to spend it!
He is making a fool out of people.
When has a Shudra ever done puja himself?
13. With no one here to teach him a lesson,
there is much impropriety going on in this town.
A man from a mean family and home,
How can he be allowed to worship the *saligram*?
14. Mean himself, he has a mean job.
He is from a mean family and from a mean house.
The Vedas and the Puranas have explicitly proclaimed,
O brothers, that a Shudra shall not touch the sacred stone'
15. After the Brahmins had thus vent their ire,
they went to stop Raidas:
'You should remain content remembering Hari's name,
but never must you worship the *saligram*.
16. If you want to live in this town,
you must not deceive anyone.'
The king tried to stop the Brahmins,
but they did not show him any respect.
Raidas told them: 'Listen, friends,
it is not important what I am or what you are.
High or low is just your invention,
only love and devotion please the Lord.'
17. They ignored the king's decree
and were only concerned with themselves.
They refused to accept the king's orders,
but threatened to kill themselves in the court.

FIVE

Then the king called Raidas,
who went to see him along with his companions.
The king said: 'Listen, Raidas:
the Brahmins are disturbed and make a lot of noise.' (Ms. 26)

1. The Dubeys, Tiwaris and Chaubeys came,
   the Vyases, Acharyas and Pathaks, too, came running.
   Young and old, all gathered together,
   leaving Raidas alone to argue.
2. They sat with the Baghela king,
   where royal decrees were issued.
   The whole town gathered to enjoy the spectacle,
   for there was no charge for this entertainment.
   The Brahmins gathered in large numbers,
   while Raidas was all alone.
3. Five landlords came and tried to protect him,
   but the Brahmins paid no heed and roared in anger.
   Then Raidas stepped forward,
   and the king and the people were pleased to see him.
4. He placed a rug on the ground and sat on it,
   like the moon that glows
   in the midst of stars and looks so attractive.
   Nothing is as great as the glory of devotion (bhajan).
5. Raidas spoke soft, calm words:
   'For what fault do you bother me?'
   The Brahmins said: 'Listen, Shudra,
   why do you disgrace our religion?
6. We are the teachers to be revered by all,
   but now people listen to what you say.
   We organize donations and worship.'
   But Raidas replied: 'Listen to me, Brahmins.
   You deceive the king and the people.
   You leave the right path and take them on the wrong path.
   Your teachings bring confusion.
   Without the name of Ram nobody can be saved.
   Look in all the sacred scriptures, and see
   if there is salvation without the Name!

Would a king ever give up his kingdom?'
Then the Brahmins replied to Raidas: (Ms. 26)

7. 'When you lay hands on the *saligram*,
Sri Jagannath, the Lord of the Universe, trembles.
When you bathe the image in holy water,
it is as if you pour vile liquor over it.
8. When you offer *tulsi, chandan,* and flowers,
there is no sin equal to that.
If you serve him breakfast (*bal bhog*), it is like shedding tears on him.
A *raj bhog* organized by you is like offering meat.
9. If you offer incense, lamp, or light,
no one will believe that any good will come of it.
Respect the rules laid down in the Shruti and Smriti.
For righteous people there is neither victory nor defeat.'
(Raidas replied)
    1. 'I do not care for victory or defeat.
    I only speak about the Supreme God (*puran Brahman*).
    2. Hari does not care for high or low.
    He is pleased only with true service.
    3. Whatever my guru told me to do,
    that way of worship (dharma) I respect.
    4. I will not give up the worship of the *saligram*;
    even death I shall accept for true service.' (Ms. 26)
10. 'What will you do with such a dharma
that will surely cast you into the pit of hell?
Your dharma simply tells you that
food should be given to everyone.
11. Remember Hari in your heart. Do not delay.
Even if it hurts control your five senses.
Do not speak ill of others.
Happily, happily sing Hari's praise.' (The Brahmins replied:)
12. 'Pay heed to what we are saying,
if you know what is good for you.'

In a low caste you were born.
You have no right to perform rituals. (Ms. 26)

Then Raidas retorted and explained:
'Brothers, true devotion remains far from you.

You are caught up in the discussion about high and low,

but the path of Hari is far from you. (Ms. 26)

13. The Bhil woman[3] offered half-eaten fruit,
knowing she had love for Hari in her heart.
Therefore, I am not afraid of sin
and I sing of Narayan with great love.'
14. The Brahmins said: 'Listen, Raidas.
Do not harbour any illusions about liberation.
In the Treta Yug, a Shudra performed ascetic penances, and
for this transgression a Brahmin had to die.[4]
15. But then the Lord shot an arrow,
that revived the Brahmin and killed the Shudra.
Since the earliest times Brahmins have been respected,
and even more so in this Kali yug.' (Ms. 26)
'I do not desire to perform asceticism or go on pilgrimage.
My refuge is Ram alone,' Raidas replied.
'Nobody will touch an Untouchable.
How can he become like a Dahma Brahmin?' (Ms. 26)
16. 'I make no distinction between high and low,
for Hari himself eats the food left by cowherds.
Even when Brahma came to eat food that had been left behind,
he did not get any because Krishna deceived him.
17. Through the mercy of the saints
and the grace of God I can talk like this.
As is clearly said in the Veda and the Bhagavata,
so has Anantadas given his story.
18. Devotion is pleasing to Ram.
No one knows the reason why.
The one who knows, finds liberation,
and then caste has no importance anymore.

Six

1. The Brahmins said, full of confidence,
'Keshav will uphold our righteousness.
The seer Bhrigu struck the Lord with his foot, and
Hari's body became even more glorious.
2. Parshuram killed all the Kshatriyas,
and gave us the right to rule on twenty-one occasions.
Nor did we disappear from the hearts of the Pandavas,
who offered food for 86,000 of us.'

3. Then Raidas said: 'Listen, Pandas.
Kicking the Lord does not make one become great.
Further, you don't know anything about ruling, and
therefore things kept turning against you.
4. With the 86,000 food offerings the sacrifice was not complete,
as Krishna's conch was blown only because of a true Shudra.
There is only one result for those who worship you:
their service takes them straight to hell.
5. You sent King Nriga to hell by pronouncing a curse on him,
but Krishna freed him.
Truly, Durvasa was your teacher, but
Hari is the refuge and rescuer of his devotees.'[5]
6. Hearing this, the Brahmins were infuriated,
as though ghee had been poured into a blazing fire.
'How can a cow and a sow be the same?
Everyone checks on her milk before drinking.
7. A fish from the Ganga does not lose its stench.
Can you produce a calf by bathing a dog?
How can a swan and a crow become equal?
And aren't glass and gold distinguished carefully?
8. There is a difference between camphor and oilcake.
Everyone knows this for sure.
Even if a Shudra masters his senses,
nobody will worship his feet!
9. Even if a Brahmin is very corrupt,
the king and the queen will honour him.'
When he heard this, Raidas, too, was angered and said:
'Hari can even abandon kings and queens.
10. He abandoned Duryodhan,
and preferred to eat the simple food of the house of Vidur.
Ram is not your private property.
Anyone giving all can have Him.

Raidas and the *Saligram*

11. Bring a *saligram* and put it here.
Who ever can summon it will be the true devotee.
It will go to the person it truly loves.'
This was the strategy Raidas employed.

12. The Brahmins agreed: 'Bring it here,
if this is what you really want!'
Raidas was struck with shyness,
as it was brought on its throne. (He prayed:)
13. 'If you are truly the Lord of the Triple World,
then come and sit in the lap of your devotee.'
The Brahmins said: 'Come here, my Lord.
We are yours, supreme Brahman.'
14. They recited the Vedas with steadfast voices,
but Keshav didn't pay any attention to them.
They repeated the Gayatri Mantra with concentrated mind,
and invoked all the other gods (dharma).
15. Then Raidas kept repeating one verse,
as the whole day passed without offering any food.
A full three and a half *pahars* had gone by,
but no one had won or lost.
16. Raidas kept offering the verse as food,
while, excited with love, tears filled his eyes.
And when Hari saw this compassionate deed,
the *saligram* leapt up into Raidas's lap.
17. The devotee Raidas kept holding it to his chest,
while the king and the people were greatly pleased.
Everyone shouted, 'well done,' and
the defeated Brahmins departed, hiding their faces.
18. They did not show their faces, hiding,
as if for six months they had been suffering from fever.
Although Raidas had won, he did not become proud,
seeing the Brahmins melting away like water from sweets.
19. In every age the Lord pats his devotees on the back.
The glory of devotion is described as endless.
Hari himself sings the praise of the greatness of devotees.
Who can be equal to them?
20. Ananta the devotee worships the Lord,
ignoring all ideas of caste.
Hari takes no account of high or low.
Real devotion gives influence over Him.

[*Jhali, the queen of Chittor, wishes to take initiation from Raidas; the Brahmins in Chittor oppose this and insist on accompanying her. Much to their rage and chagrin, Jhali takes initiation from Raidas. Their angry outrage is appeased only when the* saligram *declares Raidas to be the true devotee. Section 9 contains a long dialogue on* sagun *and* nirgun *god between Kabir and Raidas. Back home, Jhali dispatches an invitation to Raidas, inviting him to Chittor, which the guru accepts.*]

ELEVEN

5. Wandering on like this, many days passed,
while Jhali was impatient to see him.
When they had come near Chittor,
then Raidas sent two devotees.
6. The devotees came and conveyed [his] words,
and the queen was very enthusiastic:
'Blessed is this day and blessed is this hour,
when you came and gave me this message.'
7. Then Raidas approached.
At first he made a camp in a garden.
Then the queen summoned all of her ministers,
and dispatched the entire capital to his presence.
8. Both ordinary and important people went to see him,
but the Brahmins were very resentful.
While everyone was happy,
the Brahmins died of jealousy.

[*There are ten additional stanzas that are found in manuscripts 25/27 which have been omitted here*]

9. 'One is mean if his actions are mean.
One is excellent if he performs meritorious deeds.
Excellence and meanness are in one's actions.
In the human body alone there is no excellence at all.
10. Desire, anger, greed, and the nine gates,
through these all are Chamars.
One who conquers these becomes excellent
Who speaks there of Brahmins or of famous Valmikis?
11. Caste and family have no importance.
One who sings of Ram is dear to Ram.
You can achieve nothing, Brahmins.
Get up and go home.'

12. The Brahmins had been frustrated.
They became very angry and frightened the queen.
'First give us some food,
and then we will agree with whatever you want.'
13. The queen said: 'I do not like this.
Why should I feed you before my guru?'
At this, such a sharp dispute broke out
that Raidas dispatched a devotee.
14. 'For me there is neither loss nor victory.
Just do whatever will make them happy.'
The queen understood and followed his advice.
Grudgingly she decided to feed the Brahmins.
15. Without enthusiasm she called the Brahmins,
and all who were in the city came running.
The Brahmins came running in order to get food.
All together there were more than 700 of them.
16. They were very pleased at this,
eager to cook their food all day.
'If anyone dares to speak in front of us,
then we will make him fast today.' (Mss. 27, 29)
Overexcited, they prepared the cooking ground,
ordering big earthen pots to be brought.
17. They took their baths, leisurely,
while the devotees sat singing the praises of Hari.
When the food was ready they started to eat,
removing their turbans and leaving their heads bare.
18. Raidas kept his mind absorbed in meditation,
and in contemplation he transcended his body.
As in many mirrors you see the same body,
his transcending body was seen everywhere.

RAIDAS SEEN EVERYWHERE

19. He sat down to eat with everyone and
on all sides he could be seen.
Seeing this marvel, everyone was astonished.
There were as many Raidases as there were Brahmins.
20. Then someone ran to the place where Raidas was camped,
and found the devotee Raidas as well.

Everyone said, 'He is great, he is great,'
and the Brahmins hid their faces.

21. Embarrassment overwhelmed them all,
as they knew they had troubled a saint.
'If he should be angry at us,' they thought,
'he will reduce us to ashes.

22. We are sinners, he is a model devotee,
and his Lord is always present.
He is a saint, we are sinners.
We started a quarrel with a saint.
Hari is true, true are Hari's devotees'.
In this manner, the Brahmins expressed their regret.

23. 'Hail hail, the Lord is great,
and so are his servants.
Caste and family are nothing.'
Thus the Brahmins were mortified.

TWELVE

1. Then the idea came to all of them that
they should go and touch Raidas's feet.
They set off immediately, in all humility,
and asked Queen Jhali to come with them.

2. They thought: 'How can we touch his feet?
We have committed so many sins.'
From their houses to his hut, they performed full prostration,
and in this way they arrived, with fear in their hearts.

3. Then Raidas said: 'O wretched ones!
You are exalted and I come from a low caste.
How is it that you are prostrating yourselves before me?
O Brahmins, you will die of shame.'

4. The Brahmins just stood there. No words came out of their mouths,
while the Giver of Happiness gives happiness to all.
The king and the people had all come,
eager to criticize the Brahmins.

5. The Brahmins made this humble request:
'What can we do to become free from this?'
Then Raidas spoke, teaching them,
by telling the story of his previous birth.

6. 'I was a Brahmin, but did not know Hari.
Because of this I was born in a Shudra's house.'
He pulled out the sacred thread that was on his body.
Seeing this everyone came to him for protection.
7. 'Devotion has made me pure in this world.
Without devotion the entire world is a Shudra.
Caste and family have no importance.
Doing devotion one crosses over the sea of rebirth.
8. The Vedas and the Puranas all proclaim that Vishnu himself is under the sway of bhakti.
Hari himself proclaims the greatness of his devotees.
By the glory of their worship they have been placed above everything.'
9. The devotee Raidas spoke in such a manner
that everybody agreed with him.
The Brahmins said: 'You are our guru,'
and they took out their sacred threads and threw them away.
10. 'Put your hands on our foreheads, Master.
We are your servants, you are the indwelling Lord.'
Then Raidas makes them all his disciples.
Showing compassion, he placed his hands on their foreheads.
11. The king and the people were all delighted.
Shouting, 'Bravo, bravo', they felt their love swell.
People are nothing without love for the Lord.
Those who flirt with other things go to the city of Death.
12. Those who see the saints and the Lord as one,
they reach the far shore.
Anantadas has told the true story,
in which the mystery of bhakti is expressed.

NOTES

1. *The Life and Works of Raidas*, by Winand M. Callewaert and Peter G. Friedlander, New Delhi: Manohar, 1992.
2. Dhanvantari is the mythological divine physician.
3. Shabari in the *Ramayana*, the one who tasted fruit before offering it to Ram because she wanted him to eat only the sweet ones.
4. Shambhu in the *Ramayana*.
5. The first five stanzas of this section contain four references to the *Mahabharata*; the reference to Nriga is from the *Bhagavata*.

17
Rohidas the Shoemaker

MAHIPATI

This story is from one of the three volumes by Mahipati entitled Stories of Indian Saints, collected and translated by Justine E. Abbott and Narhar R. Godbole, Poona, 1933. This selection is from Mahipati's Bhaktavijaya, *# 9 in the remarkable 'Poet Saints of Maharashtra Series' published in Poona in 1933. Mahipati was an eighteenth-century* kirtankar *and his stories gain value when read or recited aloud. As in many of Mahipati's stories, there are elements of humour and also as in many the Brahmins are bested. Unlike Chokhamela, Rohidas was a Brahmin in a previous life, and here he shows his sacred thread by ripping open his chest (Mahipati writes stomach, but the illustrations depicting this incident show the thread across Ravidas's chest in the Brahmin fashion). One wonders how the stories of Ravidas reached Ahmadnagar, hundreds of miles from Varanasi, and why the spelling was changed from Raidas or Ravidas to Rohidas. There is a* palkhi *in the name of Rohidas which goes from Alandi to Pandharpur in the Pandharpur pilgrimage, and Rohidas is ever more popular among the Chambhars (Hindi: Chamar) of Maharashtra.*

ROHIDAS THE SHOEMAKER

Obeisance to Shri Ganesh; Obeisance to Radha Krishna

A Humble Trade not Blameworthy

Listeners, give close attention. Rohidas was a Vaishnava of the highest type. He was accustomed to worship Hari with feelings of love. He had put aside every wrong desire. With reverence he sang the praise for Hari. He regularly bathed and then performed the worship of Vishnu.

Although he was entangled in domestic affairs he planned acts of benevolence. To any Vaishnava who came to his house he gave a pair of shoes. The occupation of a worker in leather appears to be a low one, but there is not the least fault to be found with it. If such a one performs acts of benevolence the Pervader of the Universe will certainly be attained. Carpenters and potters who perform their accustomed tasks do so without blame, and in doing acts of benevolence the Pervader of the Universe is attained by them. Weavers and fishermen in performing their usual tasks are without blame and in performing acts of benevolence the Pervader of the Universe will be attained through their devotion. Washermen and dyers in performing their tasks are without blame and in worshipping through acts of benevolence, while in the body, the purpose of life can be attained. If there is no hypocrisy in the performers of austerities, and the acts of the Brahmins, then on account of their benevolent acts the Husband of Rukmini will certainly show His favour to them. Well, enough of all these general statements. If I should describe the characteristics of the eighteen castes my story will increase too much in length. So let my hearers give attention.

Daily Life of Rohidas

Through acts of benevolence Rohidas served the servants of Vishnu. He used to repair the worn shoes of the pilgrims. Hari is more fond of benevolent *bhaktas* than He is of His own life. At the home of the benevolent the Life of the World abides day and night. Some preach to the people and demand their services but never oblige others by giving even a little water; such a person though a learned man is a fool and ignorant. Rohidas understood this and worshipped the servants of Vishnu with reverence, realizing that earthly things are illusory. He was accustomed to rise at dawn and to take breakfast before doing other things. He first performed his bath and then worshipped Vishnu. My listeners may think this is a wrong way of doing; but Rohidas thought that if he sat down to contemplate while hungry, his mind would not be undisturbed. In this *Kali Yuga*, life is made up of food, so wise men say. When two watches of the day have passed, the body becomes exhausted. If one is hungry when sitting down to contemplate, the mind will at once wander. Rohidas understood this, and therefore he first ate; just as when one is attacked by a thief, he should first abandon the money he has and run away; or in order that a person may not suffer injury from the possession of devils, the exorciser first makes an offering to them; or when digging for a treasure, lest ghosts should persecute him a man first offers an offering as a preventive; or that the *hawaldars* (village officials) may not swear at them, men give them bribes; and so Rohidas in the same way was accustomed to make first an offering of food to his life [i.e. to sustain himself]. Then he would hasten to his bath and worship God in private. Now it happened on a certain day that this *bhakta* of Vishnu was sitting performing his worship of God. He had withdrawn to be alone with the materials of worship, and he held his fickle mind in restraint. He brought a bottle of leather and placed it there filled with water. His mat and his sacred bag and casket were also made of leather.

Leather (or Skin) All Over Creation

Rohidas was sitting down with all his vessels made of leather. Just then a Brahmin came to his house to explain to him the Calendar. The Brahmin sat down by the holy and beautiful *tulsi* altar. Rohidas at once arose and with reverence made him a *namaskar*. The Brahmin said to Rohidas,

> You are worshipping God while sitting upon a leather seat. What do you expect from that? We Brahmins worship *Shaligram*, the idol of Vishnu. How is it you have placed Him in a leather bag? How is it you have placed in a leather bag Him who dwells in Vaikunth (heaven), the Life of the World, whom yogis contemplate? How is it you have placed Him in a leather bag? He who dwells upon the sea of milk, the Recliner upon Shesha, and who cannot be described adequately by the Shastras though you might search there for Him, you have made a leather bag and placed Him within it. Shri Rang (Vishnu) who cannot be attained by ceremonial acts, by bathing at sacred places, by austerities or by sacrifices, this Dweller in Vaikunth (heaven), Terminator of the earthly existence of His *bhaktas*, how is it you have enclosed Him in that leather bag?

Hearing what the Brahmin said, Rohidas replied,

> What object have you ever seen which has not leather connected with it? Musical instruments and drums are used in the praise-service of Hari. One has never seen any of them without their being connected with leather. The black cow has a leather skin, yet her milk is holy. And in the *Panchamrit* bath (in milk, curds, ghee, sugar, and honey), it is used in the bathing of the God. Animate things that are born, those hatched from eggs, and those produced from seed, all three are covered with skin and Atmaram (God) is in them alike. Shudras, Vaishyas, Kshatriyas, and Brahmins are covered with skin.

They make drums with skin, and play them with hands covered with skin. The tongue is covered with skin. A pleasing sound comes from them that is heard by the ear which is of skin. The tongue is covered with skin and repeats the Vedas. With hands covered with skin one eats food and drinks water. And from a leather shrine (the human body) Atmaram (God) speaks with His gentle voice.

The Brahmin now replied to Rohidas, 'You are talking philosophy, but while life is in the body, the body is never defiled.' To this Rohidas answered,

If the Pervader of the Universe, the Life of the World, is in a leather bag, how can you regard Him as defiled by the leather? You considered the body of one who is conceiving or bearing a child as defiling. What good object do you see in them? The skin might be filthy and yet the good god Atmaram may be in it. Krishna who is without a spot is alike in everything.

The Brahmin now replied, 'The emblem of Vishnu (*Shaligram*) is a holy pebble and so if a shoemaker worships Him, He is defiled thereby.' Hearing the Brahmin say this, Rohidas asked, 'Who should worship the *Shaligram*? Tell me, O *Swami*.' The Brahmin replied, 'You, hundred times a fool. We alone should worship the Lord of Vaikunth (heaven). Among the four races, we Brahmins are the highest. Shri Hari is chief among the gods. The Brahmins are the highest among the four races. They alone have the authority to invest themselves with the sacred thread and they alone can worship Vishnu.'

The Brahmin's Pride Humbled

Hearing this remark, Rohidas replied, 'O Swami, I will show you my sacred thread.' Then with his sharp tool he ripped open his stomach, and showed the sacred thread within it. The Brahmin then exclaimed,

'You are indeed a *bhakta* of Vishnu. I was thoughtless and persecuted you. Gold is cast into the furnace, and thereby its value is increased. In persecuting you, I have but advanced your glory. If sandalwood is rubbed on the flat stone, its full fragrance is at once known, so in persecuting you, I have but increased your glory. When iron comes in contact with a touchstone, it at once turns into gold, so in persecuting you, I have only increased your glory. Or as stone is shaped by a chisel and then the idol of God is firmly placed, so in persecuting you, I have done what I did ignorantly. You are a supreme *bhakta* of Vishnu. Worship the *Shaligram* at your pleasure.'

Thus speaking, the good Brahmin went back to his home.

18

Ravidas in the Contemporary World

CHANDRABHAN PRASAD
& MAHESH DAHIWALE

In contrast to the lack of a contemporary role for Chokhamela and the Tamil saints in Dalit activism, Ravidas is very much an participant in Dalit thought as well as institutions, as the following essay by Chandrabhan Prasad indicates. An unpublished article by Mahesh Dahiwale that follows, provides a very different but equally passionate view of the poet-saint of the medieval period, linking Raidas to the Buddhist tradition. It may be noted that James G. Lochtefeld's paper in this volume contains an analysis of Jignasu's Buddhist portrayal of Ravidas. Dahiwale is the founder of an e-mail Buddhist Circle. Hindi quotations have been omitted in this excerpt.

The first essay by the columnist Chandrabhan Prasad, who writes in The Daily Pioneer *published from Lucknow, appeared in the Sunday edition of that paper, 7 April 2003, and refers to an upcoming conference of Dalits in Vancouver, Canada, co-sponsored by the Ravidasi Sikhs of that city. It also refers to Mayawati as chief minister of Uttar Pradesh, an office she does not occupy at the time of the editing of this volume. Prasad is perhaps the only or one of few Dalits with a regular column in an English-language newspaper in India. Kashi is the classical name for Varanasi or Banaras.*

Kashi Secured, Now for the Atlantic

CHANDRABHAN PRASAD

'How could Maya do it without the cow belt having undergone a cultural revolution?' the ecstatic D. Shyam Babu, a new-age Dalit scholar, exclaimed. We were analysing the BSP (Bahujan Samaj Party) triumph in the UP Assembly elections recently and, sitting glued to the television, watching Brahmin/Rajput/Bania MLAs pay obeisance to Kanshi Ram, founder of the BSP, and Mayawati by falling at their feet.

'Shyam, the cow belt underwent a cultural revolution 500 years ago,' I told him. Shyam thought I was joking. I said, 'Don't you know that the Dalits disciplined cow belt Brahmins in the sixteenth century itself? Rajput kings and queens prostrated before an Untouchable at the time, and a religious order practising diversity adopted a Dalit voice in its main spiritual system 300 years ago.'

I explained further: 'The cultural revolution was led by Sant Ravidas, greatest of all saints. The revolution sprang up in Kashi, cradle of the varnashram order, headquarters of Hindu religiosity, and the seat of Brahmin learning.'

Ravidas was born in AD 1378 [*sic*] in Kashi, to prosperous Untouchable parents who traded in leather. Young Ravidas rebelled against his parents' desire to make the trade his career, and left home. He erected a thatched hut, and took up shoemaking for a living. He would bestow shoes on barefoot ascetics and give money to the needy. His teachings that all men are equal before God, and that God is accessible to all, captured the people's imagination. He built a small clay-walled temple and installed a leather idol of God. God thus, for the first time, stood liberated from a brahminical prison.

Kashi's Brahmins were enraged, and petitioned the king. 'Who perceives God better, and who knows the path to redemption' were to be decided. The king organized a *shastrartha* between the saint and select Kashi pandits.

Ravidas's genius found no match. The pandits turned pale, bending before the saint in recognition of his greatness. The saint rode the royal chariot through the lanes of Kashi, the king standing by his side. That was the Dalits' first war of independence. Kashi was secured. The cow belt Brahmins never recovered from the shock, and were forced to reconcile to the Dalits' cerebral superiority.

Queen Jhali Bai of Chittor was on a pilgrimage to Kashi and, hearing of the saint's glory, expressed a desire to visit him. The royal priests accompanying her resisted the move, but the indomitable queen went ahead.

The queen, spellbound by the saint's teachings, was able to feel the difference between the barren-minded pandits and the profound

Plate 18.1: Ravidas' portrait in the hostel dining room run by Sukhadeo Ranganath Waghmare of Pune, a devotee of Ravidas, as well as a builder and an educator. The complex of the hostel includes a clinic and a temple. Photograph by Eleanor Zelliot.

Plate 18.2: The Guru Ravidas temple in Govardhanpur village, behind Banaras Hindu University in Varanasi. Photo by Eleanor Zelliot.

Plate 18.3: Saint Ravidas. Images of Guru Ravidas in the R.K. Puram temple in New Delhi. Note the photograph of Dr. B.R. Ambedkar above the image which indicates an educational institution attached to the temple. Photograph by Eleanor Zelliot.

Ravidas. She was now a disciple of the saint. Back home in Chittor, her husband was furious. How could a Rajputana kingdom accept an Untouchable as its guru? But the maharani remained unfazed. She tried to reason with her husband, and presented him a few of the saint's hymns. But the king insisted on a test, and invited Ravidas to dinner at his grand palace. The Brahmin priests refused to dine with the saint, and sat separately. To the priests' disbelief, the people serving them food all turned into Ravidas. The bewildered priests repented and collapsed at Ravidas's feet, asking for forgiveness. The king declared Ravidas his guru.

That must certainly have been the first occasion when an Untouchable crossed over the walls of untouchability by dining with a royal family. Chittor, the cradle of Rajput dominance, had fallen. Ravidas stayed on longer, with Princess Meera Bai becoming his disciple.

The wonderful religion of the Sikhs would be incomplete without the saint's thoughts, as forty-one of Ravidas's hymns form the main body of the *Guru Granth Sahib.* This is the only instance where a Dalit voice forms part of the spirituality of a major religion. Punjab, like most of north/central/western India has flourished by living and following the thoughts and teachings of Ravidas, the first ever revolutionary.

Now his followers have settled across the Atlantic and are organizing a mega event in Vancouver in April 2003, which could unleash a diversity campaign in North America, requiring MNCs in India to honour the principle of diversity for the Dalits. While speaking of revolution in eighteenth century Europe, Frederick Engels wrote: 'Every struggle against feudalism at the time had to take on a religious disguise.' Sant Ravidas, while fighting the caste system, did exactly that in India.

Ravidas and Buddhism

MAHESH DAHIWALE

Raidas was one of the greatest figures of the saint movement in the medieval period. He along with Kabir, Namdev, Chokhamela, and Dadu formed the backbone of the medieval anti-caste movement. But unlike Kabir, who comes across as a radical and, revolutionary saint, Raidas is more often than not projected as a devout Ram-worshipping saint. This creates some reservations in the minds of progressive Dalits in accepting him as one of their icons. This image, projected by Brahminical writers, is an illusion, as we shall see.

Raidas belonged to the Chamar community which, like all Dalit communities, is Buddhist in origin. Contrary to popular belief, the term Chamar is not derived from *charm* (leather) but from the Pali word *chivar*, which means a *bhikkhu's* robes.

As opined by Buddhist scholars such as Jyotheedas, Anagarika Dharmapal, and Babasaheb Ambedkar, the Untouchables were Buddhist communities that continued to practise Buddhism after its decline and were, therefore, isolated as Untouchables by the anti-Buddhist Brahmins. Raidas, whose period is believed to be between 1450 and 1520, lived about 300 to 400 years after the decline of Buddhism in northern India. It is difficult to believe that he remained uninfluenced by the Buddhist thought that he had inherited from his community. Raidas's works and his life reflect a Buddhist influence. In fact, the miracles and myths associated with his life point to a Brahminical plot to incorporate him into the Vaishnava fold and to deny his Buddhist thought.

A look at his work also points to the frequent use of Buddhist terms and symbols. The well-known Hindi writer Hazari Prasad Dvivedi has noted the influence of Vajrayana Buddhism on Raidas.

Raidas's basic teachings are:

1. Equality of mankind, rejection of brahminical *varnashrama*
2. Equality of man and woman
3. Rejection of the authority of the Vedas
4. Rejection of rituals and bathing in sacred rivers
5. Emphasis on morality (*shila*)

All these teachings are very consistent with Buddhist thought and are anti-brahminical.

The essential features of Buddhism are equality, morality, universal love, meditation, dependent origination, impermanence, the erasing of the self, and the eight-fold path.

While searching for Buddhist concepts in Raidas's teachings, it should be remembered that by the twelfth-century Buddhism had been eroded in north India. Brahminism, with the help of Islam, had destroyed Buddhism by the twelfth century in northern India. Buddhists were made Untouchables with no right to read, and therefore with no right to preserve these traditions. Buddhism was also transformed in the

1800-1900 years following Gautama Buddha. Mahayana had transformed into Vajrayana, which changed to *Sahajyan*, which further gave rise to the *Siddhas* and then to the Nath sect. The medieval saints were products of the Nath sect, which was Buddhist in origin. The influence of *Sahajyan* and *Siddha* teachings and symbols are present in the teachings of Raidas. Words such as *man*, *chit*, *sahaj*, *sunya*, and *samadhi* are frequently used, which suggest Buddhist/*Sahajyan* influence.

Raidas refers to *sahaj* on numerous occasions. One term which he uses is *sahaj sunya*; the term *sunya*, the void, is like *sahaj*, one which has been important since the time of Vajrayana Buddhism. It is a symbol for the ultimate reality in both Buddhist and saint literature. When Raidas refers to *sahaj sunya*, he refers to a state of mental absorption. He often speaks about this state by using esoteric language, which demonstrates the origins of this concept in the yogic/Buddhist tradition.

19

Bhakti Voices on Untouchability

NAMMALVAR (*c.* 880–930)

Nammalvar is the most beloved of all the alvars. A Shudra with Brahmin disciples, he is said to have been a yogi from his birth. He composed a great number of hymns, varied in style and substance. He is one of a very few saints to merit an entire book of translations. See A.K. Ramanujan below:

The four castes
    uphold all clans;
go down, far down
    to the lowliest outcastes
        of outcastes:

if they are the intimate henchmen
    of our lord
        with the wheel in his right hand,
        his body dark as blue sapphire,

then even the slaves of their slaves
    are our masters.[1]

BASAVANNA (1106–1167)

The twelfth-century saint-poet from Karnataka was arguably the most radical of all bhakti poets in terms of caste. As Godwin Shiri writes,

'Basava's identification with Untouchables was unreserved and knew no bounds . . . we see how uncomfortable he was feeling within himself because of his own Brahmin roots. "I have had my birth in this obnoxious caste. . . . Is this my lot," he lamented. . . . In an eager bid to identify himself with Dalits and *Shivabhaktas* of Dalit origin, he claimed that he himself was born in a Dalit family. He declared that he was very proud and grateful to be part of the *Shivabhakta* cobbler Chennayya's family. . . . He claimed that cobbler Chennayya was his spiritual guru who had washed off his dirt—the taint of caste. . . . He declared that *Madivala* [washerman] Machaiah was a true embodiment of God himself. . . . "What if he knows the four Vedas? Without *Linga*, he is a low-born man. What if he is an outcaste? With *Linga* he is a holy place!""[2]

Basava himself still excites ideas of equality. A play by Girish Karnad, *Tale Danda* (1993) concerns the marriage of a Brahmin and an Untouchable under the care of Basava, and the terrible punishment that ensues. The Lingayats, however, who emerged from the movement, are not a reformist group. There are some of Basavanna's poems that have been translated into English that tell of his attitude toward caste. A fragment of one is:

> It is said:
> A man is born a Shudra;
> he becomes twice-born by his deeds;
> he becomes a scholar by his lore;
> he becomes a Brahmin who walks the Brahmin way.
>
> It is said:
> The man in whom there is no Brahman is low born.
> Therefore, O Lord of the Meeting River,
>
> I say:
> The Brahmin is the ass who carries the Veda as load.[3]

KALAVVE (*c.* TWELFTH CENTURY)

Kadire Kayakade Kalavve, a spinner, part of the Basavanna Virashaivite movement, wrote powerful anti-brahminical verse. Vijaya Ramaswamy[4] has translated one of these poems that is specifically about Madigas, one of the lowest of the Untouchable castes in Karnataka and Andhra. The poem criticizes Brahmins with, according to Ramaswamy, 'somewhat curious logic'. The Kannada source is Hiremath 1968: 217: 101:

Those who eat cock, fish and parrot
are regarded as high caste but
those Madigas who eat beef of that
cow whose milk is offered
by Brahmins to Siva,
why are they alone polluting?
The darbha grass Brahmins eat
is licked by dogs while the cow
Madigas eat is worshipped by Brahmins.
The Madiga is superior to the Brahmin.

JANABAI (FOURTEENTH CENTURY)

The servant of Namdev, Janabai, wrote an *abhanga* that is illustrated on large posters sold during pilgrimage time and which indicates Vithoba's love for all his disciples. Note that the Untouchable Chokhamela is described as being in Vithoba's heart:

My Vitthal has many children
with him is a merry crowd,
Nivritti rides on his shoulder
he holds Sopan by the hand,
Jnaneswar walks in front,
beautiful Muktabai close behind,
Gora the potter rides his hip,
Chokha in his very heart,
Banka clings to his waist,
Nama holds his smallest finger.

Jani says, O Gopala,
it is a festival of your dear ones.[5]

KANAKA (SIXTEENTH CENTURY)

The sixteenth-century Kanaka or Kanakadasa was low caste but not Untouchable. He wrote boldly of many matters, and the following song is about *kula*, which may be translated as family, community, or caste:

They talk of *kula*
times without number.

Pray, tell me
what is the *kula* of men
who have felt real bliss?

When a lotus is born in mire,
do they not bring it
and offer it to the Almighty?
Do not the gods of the earth
drink the milk
which comes from the flesh of the cow?

Do they not besmear
their bodies with deer musk?

What is the caste of God Narayana?
and Siva?
What is the caste of Atman:
and of Jiva?
Why talk of *kula*
when God has blessed you?[6]

KABIR (1440–1518)

Linda Hess has translated a song by Kabir which shows that the iconoclastic Kabir 'has proved a radical equality: not only of all people, but of all substances and interactions'.[7] The eighty-four hundred thousand vessels represent the traditional number of lives an individual must live before he or she can attain salvation. Maya is, of course, here 'illusion'.

Pandit, look in your heart for knowledge.
Tell me where untouchability
came from, since you believe in it.
Mix red juice, white juice and air—
a body bakes in a body.
As soon as the eight lotuses are ready, it comes
into the world. Then what's
untouchable?
Eighty-four hundred thousand vessels

decay into dust, while the potter
keeps slapping clay
on the wheel, and with a touch
cuts each one off.
We eat by touching, we wash
by touching, from a touch
the world was born.
So who's untouched? asks Kabir.
Only he
who has no taint of Maya.

EKNATH (1548–1600) AS A MAHAR

One of the most remarkable notes on the bhakti view of untouchability comes in the Brahmin Eknath's sixteenth-century *bharuds* (drama poems), written in the voice of a Mahar. The forty-seven *bharuds* spoken as a Mahar represent a greater number by far than those of any other of Eknath's voices, those of women, Muslims, wandering fortune-tellers, etc. Many of these simply use the Mahar duties as metaphors, as in: 'I sweep the four Vedas, I collect the rubbish of the six Shastras, I gather together all the Puranas, I bring this to the street of the Sants.' Others stress the common bhakti theme that anyone, even a Mahar, can achieve wisdom through bhakti. The Mahar, a scorned and feared village figure, can also deliver harsh bhakti messages about the end of life of those who do not take refuge in bhakti. In one complex and at times obscure *bharud*, Eknath gives the Mahar three stanzas which seem to protest his place in village life and to demand respect in remarkably vivid terms:

. . . don't give me that scornful sidelong glance!

I do more than my routine work.
I answer to anyone who comes or goes.
I guard the houses of all the villagers.
  Is this hard life such a small thing,
  O my masters?

I must get firewood for so many people.
It's me who supplies the bones and the horns.

I suffer the yoke of the dirtiest of work.
    Is all this such a small thing,
    O my masters?

My fate is tethering pegs, hobbles, feed bags.
Soul weary in this forced labour,
I roam eighty-four hundred thousand villages.
    Is this sorrow such a small thing,
    O my masters?[8]

TUKARAM (1598–1649)

Tukaram, the most beloved saint-poet of Maharashtra, wrote hundreds of *abhangas*, many of which were anti-orthodoxy and anti-caste. The following excerpt from #4299 in the Government of Maharashtra's collection of Tukaram's *Gatha* has been translated by Bharat Patankar and Gail Omvedt:

Who is purified by pride of *varna*?
Tell me if you know!
Untouchables are saved by hymns to Hari,
legendary stories become their bards.
Tuladhar Vaishya, the potmaker Gora,
the leatherworker Rohidas,
the Momin Kabir, Latif the Muslim,
the barber Sena are Vishnudasis.
Kanhopatra, Khodu, cotton-carder Dadu
sing hymns to Hari without discord.
Banka, Chokhamela, by caste Mahar,
have united with the Lord.
What is the worth of Nama's Jani
when Pandhari's lord eats in her company?
Can you tell the lineage of Mairala?
What greatness did he have, do tell!
Vishnu's servants have no caste,
the Veda's science so decrees.
Tuka says, which of your books
have saved the fallen? I know of none.

THE CHANDALA'S SONG

In an article entitled 'The Candala's Song',[9] Guy Welbon describes a temple festival drama in Tirukkurungudi, Tamil Nadu. The Sanskrit text which is at the core of that festival involves a Chandala devotee of Vishnu who is assaulted by a demon (a Brahmin in an earlier birth) while on his way to sing before the image of Vishnu. He is released to sing his song on the promise of returning to the demon and offering to him the merit of that praise to Vishnu. In the end, both demon and Untouchable are assured of rebirth as Brahmins. Devadasis perform the roles of the Chandala and of Vishnu. A non-Brahmin plays the leading role, that of the *rakshasa*, the demon. The story is found in the *Kasika Purana*. Much stress in the drama is on the Vaishnava Chandala's keeping his word, and the Untouchable singer becomes a Brahmin 'because of faultless action'.

There is no current Tamil caste named Chandala, which is the earliest term we know for those considered to be Untouchable, a term much used in the *Manusmriti*. There seems to be no connection between the tale of the devout singer and the ability of Untouchables to enter the temple. And there seems to be no overt moral that 'even a Chandala can be devout'. The steadfastness of the *bhakta* of Vishnu, whoever he is, seems to be the point, but it is interesting that the steadfast one is an Untouchable.

NOTES

1. *Hymns for the Drowning: Poems for Visnu by Nammalvar*, translated from the Tamil by A.K. Ramanujan, Princeton: Princeton University Press, 1981, p. 61.
2. 'Basava, Casteism and Untouchables', by Godwin Shiri, in *Religion and Society*, vol. XXXIX, nos. 2 and 3, June–Sept. 1992, pp. 20–1.
3. *The Lord of the Meeting Rivers: Devotional Poems of Basavanna*, translated by K.V. Zvelebil, New Delhi: Motilal Banarsidass, 1984, p. 90.
4. Vijaya Ramaswamy, *Divinity and Deviance: Women in Virasaivism*, New Delhi: Oxford University Press, 1966, p. 56.
5. Translated by Sarah Sellegren and S.G. Tulpule in 'Janabai and Kanhopatra: A Study of Two Women Saints', in *Images of Women in Maharashtrian Literature and Religion*, edited by Anne Feldhaus, Albany: State University of New York Press, 1996, p. 218.
6. M. Sivaramkrishna and Sumita Roy, *Poet Saints of India*, New Delhi: Sterling Paperbacks, 1998, p. 184.
7. *The Bijak of Kabir*, translated by Linda Hess and Sukhdev Singh, San Francisco: North Point Press, 1983, p. 18. The poem appears on pp. 17 and 55.

8. From *bharud* 3892 in the *Srisakalsantgatha*, adapted from Eleanor Zelliot's article, 'Eknath's Bharuds: The Sant as Link between Cultures', in *The Sants: Studies in a Devotional Tradition of India*, edited by Karine Schomer and W.H. McLeod, Berkeley: Religious Studies Series, New Delhi: Motilal Banarsidass, 1987, pp. 91–110.
9. *Religious Festivals in South India and Sri Lanka*, edited by Guy Welbon and Glenn E. Yocum, New Delhi: Manohar, 1982, pp. 77–100.

Glossary

(Tamil words are indicated by Tam.; all other words are Marathi or Hindi or both, based on Sanskrit.)

abhanga (abhaṅga)—literally unbroken. A poetic form used by the Marathi saint-poets.

acharya (āchārya)—leader or teacher, the term the Shaiva Siddhanta and Shrivaishna philosophical schools use to designate their gurus.

Adi Granth (Ādigranth)—literally, original or first book. The sacred writings of the Sikh religion. Poems of Ravidas are included.

advaita vedanta (advaita vedānta)—literally non-dualism; end of the Vedas. The philosophy expounded by Shankaracharya (788-820), now the dominant Brahminical school.

agama (āgama)—a text or manual in Sanskrit giving instructions and philosophical meanings for the performance of rituals to Shiva. There are traditionally 28 agamas in the Shaiva Siddhanta philosophical school of the medieval period.

ajapajap/jap (ajapajap/jap)—the technique of silent or internal meditation upon God.

alvar (āḻvar, Tam.)—literally 'one who is drowning.' Used for the twelve poet-saints whose poems in praise of Vishnu form the *Nalayira Tiviya Pirapantam.*

Amar Citra Kathā.—literally immortal picture story. A very popular comic book series on gods and goddesses and epic and Puranic heroes and heroines.

amrita (amṛta)—literally nectar, i.e. the nectar of immortality.

anahat nad (anāhat nād)—the 'unstruck sound' heard at the highest stages of meditation.

Anantadas (Ānantadās)—sixteenth-century author of the *Raidas Parchai* and 'introductions' to other bhakti saints. His work exists only in manuscript form.

apana (apāna)—the air of the lower part of the bodily trunk.

ashram (āśrama)—traditionally the four stages of a twice-born Hindu's life; also a retreat or center of a religious community.

atman (ātman)—the individual soul whose nature is Brahman according to Vedantic philosophy.

avatar (avatār)—an incarnation or manifestation. Krishna and Rama are two of the ten avatars of Vishnu.

bani (bāni)—speech.

Bhadve (Bhadve)—the priests of the Vithoba temple in Pandharpur, usually not members of the Varkari panth (q.v.).

Basava, Basavanna (Basavaṇṇa) (1106-67)—poet, saint, and founder of the sect which became the Lingayats, q.v.

bhagat (bhagat)—a devotee, used in Hindi bhakti.

bhajan (bhajan)—a devotional singing session using the hymns of the saint-poets.

bhakta (bhakta)—a devotee, one who follows the bhakti marg or way.

bhakti (bhakti)—devotion. From Sanskrit bhaj, to share, partake, participate.

Brahmin (Brāhmaṇ)—a member of the priestly class, not to be confused with brahman—the world spirit.

cankam (caṅkam, Tam.)—academy or community. Tradition says there were three successive ancient academies of Tamil poets.

cannati (cannati, Tam. from sannidhi, Sanskrit)—a place where the divine presence is perceived.

Cekkilar (Cēkkilar, Tam.)—the author of the *Periya Puranam* hagiography of the 63 Shaivite Tamil saints. He was probably a minister to the twelfth-century Chola king Kulottunga II. Sometimes spelled Sekkizhaar.

Chamar (Camār)—the largest Untouchable caste, spread throughout the north in many divisions, whose traditional duty is work with leather. Chambhar (Cambhār) in Marathi.

Chandala (Caṇḍāla)—a word used for burning ground attendants and other low workers in Sanskrit texts, synonym for Untouchable.

chit (cit)—pure consciousness in the Samkhya philosophical system.

chitta (citta)—mind or the sense faculties.

Chola (Cōḻa, Tam.)—an imperial dynasty in the Tamil lands rising to prominence about 870 CE.

darshan (darśan)—a sight of a God or a saintly being.

dharma (dharma)—duty, law, righteousness, code of conduct, religion.

dindi (dinḍi)—a group of devotees usually from one caste or village who are part of a larger *palkhi* going to Pandharpur on pilgrimage.

Divya Suri Caritam (Divyasūricaritam)—The Sacred Life, title of a Sanskrit biography of the alvars and early acharyas written between the twelfth and early fifteenth centuries CE.

ekadashi (ekādaśī)—the eleventh day of either the dark or the light fortnight of the lunar month.

gopi (gopī)—a female cow herder.

himsa (himsā)—harm, violence.

Indra (Indra)—king of the gods in Hindu mythology, not a subject for devotion but an actor in the legends of saints' lives.

jiv (jīv)—the individual life, life force in general, soul.

jnana (jñāna)—knowledge.

kirtan (kīrtan)—a sermon interspersed with devotional singing, also congregational singing. A kirtankar is an acknowledge leader of the kirtan.

kulam (kulam, Tam.)—family, community. In the discussion of Untouchable saints, the term takes on overtones of caste. Nandanar was of the Pulai kulam, a community of agricultural and leather workers; Tiruppan Alvar was a member of the Panar music community.

Lingayat (Liṅgāyat)—members of the bhakti cult begun by Basavanna in the twelfth century, chiefly in Karnataka, now similar to a caste. Also known as Virshaiva (Virasaiva).

madhura (madhura)—romantic love. Madhura bhakti is a form of bhakti in which the individual soul and God are lovers.

Mahar (Mahār)—the largest Untouchable caste in Maharashtra with duties as servants of the village.

Mahipati (Mahīpati) (1715–90)—Brahman biographer of the saints in Maharashtra and the Hindi speaking north. He was a devout bhakta and kirtankar, the author of three collections of legends.

malam (mala) Skt.; malam Tam.)—dirt or fault, with specific philosophical meanings. Tiruppan alvar describes Vishnu as vimalan, the prefix of ni negating the meaning and indicating one free of fault.

man unmani (man unmani)—the destruction of the mind, i.e. the final state in the Hatha-yoga system.

Manam (Manas, Skt.; Manam, Tam.)—mind or heart. The poems of the Nayanar frequently describe Shiva as 'in my mind/heart'.

Manipravala (Maṇipravala, Tam.)—a hybrid language made up of Tamil and Sanskrit, literally meaning jewels and coral.

mat (mat)—idea, opinion; sant mat refers to the teachings of the Sants.

mai-bap (māybāp)—literally mother-father, used for a superior authority. A traditional Mahar greeting for god or higher castes.

maya (māyā)—cosmic illusion.

muvar (muvar, Tam.)—the three, used to denote the three most famous Tamil Shaiva bhakti authors, Campantrar, Appar and Cuntarar.

Nābhadas (Nabhadās)—the first Hindi (or Braj Bhasa) biographer of Ravidas and the author of 200 biographies or portraints of saints in the *Bhaktamal*—the garland of bhaktas.

nam-smaran (nāmasmaraṅ)—the worship of God with either a chanting or a silent repetition of the name of God.

Nandanar (Nantanar, Tam.)—probably the only Untouchable saint among the sixty-three saints, worshippers of Shiva called the Nayanars. His story is told in the Periya Puranam, where he is called Tirunalaippovar, 'the holy one who will go tomorrow', an allusion to his long put off desire to see Shiva at Chidambaram. There is no record of his songs but his legend is important, especially in the nineteenth and twentieth centuries.

Nayanar (Nāyaṉar)—the sixty-three canonized saints who worshipped Shiva.

nirgun (nirguṇa)—literally 'without attributes', used for the formless

indescribable divine. Nirguna saints are those who do not worship a specific form of God.
pad (pad)—a poetic measure or verse, used in the Hindi tradition.
palkhi (pālkhi)—the palanquin carrying silver representations of the saint-poet's footprints.
Pandharpur (Paṇḍharpūr)—a town in south-east Maharashtra whose Vithoba temple is the center of the varkari panth.
panth (paṁth)—religious movement or order, as in varkari panth or the Sikh panth.
paramatman (paramātman)—the supreme Soul.
parampara (paramparā)—a spiritual lineage or tradition.
patikam (patikam, Tam.)—a group of verses, usually ten or eleven, in the Shaiva bhakti hymns.
Periya Puranam (Pĕriya Purāṇam, Tam.)—a hagiography in Tamil about the Nayanar, attributed to Cekkilar.
prakruti (prakṛti)—usually translated as 'nature'. See purusha.
prana (prāṇa)—breath. pranayam (pranayam) is breath control.
Priyadas (Priyadās)—eighteenth-century author of the Bhaktirasabodhini (knowledge of the essence of bhakti), containing stories of the Hindi speaking bhaktas.
puja (pūjā)—worship involving ritual acts, prayer.
Puranas (Purāṇas)—literally meaning old; the later sacred texts in Sanskrit, many containing stories of Gods and kings.
purusha (puruṣa)—the masculine spiritual substance which, alone with the feminine prakruti (q.v.) is the organizing principle of the world.
Rai Das Parcai (Rai Dās Parcaī) Introduction to Rai Das, composed late sixteenth by Anantadas.
Ramananda (Rāmānanda)—a fifteenth-century saint-reformer, traditionally a spiritual descendant of the great philosopher Ramanuja and also traditionally the guru of Kabir and Ravidas.
sadguru (sadguru)—the true guru, the Divine.
sadhana (sādhanā)—religious or spiritual discipline.
sadhu (sādhu)—a holy man, usually a wandering mendicant.
sagun (saguṇa)—literally 'with attributes' used for a God who can be described, given qualities such as loving or rewarding, or attributes such as three faces, four arms, weapons, etc.
sahib (sāhib)—lord, either divine or human.
sakhya (sakhya)—love based on friendship.
sampradaya (saṁpradāya)—a sect, a panth (q.v.), a tradition.
sant (saṅt)—an ascetic, a holy person, a devotee, usually used for 'saints' in the Hindi tradition.
Sesha (Śeṣa, Tam.)—servant, slave, 'owned by the Lord', the word Shrivaishnavas use to describe the alvar bhaktas.
shabda (śabda)—literally word. In the Sant movement it refers to the guru's word which leads to divine revelation.
Shaiva Siddhanta (Śaiva Śiddhānta)—the end or culmination of knowledge of Shiva, a philosophical school which, in the medieval period (*c.* tenth-

fourteenth centuries) became increasingly predominant in Tamil country. In the fourteenth century philosophers began to write their texts, known as Shastras, in Tamil.

Shrivaishnava (Śrīvaiṣṇava)—a religious and philosophical school in Tamil Nadu, originating in medieval times, whose members wrote or collected commentaries on the poetry of the Vaishnava bhaktas. The theology of the Shrivaishnavas is drawn on the work of Ramanuja.

Shudra (Sūdra)—the lowest of the four varnas; traditionally, those who served the three higher varnas of 'Brahmin, Kshatriya and Vaishya'. In the South and to a lesser extent in Maharashtra, all non-Brahmans are considered to be Shudras or a group below Shudras, those without varna or Untouchables.

swarup (svarup)—one's own form, natural and real figure.

Tamil (Tamil)—the name of the mother tongue spoken in the south-east area of India now called Tamil Nadu, the land of Tamil. The Tamil language is part of the Dravidian group which includes Malayalam, Kannada and Telugu and is held to be the oldest vernacular (as opposed to the literary language of Sanskrit) in India.

Tiru (Tiru, Tam.)—a prefix meaning holy or sacred, comparable to the Sanskrit prefix ṣhri (sri).

Tiruppan alvar (Tiruppān āḻvār, Tam.)—The name means 'the Vaishnava saint who belongs to the panar caste. He composed the Amal-anatipiran which is included in the Nalayira Tiviya Pirapantam. Pan is an ancient Tamil system of music and the panan or panar were an ancient class of Tamil bards or minstrels.

Tontar (Tontar, Tam.)—slave or servant, often used in reference to the bhaktas of Shiva.

Varkari (Vārkari)—a pilgrim to Pandharpur, a member of the Varkari panth centered on the worship of Vithoba.

varna (varṇa), literally color, covering. The classical varnashramadharma contains four castes or classes, Brahmin, Kshatriya, Vaishya, Shudra. Untouchables are sometimes referred to as avarna, without varna.

vatsalya (valsalya)—parental love.

viraha (viraha)—separation from one's beloved. Viraha bhakti describes the bhaktas longing for union with God.

watan (vatan)—a piece of land given to Mahar families who were official village servants.

yal (yal, Tam.)—an ancient Tamil stringed instrument, comparable to a lute or a vina; Tiruppan alvar played this instrument.

Contributors

ANANTADAS was a sixteenth century bhakta who claimed to be in a line of spiritual descent from Ramananda. His *Kabir Parachai* is the oldest collection of legends about that important saint. His account of the cobbler Ravidas is dated to 1588, and in his version Ravidas was a Brahmin in a previous life.

MAHESH DAHIWALE, who hails from Maharashtra, is a graduate in Electronic Engineering from Mumbai University. While working as a Section Officer in the Ministry of Commerce in New Delhi, he coordinated a website for the 'Buddhist Circle'. He is now centered in Pune, working with *Lokamitra* in the Buddhist organization Jambudvipa.

STEVEN P. HOPKINS teaches in the Religion Department at Swarthmore College in Swarthmore, Pennsylvania. He is the author of *Singing the Body of God: The Hymns of Vedantadesika in Their South Indian Tradition* (New Delhi: Oxford University Press, 2002) and with John B. Carman he has co-edited *Tracing Common Themes: Comparative Courses in the Study of Religion* (Atlanta: Scholars Press, 1991). He has contributed to *Bibliography: Love in India*, and has presented papers at the Association for Asian Studies (AAS) and the American Association of Religion meetings on the theme of devotional tradition.

JAMES G. LOCHTEFELD teaches in the Department of Religion, Carthage College in Kenosha, Wisconsin and is active in the Asia Network programmes. A graduate of Harvard Divinity School, the University of Washington, and Columbia University, his research and writing centres on the interaction and interrelationships between texts, tradition, and modern Hindu life. His recent visits to India have involved the study of pilgrimage. He is the author of the two-volume set, *The Illustrated Encyclopedia of Hinduism* (New York: Rosen Publishing, 2001, 2002).

MAHIPATI (1715-1790) was the most prominent of all the Marathi hagiographers. He lived near Ahmednagar and devoted his life to performing *kirtanas* on the lives of the saints. He produced four volumes of the lives of the saints, both those in Maharashtra and some in the Hindi North.

V.L. MANJUL retired as Head Librarian, Bhandarkar Oriental Institute, Pune, but continues to write and to aid a great many researchers in Pune. He is co-editor of a collection of articles about the poet-saint Chokhamela. Manjul is also a collector and cataloguer of Marathi-language manuscripts related to religion, especially bhakti.

ROHINI MOKASHI-PUNEKAR teaches at the Department of Humanities and Social Sciences, Indian Institute of Technology, Guwahati, Assam. She has earlier taught at St. Xavier's College, Ahmedabad. Educated at the Universities of Mysore and Gujarat, she worked on contemporary British fiction for her Ph.D. Her areas of research include bhakti literature as well as postcolonial and cultural studies, fields in which she has published several papers. Her book of translations of Chokhamela's poems, *On the Threshold: Songs of Chokhamela*, was published in 2002 by The Book Review Literary Trust, New Delhi which was republished with additional translations, as a world edition by the International Sacred Literature Trust in cooperation with the Alta Mira Press, London and New York. She also reviews for *The Book Review*, New Delhi and previously before it shut office, for *The Indian Review of Books*, Chennai.

ANNE MURPHY is a Ph.D. candidate in South Asia religions at Columbia University, New York. Her dissertation will address historical representation, material and textual, in the Sikh tradition. She is interested in material forms of history, specifically objects and sacred sites related primarily to the Gurus, and how these work as evidence in history, including the increased importance of the sites in the nineteenth century under the British. She works mainly in Hindi, Punjabi, and Urdu and has added Persian in the summer of 2003. She has translated the Ravidas poems in this volume specifically for this publication.

VASUDHA NARAYANAN is a Professor of Religion at the University of Florida and was President of the American Academy of Religion (2001–2). Educated at the Universities of Madras and Bombay and Harvard University, she has written five books and over seventy articles. Among her books relating to bhakti are *The Way and the Goal: Expressions of Devotion in the Early Srivaisnava Tradition* (Cambridge, Mass.: Center for the Study of World Religions, Harvard University, 1987); *The Tamil Veda: Pillan's Interpretation of the Tiruvaymoli* (with John Carman) (Chicago: University of Chicago, 1989); and *The Vernacular Veda: Revelation, Recitation and Ritual* (Columbia, SC: University of South Carolina Press, 1994). She is now working on a study of Hindu traditions in the United States.

CHANDRABHAN PRASAD comes from a middle class Dalit family in an eastern Uttar Pradesh village. He has an MA in International Politics and an M.Phil. on China's Technology Acquisition from Jawaharlal Nehru University. He is now a columnist for the English daily *Pioneer*, the only Dalit columnist in a major English newspaper. In an interview he said, 'I believe in Ambedkarism, Dalits' intelligence, democracy, science and the Indian State. Call these my gods and goddesses.'

KAREN PECHILIS PRENTISS analyses the story of Nandanar in her book *The Embodiment of Bhakti*, New York: Oxford University Press, 1999. One of the original panel members at the Association of Asian Studies, she began the same year to teach at the Religion Department, Drew University. She has recently been appointed the NEH Distinguished Teaching Professor and Director of the Humanities at Drew University. She received a Fulbright fellowship in 2002–3 to pursue her study 'Karaikkal Ammaiyar: The Three Lives of a Woman Saint'. The article and translation in this volume have been edited from her early work by Rohini Mokashi-Punekar.

ANIL SAPKAL teaches Marathi at Fergusson College, Pune. His Ph.D. is from the University of Pune. Under the name of Kumar Anil, Sapkal is active in the field of mass communication. He is associated with Dalit theatre, and has written scripts for Marathi films, including *Gabhara*, and is also a creative writer for both adults and children. A video film on Shantabai Dani, entitled simply *Shantabai*, commemorates that late well-known Dalit educator, and has been prepared for public use in English, Marathi, and Hindi.

JOSEPH SCHALLER teaches at Nazareth College in Rochester, Pennsylvania and has also taught at the University of California, Berkeley and at Carleton College. A Ph.D. from the University of California at Berkeley, his dissertation is on the poet Ravidas. A participant in the original panel on Untouchable Saints, he published his first article on Ravidas in a volume edited by David Lorenzen, *Bhakti Religion in North India: Community, Identity and Political Action* (Albany: State University of New York Press, 1995).

LYNN VINCENTNATHAN teaches in the Anthropology Department, University of Texas-Pan American. Her Ph.D. is from the University of Wisconsin, Madison on 'Harijan Subculture and Self-Esteem Management in a South Indian Community'. She has published on both Harijan subcultures and Untouchable concepts of personhood and society. She has also done a study with S. George Vincentnathan on attitudes toward the aged in three Untouchable communities.

ELEANOR ZELLIOT has studied the Ambedkar movement in all its historical, social, and cultural facets, and also works in the field of medieval bhakti. She has written some eighty articles on these subjects, some of which are gathered in *From Untouchable to Dalit: Essays on the Ambedkar Movement* (New Delhi: Manohar, 1992, 3rd edn. 2001). She has also written introductions for Vasant Moon's *Growing Up Untouchable*, translated by Gail Omvedt (Lanham, Maryland: Rowman & Littlefield, 2001), and Detlef Kantowsky's *Buddhists in India Today*, translated by Hans-Georg Tuerstig (New Delhi: Manohar, 2003). She retired from the History Department of Carleton College in 1997.

Bibliography

Sanskrit

Divyasuricaritam, edited by T.A. Sampath Kumaracharya and K.K.A. Venkatachari, with a Hindi translation by Pandit Madhavacharya, Bombay: Ananthacharya Research Institute, Series 2, 1978.

Tamil/Manipravala

Alvarkal Vaipavam, edited by R. Kannan Swami, Madras, 1987.

Cekkilar Cuvamikal Ennum Arunmolithevar Aruliya Tiruttontar Puranam, vol. 2, edited by C.K. Cuppiramaniya Mataliyar, Coimbatore: Kovait Tamil Cankam, 1968.

Kuruparamparaprapavam, Tenkalai, edited by S. Kirusnaswami Ayyankar, Tirucchi, 1968.

Munivahanapokam, Madras: Independent Esoteric Treatises, 1974.

Nalayire Tivya Prapantam, edited and commented by K.P.B. Annankaracharya, Madras: V.N. Devnathan, 1971.

Periya Tirumutiyataivu, edited by S. Kirusnaswami Ayyankar, included in the Tenkalai edition of *Kuruparamparaprapavam*, edited by S. Kirusnaswami Ayyankar, Tirucchi, 1968.

Periya Puranam: Ilakkia Chorpozhivu, edited by Kandaswamy Kavirayar, M.R. Vidwan, Madurai: Parvathi Pathippaham, 1978.

Marathi

Chokhamela yancha Abhanga Gatha, Bombay: Balkrishna Lakshman Pathak, 1950.

Kadam, S.B., *Shri Sant Chokhamela: Charitra ani Abhang*, Mumbai: Shabdalay Prakashan, 1969, reprinted in 1998 by Balchandra Nemade.

Sant Cokhamela Vividh Darshan, edited by Eleanor Zelliot and V.L. Manjul, Pune: Sugawa Prakashan, 2002. Includes the original Marathi versions of Sapkal, 'Marathi Natak va Citrapath', and Manjul, 'Pandharpuraca Vitalnara Dev Ghagarit Sathvila'.

Srisakalsantgatha, vol. I. Collected by Srinanamaharaj Sakhre, edited by Kashinath Anant Joshi, Pune: Srisantwangmaya Prakashan Mandir, 1967 (1923).

Hindi

Anantdas, *Raidas Parchai*, unpublished manuscript.

Chaturvedi, P., *Uttari Bharat ki Sant Parampara*, Allahabad: Leader Press, 1951.

Bahura, G.N. and K. Bryant, *Pada Suradasa Ji Ki*, Jaipur: Maharaja Sawai Man Singh II Museum, 1982.

Jijnasu, C., *Sant Pravar Raidas Saheb*, Lucknow: Bahujana Kalyan Prakashan, 1956.

Nabhadas, *Sribhaktamal*, with commentary in poetry by Priyadas and in prose by Roop Kala, Lucknow: Tejkumar Press, 1964.

Singh, P.G., *Sant Ravidas, Vicarak aur Kavi*, Jullundur: Nav Chintan Prakashan, 1977.

English

According to Tradition: Hagiographical Writing in India, edited by Winand Callewaert and Rupert Snell, Wiesbaden: Harrassowitz Verlag, 1994.

Adi Granth, or the Holy Scriptures of the Sikhs, translated by Ernest Trumpp, London: W.H. Allen, 1877.

Adi Granth: Selections from the Sacred Writings of the Sikhs, translated by Trilochan Singh et al., London: G. Allen & Unwin, 1960.

Arunachalam, M., *Harijan Saints of Tamilnadu*, Tiruchitrambalam, 1977.

Bhakti Religion in North India: Community Identity and Political Action, edited by David N. Lorenzen, Albany: State University of New York Press, 1995.

Bhakti Studies, edited by G.M. Bailey and I. Kesarcodi-Watson, Bangalore: Sterling Publishers, 1992.

Callewaert, Winand M., *The Sarvagi of Gopaldas: A 17th Century Anthology of Bhakti Literature*, New Delhi: Manohar, 1993.

——, *The Hagiographies of Anantadas*, London: Curzon, 2000.

Callewaert, Winand M. and Peter G. Friedlander, *The Life and Works of Raidas*, New Delhi: Manohar, 1992.

Cutler, Norman J., *Songs of Experience: The Poetics of Tamil Devotion*, Bloomington: Indiana University Press, 1987.

Darshan Singh, *A Study of Bhakta Ravidasa*, Patiala: Publication Bureau, Punjabi University, Foreword by L.M. Joshi, 1981.

Dass, Nirmal, *Songs of the Saints from the Adi Granth*, Albany: State University of New York Press, 2000.

Dehejia, Vidya, *Slaves of the Lord: The Path of the Tamil Saints*, New Delhi: Munshiram Manoharlal, 1988.

Deleury, G.A., *The Cult of Vithoba*, Pune: Deccan College Postgraduate and Research Institute, 1960.

Dumont, Louis, *Homo Hierarchicus*, translated by Mark Sainsbury, Chicago: University of Chicago Press, 1970.

Fuller, C.J., *The Camphor Flame: Popular Hinduism and Society in India*, Princeton: Princeton University Press, 1992.

Gnanambal, K., 'Srivaishnavas and their Religious Institutions', in *Bulletin of the Anthropological Survey of India*, vol. 20, no. 3, 1971.

Gokhale-Turner, Jayashree B., 'Bhakti or Vidroha: Continuity and Change in Dalit Sahitya', in *Tradition and Modernity in Bhakti Movements*, Leiden: E.J. Brill, 1981.

The Golden Anthology of Ancient Tamil Literature, 3 vols., translated by Nalladai R. Balakrishna Mudaliyar, Tinnevelly: South India Shaiva Siddhanta Works Publishing Society, 1959–60.

Govindachari, Alkondaville, *Life of Ramanuja*, Madras, 1906.

Hardy, Friedhelm, *Viraha Bhakti: The Early History of Krishna Devotion in South India*, London: Oxford University Press, 1983.

——, 'Tiruppan-Alvar: The Untouchable Who Rode Piggy-Back on the Brahmin', in *Devotion Divine: Bhakti Traditions from the Regions of India: Studies in Honour of Charlotte Vaudeville*, edited by Diana L. Eck and Francoise Mallison, Groningen: Egbert Forsten, and Paris: Ecole Francaise d'Extreme-Orient, 1991.

——, *The Religious Culture of India: Power, Love and Wisdom*, Cambridge Studies in Religious Tradition, 1994.

Hart, George L. III, *The Poems of Ancient Tamil: Their Milieu and their Sanskrit Counterparts*, Berkeley, California: University of California Press, 1975.

Hawley, John Stratton, and Mark Juergensmeyer, *Songs of the Saints of India*, New York: Oxford University Press, 1988. Text and Notes by Hawley, translations by Hawley and Juergensmeyer.

Hopkins, Steven P., 'In Love with the Body of God: Eros and the Praise of Icons in South Indian Devotion', *Journal of Vaisnava Studies*, vol. 2, no. 1, 1993, pp. 17–54.

Kabir, *The Bijak of Kabir*, translated by Linda Hess and Sukhdev Singh, San Francisco: North Point Press, 1983.

Karnad, Girish, *Tale-Danda* (Death by Beheading), translated from the Kannada by the author, Delhi: Ravi Dayal, 1993.

Karve, Irawati, 'On the Road: A Maharashtrian Pilgrimage', in *The Experience of Hinduism*, edited by Eleanor Zelliot and Maxine Berntsen, Albany: State University of New York Press, 1988.

Khare, R.S., *The Untouchable as Himself: Ideology, Identity, and Pragmatism among the Lucknow Chamars*, Cambridge: Cambridge University Press, 1984.

Kincaid, C.A., *Tales of the Saints of Pandharpur*, Bombay: Oxford University Press, 1919.

Lakshamma, G., *The Impact of Ramanuja's Teaching on Life and Conditions in Society*, Delhi: Sundeep Prakashan, 1990.

Lochtefeld, James G., 'The Saintly Camar: Perspectives on the Life of Ravidas', *ARC, the Journal of the Faculty of Religious Studies*, McGill University, vol. 26, 1998, pp. 63–82.

Lorenzen, David, *Kabir Legends and Ananta-Das's Kabir Parachai*, Albany: State University of New York Press, 1991.

Lutgendorf, Philip, 'Medieval Devotional Traditions: An Annotated Survey of Recent Scholarship', in *The Study of Hinduism*, edited by Arvind Sharma, Columbia: University of South Carolina Press, 2003.

Manickam, Sundararaj, *Nandanar, the Dalit Martyr: A Historical Reconstruction of His Times*, Madras: Christian Literature Society, 1990.

Mahipati, *Stories of Indian Saints*, translated by Justin E. Abbott and N.B. Godbole, 2 vols., nos. 9 and 10, in The Poet Saints of Maharashtra Series, Poona, 1933, 1934. Reprinted in one volume by Motilal Banarsidass, Delhi, in 1982.

Mate, M.S., *Temples and Legends of Maharashtra*, Bombay: Bharatiya Vidya Bhavan, 1962. See 'Pandharpur', pp. 188–219.

Medieval Bhakti Movements in India: Sri Caitanya Quincentenary Commemoration Volume, edited by N.N. Bhattacharyya, New Delhi: Munshiram Manoharlal, 1989.

Moffat, Michael, *An Untouchable Community in South India: Structure and Consensus*, Englewood Cliffs: Prentice Hall, 1979.

Mokashi-Punekar, Rohini, *On the Threshold: Songs of Chokhamela*, New Delhi: Book Review Literary Trust, 2002. Republished with additional translations in April 2005 by the Alta Mira Press in cooperation with the International Sacred Literature Trust, UK, USA and Canada.

Narayanan, Vasudha, *The Vernacular Veda: Revelation, Recitation and Ritual*, Columbia, SC: University of South Carolina Press, 1994. See especially Chapter 5.

Nilakanta Sastri, K.A. and G. Srinivaschari, *Advanced History of India*, Bombay: Allied Publishers, 1970.

Pai, Anant, ed., 'Guru Ravidas', Amar Chitra Katha Series, no. 350, Bombay: IBH Publisher Pvt. Ltd., 1988.

Parthasarathy, Indira, *Legend of Nandan (Nandan Kathai)*, translated from the Tamil by C.T. Indra, New Delhi: Oxford University Press, 2003. Originally published in 1978.

Peterson, Indira Viswanath, *Poems to Siva: The Hymns of the Tamil Saints*, Princeton: Princeton University Press, 1989.

Poet-Saints of India, edited by M. Sivaramkrishna and Sumita Roy, New Delhi: Sterling Paperbacks, 1996, rpt. 1998.

Prentiss, Karen Pechilis, *The Embodiment of Bhakti*, New York: Oxford University Press, 1990.

Rajam, S. and Prema Nandakumar, *Periapuranam in Pictures*, Madras: International Society for the Investigation of Ancient Civilization, 1993.

Ramanujan, A.K., *Hymns for the Drowning: Poems for Vishnu by Nammalvar*, Princeton: Princeton University Press, 1981.

Ramaswamy, Vijaya, *Divinity and Deviance: Women in Virasaivism*, New Delhi: Oxford University Press, 1996.

Ranade, R.D., *Pathway to God in Marathi Literature*, Bombay: Bharatiya Vidya Bhavan, 1961.

The Sants: Studies in a Devotional Tradition of India, edited by Karine Schomer and W.H. McLeod, Berkeley, California: Religious Studies Series, and New Delhi: Motilal Banarsidass, 1987.

Sardar, G.B., *The Saint-Poets of Maharashtra (Their Impact on Society)*, translated from the Marathi by Kumud Mehta, Bombay: Orient Longman, 1969.

Schaller, Joseph, 'Sanskritization, Caste Uplift, and Social Dissidence in the *Sant* Ravidas Panth', in *Bhakti Religion in North India: Community Identity and Political Action*, edited by David N. Lorenzen, Albany: State University of New York Press, 1995, pp. 94–119.

Sekkizhar's *Periya Puranam*, part I, translated by T.N. Ramachandran, Tanjavur: Tamil University, 1990.

Sellegren, Sarah, 'Janabai and Kanhopatra: A Study of Two Woman Saints', in *Images of Women in Maharashtrian Literature and Religion*, edited by Anne Feldhaus, Albany: State University of New York Press, 1996, pp. 213–38.

Sharma, Krishna, *Bhakti and the Bhakti Movement: A New Perspective: A Study in the History of Ideas*, New Delhi: Munshiram Manoharlal, 1987.

Shiri, Godwin, 'Basava, Casteism and Untouchables', *Religion and Society*, vol. 39, nos. 2 & 3, June–Sept. 1992, pp. 17–24.

Shyamlal, 'Maharishi Naval: A Bhangi Saint-Reformer of Rajasthan', in *Scheduled Caste and Scheduled Tribes in India: A Socio-Economic Profile*, edited by H.C. Upadhyay, New Delhi: Anmol Publications, 1991, pp. 311–22

Subramanian, V.K., *Sacred Songs of India*, 3 vols., New Delhi: Abhinav, 2001.

Tradition and Modernity in Bhakti Movements, edited by Jayant Lele, Leiden: E.J. Brill, 1982.

Tulpule, Shankar Gopal, *Classical Marathi Literature*, vol. IX, in the History of Indian Literature Series, Wiesbaden: Otto Harrassowitz, 1979.

Upadhyaya, K.N., *Guru Ravidas, Life and Teachings*, Beas: Radha Soami Satsang, 1982.

Vanmikananathan, G., *Periya Puranam: A Tamil Classic on the Great Saiva Saints of South India by Sekkizharr*, condensed English Version Madras: Sri Ramakrishna Math, 1985.

Varadachari, K.C., *Alvars of South India*, Bombay: Bharatiya Vidya Bhavan, 1966.

Vaudeville, Charlotte, 'Chokhamela: An Untouchable Saint of Maharashtra', in South Asian Digest of Regional Writing, vol. 6: *Bhakti in South Asian Regional Literature*, Heidelberg, 1977.

——, *Kabir*, vol. 1, London: Oxford University Press, 1974.

Vincentnathan, Lynn, 'Nandanar: Untouchable Saint and Caste Hindu Anomaly', in *Ethos*, vol. 21, no. 2, 1993, pp. 154–79.

Warder, A.K., *Indian Kavya Literature*, vol. 1: *Literary Criticism*, New Delhi: Motilal Banarsidass, 1972, 1989.

Younger, Paul, *The Home of Dancing Sivan: The Traditions of the Hindu Temple in Citamparam*, New York: Oxford University Press, 1995.

Zelliot, Eleanor, 'The Medieval Bhakti Movement in History: An Essay on the Literature in English', in *Hinduism: New Essays in the History of Religions*, edited by Bardwell L. Smith, Leiden: E.J. Brill, 1976.

——, 'Chokhamela and Eknath: Two Bhakti Modes of Legitimacy for Modern Change', in *From Untouchable to Dalit: Essays on the Ambedkar Movement*, New Delhi: Manohar, 3rd edn. 2001. First published 1981.

——, 'Chokhamela: Piety and Protest', in *Bhakti Religion in North India: Community Identity and Political Action*, edited by David N. Lorenzen, Albany: State University of New York Press, 1995, pp. 212–20.

Index